SHAMBHALA DRAGON EDITIONS

The dragon is an age-old symbol of the highest spiritual essence, embodying wisdom, strength, and the divine power of transformation. In this spirit, Shambhala Dragon Editions offers a treasury of readings in the sacred knowledge of Asia. In presenting the works of authors both ancient and modern, we seek to make these teachings accessible to lovers of wisdom everywhere.

Each Shambhala Dragon Edition features Smyth-sewn binding and is printed on acid-free paper.

Great Swan

Meetings with Ramakrishna

LEX HIXON

SHAMBHALA *Boston & London* 1992

Shambhala Publications, Inc.
Horticultural Hall
300 Massachusetts Avenue
Boston, Massachusetts 02115

Shambhala Publications, Inc.
Random Century House
20 Vauxhall Bridge Road
London SW1V 2SA

9 8 7 6 5 4 3 2 1

First Edition
Printed in the United States of America on acid-free paper

Distributed in the United States by Random House
and in Canada by Random House of Canada Ltd.
Distributed in the United Kingom by Element Books Ltd.

Library of Congress Cataloging-in-Publication Data

Hixon, Lex.
  Great swan: meetings with Ramakrishna / Lex Hixon. — 1st ed.
      p.   cm. — (Shambhala dragon editions)
    ISBN 0-87773-660-X (pbk.: alk. paper)
    1. Ramakrishna, 1836–1886.   2. Ramakrishna Mission—Biography.
  3. Hindus—India—Biography.   I. Title.
  BL1280.292.R36H59   1992
  294.5'55'092—dc20   91-53228
    [B]   CIP

Contents

Preface   vii
Introduction   xi

1 INITIAL ENCOUNTER
Visiting Dakshineswar Garden on the Ganges
Near Calcutta   1

2 FACE TO FACE WITH THE DIVINE DANCER   14

3 ANCIENT SAGE MEETS MODERN PANDIT
Ramakrishna and Vidyasagar   19

4 FROM THE GOD-MAN'S TREASURY OF SECRETS   28

5 THE TASTE OF SUGAR
Boating on the Ganges with Keshab Sen   33

6 ONE HEMP-SMOKER RECOGNIZES ANOTHER   38

7 THE SAGE OPENS A GAP IN THE NET
OF CONVENTION   45

8 THE BLISS OF RAMAKRISHNA'S BIRTHDAY   51

9 THE NEW DISPENSATION
Harmony of All Religions   56

10 CRY WITH AN INFINITE CRY
The Master Responds to Burning Questions   62

11 TIMELESS MAN MEETS CONTEMPORARY MAN
Ramakrishna and Bankim Chandra   70

12 RAMAKRISHNA RELATES HIS INTIMATE
EXPERIENCES   80

13 RADHA AND KRISHNA IN MYSTIC UNION
The Festival at Panihati   93

14 MEETING MOTHER SARADA
Where There Is Shiva, There Is Shakti   100

15 THE MASTER EXPOUNDS ADVAITA VEDANTA   107

16 THE MYSTERY OF NARENDRA AND THE VOW
OF SPIRITUAL COMPLETION   113

17 TWO GREAT SOULS
Ramakrishna's Last Meeting with Keshab Sen   120

18 THE PARAMAHAMSA TRANSMITS
SPIRITUAL INTENSITY
O Brother Madhusudana, Please Come!   140

19 THE IDEAL OF FEMININE LOVE   149

20 AVATARA MEETS WANDERING SADHU   155

21 THE MOOD OF THE DIVINE CHILD
Ramakrishna Breaks His Arm   161

22 UPWARD-FLOWING ENERGY OF KUNDALINI   167

23 SECRET RHYTHM OF THE WISDOM MOTHER   173

24 SPECIAL WORSHIP OF KALI
The Master Meets a Young Actor   182

25 GREAT SWAN MEETS ORTHODOX PANDIT
Ramakrishna and Shashadhar   193

26 RAMAKRISHNA SINGS THE TANTRIC
TRANSMISSION   202

27 THE MASTER'S TERMINAL ILLNESS
His Friendship with the Humanist, Dr. Sarkar   212

28 MY PLAY IS OVER   219

29 THE MASTER TRANSFORMS DR. SARKAR   222

30 RAMAKRISHNA AND LORD BUDDHA   233

31 THE MOOD OF FORMLESSNESS
The Master Gives Away His Treasures   241

32 UNIVERSAL VICTORY
The Passing Away of Ramakrishna   245

33 DIVINE COMMUNION   250

Index   309

Preface

Ramakrishna's life enables us to see God face to face.
—*Mahatma Gandhi*

BY MEETING RAMAKRISHNA, which is possible here and now, we enter a unique realm of experience where the Wisdom Goddess reigns—the one Ramakrishna calls *my blissful Mother*. The wonderful nature of this realm cannot be analyzed, yet it describes itself. The present volume contains that mysterious description—not only in words, which are merely instruments, but as the living presence of Ramakrishna Paramahamsa, the Great Swan, the God-intoxicated sage of Bengal.

We are peacefully gathered together, beyond the reach of philosophy or theology, here in the sage's room at the Dakshineswar Temple Garden beside the sacred river Ganges. Joyfully we contemplate and participate in his adventuresome life and animated conversations. The details are concrete, cultural, earthly. Yet they achieve the impossible—they transmit the experience of supreme Reality.

The pages of this book, as well as the actual, historical conversations and events that they depict, are part of a timeless current that embodied itself in India from 1836 to 1886 as Ramakrishna Paramahamsa. Whatever our background may be, we can swim in this refreshing, surprising current of love and wisdom to be awakened and renewed.

This is not a conventional biography but a workbook. Ramakrishna comes along with these pages—to work side by side with us, clarifying our general understanding of religion as well as initiating or intensifying our particular experience of the mystic path. Ramakrishna laughs and weeps with us. He leads us into ecstasy. This workbook will be useful to every seeker of Truth along every way, because the Paramahamsa accepts and merges with every authentic sacred tradition. The atmosphere that surrounds the sage is intensely Indian, completely non-European, yet Ramakrishna mysteriously provides a master key that opens all cultures and all hearts.

The author must now step aside, as he attempts to do throughout these conversations and existential encounters, allowing Ramakrishna himself to describe the path and to invoke the Truth with great humor and with palpable initiatory power. This book is not invention, but simply the original diamond, placed in a new linguistic setting for the global civilization of the twenty-first century.

RAMAKRISHNA The sensitive mother presents various preparations of fish to her hungry children—plain and bland or rich and spicy, depending on their tastes and their powers of digestion. Just so, the Mother of the Universe reveals various spiritual practices. This child enjoys every one of Her delicious dishes without exception.

Whether you follow the ideal of the Personal God or the impersonal Truth, you will certainly realize the One Reality, provided that you experience profound longing. The same cake tastes sweet from every direction.

Place your devotion whole-heartedly at the service of the ideal most natural to your being, but know with unwavering certainty that all spiritual ideals are expressions of the same supreme Presence. Do not allow the slightest trace of malice to enter your mind toward any manifestation of God or toward any practitioner who attempts to live in harmony with that Divine Manifestation. Kali, Krishna, Buddha, Christ, Allah—these are all full expressions of the same indivisible Consciousness and Bliss. These are revelatory initiatives of Divine Reality, not manmade notions. Blessed is the soul who has known that all is one, that all jackals howl essentially alike.

The ecstatic lover has burning faith in every Divine Manifestation—as formless Radiance, as various Forms or Attributes, as Divine Incarnations like Rama and Krishna, and as the Goddess of Wisdom, who is beyond form and formlessness, containing both in Her mystic Womb.

Meet as many adepts from various paths as you can. Love these persons, receive their initiations, and passionately practice their disciplines. But enter your own inner chamber of primordial awareness to enjoy selfless peace and delight.

Everyone will attain God-consciousness and be liberated. Some receive their meal early in the morning, others at noon, still others not until evening. But none will go hungry. Without any exception, all living beings will eventually know their own true nature to be timeless awareness.

Ramakrishna is the *paramahamsa*, or Great Swan, who can separate out the milk of Truth which has become diluted by the water of personal and cultural habits, opinions, and conventions. As the blissful sage proclaims: "Some persons have heard about milk, others have seen milk, while others have actually tasted milk. Still others can drink milk whenever they wish and can offer it freely to humankind." May we ascend together through these four levels of maturity, described so simply by the God-intoxicated child of Bengal.

Introduction

In the spiritual firmament, Sri Ramakrishna is a waxing crescent.
—*Nikhilananda*

AN EYEWITNESS TO the teaching of Ramakrishna reports that his linguistic style was unique, even to those who spoke Bengali. It was not literally translatable into English or any other language. The ecstatic sage communicated in terse, aphoristic phrases, containing only three or four words each—phrases with minimal grammatical or logical structure. Yet these inspired utterances of the Master were rich with meaning. Swami Vivekananda, the successor of Ramakrishna and the transmitter of his universal message, maintained that he could expand for three days upon even a single phrase.

Adding to the difficulty of translation, Ramakrishna Paramahamsa spoke a colorful village Bengali, replete with obscure local words and idioms. He also interspersed his teachings with technical Sanskrit terms from various strands of Hindu yoga and philosophy. He made extensive references as well to the complex realm of sacred history, as recorded by the Vedas, Puranas, and Tantras.

The only option in the face of this linguistic situation is to paraphrase the utterances of Ramakrishna, adding selective commentary and explication of the various contexts of meaning through which the sage moved so freely, rapidly, and unpredictably. He never presented a general philosophy or theology, but only specific teachings for specific individuals at specific points in their development. His conversations consisted of quantum leaps between the apparently inexhaustible variety of his ecstatic moods. The term *ecstasy*, used so frequently in this text, carries its etymological meaning *ex-stasis,* "standing outside"—beyond the habitual, conventional categories of thought and perception called *self* and *world.* Ramakrishna's life was a constant exploration and expression of various levels and dimensions of ecstasy.

The attempt to approximate Ramakrishna's oral transmission in literary form began with the original *Kathamrita* of Mahendranath Gupta, a beloved disciple of the Master who was expressly chosen for this function. Ramakrishna informed Mahendra, who was trained in the literatures of East and West, that the Divine Mother had granted this young headmaster of a school in Calcutta certain special powers in order to transmit Her Wisdom, flowing so abundantly through the Paramahamsa. Some years before Mahendra encountered Ramakrishna, he began the discipline of daily journal keeping, sharpening his memory, his powers of observation, his gift for verbal expression. The Paramahamsa used to review key points with Mahendra, requesting the young scholar to repeat certain teaching-stories and correcting him on subtle shades of interpretation. For example, Ramakrishna asked Mahendra whether he thought his master was completely egoless. Mahendra replied: "Sir, you purposely keep a trace of ego so that you can enjoy the company and conversation of the lovers of God." Ramakrishna corrected him: "No. It is Divine Mother alone who keeps this provisional ego in me."

Mahendra was trained and prepared on many levels to write his *Kathamrita,* or *Ocean of Nectar,* as he entitled this multivolume diary of encounters and conversations with Ramakrishna which he personally witnessed. According to Sarada Devi, Ramakrishna's wife and spiritual consort, the *Kathamrita* genuinely reflects the atmosphere and content of the Paramahamsa's teaching. But it is only a reflection, a translation into literary Bengali of condensed and often enigmatic phrases which were not delivered in a linear manner but depended for their meaning and emotional impact on the Master's subtle gestures and powerful spiritual presence. Mahendra had to provide certain logical links and contextual descriptions—including the appearance of the Paramahamsa, the nature of his ecstasy, the atmosphere of the Temple Garden, the mood of the visitors. This task the author of the *Kathamrita,* who refers to himself humbly as M, performed with beauty and subtlety. This root text of Ramakrishna's oral teaching is not a dry stenographic report but a contemplative reconstruction by a sensitive eyewitness.

The next step in the history of this challenging literary project—recording in prose the divine epiphany called Ramakrishna—was the translation of M's *Kathamrita* from Bengali into English. The resulting masterwork, *The Gospel of Sri Ramakrishna,* was published in the United States in 1942 by its author, Swami Nikhilananda of the Ramakrishna Order of Monks. This gifted and affable Swami, who lived and taught for more than forty years in New York City, was a direct disciple of Sarada Devi and a monastic disciple of Swami Saradananda. Saradananda was intimate as a young man with Ramakrishna and authored the other classic Bengali work in this tradition, the definitive spiritual biography of the God-man, *Lilaprasanga,* translated into English as *The Great Master*.

Swami Nikhilananda possessed literary as well as spiritual gifts. A journalist in his premonastic days, he had already written the first full-length English biography of Ramakrishna when he began work on the translation of M's account with Margaret Wilson, daughter of President Woodrow Wilson. She helped the Swami refine his somewhat Victorian literary style into flowing American English. The mystic hymns that abound in the text were put into free verse by the Swami's close friend and disciple, the American poet John Moffitt. The scholar Joseph Campbell helped with the editing of the manuscript. This open spirit of collaboration between East and West produced an excellent literary result, with Swami Nikhilananda himself making the important spiritual decisions behind the translation.

For example, Ramakrishna constantly used the Bengali phrase *kamini kanchan* to indicate the habitual drives of sexuality and possessiveness. This phrase became his shorthand description for the entire conventional world. To suggest the atmosphere of Ramakrishna's colorful language, Swami Nikhilananda chose to retain this phrase in its literal translation as "woman and gold." As a result, almost every page of the thousand-page *Gospel of Sri Ramakrishna* mentions "renunciation of woman and gold." Through footnotes, the Swami explained that Ramakrishna taught his female disciples to renounce "man and gold," assuring the reading public that the Paramahamsa worshiped woman rather than rejecting or denigrating her. In any work of translation, particularly of such rich and subtle teaching, one is faced with many difficult literary and spiritual decisions. A different approach is taken by the present work. There is no single correct answer.

Mature practitioners, knowledgeable about the Ramakrishna lineage, have deeply appreciated Nikhilananda's *Gospel,* as it is called for short. It is widely regarded as a spiritually authentic and powerful rendering of the *Kathamrita* into dignified English. English-speaking readers from all over the world have found the *Gospel* stylistically satisfying as well as spiritually inspiring. But the *Gospel* certainly does not represent Ramakrishna speaking in terse, enigmatic, ungrammatical phrases. The blissful sage speaks highly intelligible and intelligent English.

Mahendra tried his hand at a brief English version of his own Bengali diaries, now available as *The Condensed Gospel of Sri Ramakrishna.* The literary atmosphere of this book is charming but less universal than the *Gospel* produced by Swami Nikhilananda and his American collaborators. Mahendra was very fond of Nikhilananda and blessed him heartily when the young monk was sent to America by his Order in 1930, proclaiming: "Wherever you go, you will be victorious!" Perhaps Mahendra intuited that the gifted young Swami would someday present his *Kathamrita* to the entire English-speaking world.

Nikhilananda deleted some of M's original commentary in his version, perhaps in order to reduce the five Bengali volumes to a single volume in English, but also because M was writing for Bengal and Nikhilananda was writing for Western culture.

The next step in this historical process will be taken by authors who attempt to bring the conversations and encounters with Ramakrishna into their own native languages. These efforts will involve numerous literary and spiritual decisions about presentation, commentary, contextualization, translation. These authors will write from different levels of contemplative maturity and scholarly knowledge. They will each espouse a different understanding of the spiritual needs of their own culture and the way that Ramakrishna's teachings speak to these needs.

Neither the *Kathamrita* nor the *Gospel of Sri Ramakrishna* will be outmoded or replaced by ongoing efforts at transcribing and assimilating the Master's powerful words, whether into English or into any other language. Each generation will produce its own versions of the root text. Some will be more successful than others, but each will be useful in awakening sincere minds and hearts to the universal message of the blissful sage of Bengal—a message of love, harmony, and freedom.

While composing this present version, *Great Swan: Meetings with Ramakrishna,* I have worked not from M's Bengali text but from certain passages in the *Gospel of Sri Ramakrishna,* enriching them further with references to the entire Ramakrishna literature, including more detailed descriptions of the Paramahamsa and his environment. For example, neither the *Kathamrita* nor the *Gospel* presents a conversation with Sarada Devi, the enlightened wife of Ramakrishna who remained, after his death in 1886, as the spiritual guide of his movement for thirty-four years until her passing in 1920. I have included in this book the sense of her essential and prominent although subtle presence at the side of her husband, synthesizing a conversation with her from teachings recorded in *Holy Mother,* the standard English biography by Swami Nikhilananda. This gives a wider scope to the present version of Ramakrishna's conversations. There are many other aspects and events of the Paramahamsa's holy life, however, which I have barely been able to touch, because my intention was to write a three-hundred-page book, not one of a thousand pages or more. *Great Swan* can be regarded as a contemporary commentary on *The Gospel of Sri Ramakrishna* and *The Great Master,* the root texts of this fruitful spiritual lineage.

Through my study and practice of Islamic Sufism and Tibetan Buddhism, I have been able to understand the teachings of Ramakrishna on *bhakti* and *tantra* from a wider perspective. My study of Sanskrit and my doctoral dissertation at Columbia University on the Advaita Vedanta of Gaudapada, has enabled me to appreciate more deeply the Master's universal Vedantic approach. But far more precious than these studies were my years of friendship with Swami Nikhilananda himself.

For seven years until his passing away, I associated closely with the Swami, having received formal initiation from him in 1965. I was blessed to hear his oral commentary on both the *Gospel* and *The Great Master.* I also received many corrections and scoldings from him, which I now cherish, as he firmly predicted I would. He was the person who insisted I study for the doctorate, remarking simply: "You will have to read very widely." Initiatory instructions from other Ramakrishna Order monks, Swami Prabhavananda and Swami Asheshananda, as well as Mother Gayatri Devi, who represents the line of Swami Paramananda, have been important for the development of my understanding.

Twenty-five years of personal meditation on Ramakrishna Paramahamsa and on the entire *mandala* of remarkable souls who incarnated with him has given me the insight and courage to write this book. I have not departed in essence from any of the teachings I received through the kindness of Swami Nikhilananda. My interpretation of Ramakrishna is not my own.

Great Swan presents a dramatized first-person portrait of the Goddess-worshiping sage for the twenty-first European century, the second century of Ramakrishna's Descent. Its content is not controversial, remaining firmly grounded in published eyewitness accounts. Particularly useful is *Ramakrishna as We Saw Him* by Swami Chetanananda, a recent compendium of authentic reminiscences, many available before only in Bengali sources or in obscure English-language journals.

What may be controversial, however, is the literary style in which Ramakrishna's words are expressed. He speaks a language in some ways similar to that of a contemporary, highly educated person. I made the decision not to attempt to reproduce the terse, enigmatic Paramahamsa, but to unfold some of the rich meanings intended by his original words. Ramakrishna's words were not really simple after all. His teachings abound with technical terms that refer to advanced philosophical understanding as well as parables that condense a vast amount of subtlety and sophistication.

For example, the God-intoxicated sage used to proclaim: *"Brahman* is *shakti* and manifests as Gauranga." Here is the sense and spirit of this utterance: "The transparent Ground of Being manifests as the primordial Divine Energy—creating, sustaining, and dissolving all worlds—and also condenses completely into human form as various Divine Incarnations." In this paraphrase, we have lost some of the charm of his words, but we have the clear meaning of his teaching.

I have tried to convey, through my chosen literary form, a spiritual atmosphere which is authentically that of the Paramahamsa, who was emphatically not an unsophisticated village man, although he may have sometimes appeared that way. Ramakrishna was constantly operating at the highest level of philosophical and religious refinement and universality. He remembered every Sanskrit scripture he heard chanted, even once, as well as every mystic hymn in Bengali and Hindi. In secular Western terms, he was a genius. Thus, even the most advanced literary expression of which I am capable is inadequate to express the subtlety of insight hinted at by his words. And herein lies the relevance of this book. Ramakrishna is not a quaint person from an ancient culture, representing a particular religious background, but an Einstein of the planetary civilization of the near future.

What or who Ramakrishna is can only be intimated by his own startling words, actions, and experiences. This is what *Great Swan* is all about. It is not a volume of philosophy, theology, or anthropology. Nor is it a book *about* Ramakrishna, but simply *is* Ramakrishna at play, continuing to express nondual Reality spontaneously, offering guidance, inspiration, and initiation to subsequent generations of Truth seekers and lovers of God. To immerse mind and heart in these selected conversations provides a vivid experience—sweet, astonishing, spiritually intoxicating. Welcome to Ramakrishna's unmistakable, inimitable presence.

Great Swan

Initial Encounter

Visiting Dakshineswar Garden
on the Ganges Near Calcutta

Is Dakshineswar an ordinary place? It is heaven on earth.

—Shivananda

Ramakrishna's life is a breathing, blazing Upanishad.

—Premananda

Here all the doors are open.

—Ramakrishna Paramahamsa

A PARAMAHAMSA, or great swan, is a true human being: one who has realized the timeless nature of awareness, one who has awakened with relaxed delight to the indescribable, the inconceivable, the inexpressible, one who has attained the goal of spiritual evolution. To meet and communicate with a *paramahamsa* is to perceive through the eyes of every sacred scripture revealed during the long history of humanity. To breathe the healing atmosphere of bliss and illumination that surrounds such a person and to hear the resonant words of a *paramahamsa* in intimate conversation is to commune with every saint of love, every wise sage, every mystic poet. This fully awakened being is a confluence of all the lineages of sacramental power—initiatory successions that have been cherished and carefully transmitted by generations of disciplined practitioners.

Where can we encounter a true human being? The Great Swan, Ramakrishna Paramahamsa, abides in a sacred garden dedicated to Goddess Kali, Great Mother of the Universe. Hidden within the perennially ancient realm of India, he lives peacefully, roaming and dancing through twenty acres of consecrated land along the Ganges River, just north of modern

Calcutta. He converses for hours on end with his spiritual friends, who remain fascinated by the luminous flow of words and silences. Shall we visit these hallowed grounds to meet with the Great Swan?

Ramakrishna teaches that the closer one comes to Mother Ganga, the river of transcendent peace, the more one experiences Her delicious tranquillity, Her subtle coolness that alleviates disease, suffering, and anxiety. As we now approach Dakshineswar Garden, we begin to intone spontaneously SHANTI SHANTI SHANTI—peace, peace, peace. May the perfect peace of knowing the one Presence permeate us, through and through, pervading all space and illuminating conscious beings everywhere!

Arriving at the impressive main gate of the Temple Garden along the dusty highway from the conventional world, the crowded city of Calcutta, we proceed directly to the chamber of Ramakrishna, moving through exalted architecture and beside abundantly flowering gardens—a natural offering of the earth to the sublime Wisdom Goddess enshrined here. Even the nine domes of the Kali Temple seem to bloom from this rich, sacred soil.

The Paramahamsa's room is always open. He cherishes no sense of separate, private, personal space. We find him seated comfortably on a common wood-frame bed facing east, his wonderful eyes gazing into the perpetual dawn of Divine Wisdom. Smiling with delight, experiencing only the innate bliss of primordial awareness, Ramakrishna Paramahamsa is conversing with his friends about Divine Reality—its play as the universe, its compassionate manifestation through various traditional religious forms, its nature as formless radiance that shines at the heart of every conscious being, and its essence that can never be touched by speech or mind. This is the sage's only subject of conversation, yet his approach to it is constantly new and unpredictable.

Welcoming and treating all visitors as messengers from his Divine Beloved, or even as direct manifestations of the Beloved, Ramakrishna talks and laughs with them—communing as well in radiant silence—for more than twenty hours every day. He feasts with these forms of his Beloved, dances and sings with them, rests with them on white cloths spread over the cool stone floor during the heat of the afternoon, keeps vigil with them at the mystic midnight hour, worships with them in the Temple of the Universal Mother, withdrawing alone to the pine grove only to answer the call of nature.

In the delicate early morning light and again at twilight, the Paramahamsa burns incense in his room, bowing humbly and devotedly before sacred images and symbols from the diverse religious traditions of humanity. After chanting various beautiful Divine Names in a melodious voice and dancing gracefully, he sits at ease in his natural state of total illumination, radiating a mother's tender concern for all conscious beings, with whom he identifies his own being constantly and completely. His blessed wife, Mother Sarada, who lives almost invisibly in the small music pavilion just north of the Master's room, has experienced her husband's blissful presence even in the ants that abound in the Temple Garden. She treats all sentient beings with loving respect, for to her they manifest the indivisible Consciousness that she and Ramakrishna simply call *Ma*, Mother. At this Temple Garden of the Great Goddess, a timeless festival is blossoming, night and day, around these enlightened twin souls, Ramakrishna and Sarada.

Ramakrishna's room is immediately familiar to us. Even our childhood homes seem strange and foreign by comparison. This mysterious chamber of the Great Swan, though physically small, appears vast to the eyes of the heart—a palace of the highest realization, a paradise of ecstasy where the Paramahamsa ceaselessly sings:

> Become drunk, O mind,
> with the wine of bliss.
> Fall upon the sacred earth
> weeping and chanting the holy Name.
> Fill space with your lion's roar,
> whirling round and round,
> both arms raised high,
> giving away the *mahamantra*
> to all conscious beings.
> Transform limited desire
> into the radiance of Krishna,
> and swim night and day
> in the wild sea of rapture.
> The universe is now submerged
> beneath waves of ecstatic love.

The dozen people we find seated here on the floor, raptly listening to the Paramahamsa as he sings traditional hymns of mystic union, represent the millions of sincere aspirants among humanity. The place is swept so clean by the sage that one can eat grapes from the floor that are scattered from the wooden throne of this humble sovereign of Divine Love. As Ramakrishna remarks: "I cherish only two desires—to be the king of ecstatic lovers and never to become a cross, dry ascetic."

Some visitors tumble on this hallowed floor as they laugh with abandon at the Master's unconventional humor, which transcends every proper boundary. Others sink down upon this heavenly floor, lost in ecstasy, during the intoxicating chanting of Divine Names or the absorbing rendition of mystic hymns. Ramakrishna requests some of his visitors to spread mats and sleep for an hour on this peaceful floor when they arrive at the Temple Garden in the evening after a long working day. Many devotees bow and touch their foreheads to this fragrant floor, impregnated over the years by incense, when greeting or taking leave of the Great Swan. This holy floor is also blessed by the touch of Ramakrishna's own forehead as he prostrates before his visitors, whom he worships as part of one encompassing Divine Manifestation. He also prostrates spontaneously in the direction of the Kali Temple, expressing the overwhelming attraction of a divine child for its Divine Mother.

Scholars, philosophers, social leaders, artists, and revolutionaries sit on this floor for hours, temporarily free from their limited responsibilities and thirstily drinking in the surprising responses of the sage to their most burning questions. Ramakrishna serves his visitors with sweets that he orders from a local shop or that have been ceremonially offered in the Kali Temple. Mother Sarada feeds them meals that she prepares with her own hands and brings from her residence in the Nahabat, silently walking the garden path. To refresh his visitors, the Paramahamsa humbly and graciously pours Ganges water from a large earthenware jar kept in the corner of the bare room. He opens his umbrella and places it in the western door to shield the eyes of his visitors from the harsh glare of the afternoon sun. He stands respectfully whenever his visitors leave, fervently repeating: "Divine Mother will bless you!" Again and again, the childlike sage teaches: "One cannot recognize God, the Simple One, unless one is simple."

Medical doctors, lawyers, magistrates and other Europeanized professionals lose their disciplined sense of time in the timeless precinct of this chamber overlooking the holy river, this heaven for the lovers of God, this vast ocean for the knowers of Oneness. Simple villagers feel completely at ease here beside wealthy aristrocrats, university professors, government officials. Radical young persons unusually gifted in music, vision, or insight also gather here, vowing in the presence of this great fire of consecration, Ramakrishna Paramahamsa, to renounce the conventional world and devote their entire lives, breath by breath, to the expression of the highest spiritual ideals—whether as contemplatives retired from social responsibility or as loving revolutionaries, active in renewing the fabric of social and religious institutions. In his charming, playful manner, which bears no resemblance to preaching, Ramakrishna teaches these avid young students never to compromise their high aspirations—whatever they may be, springing from whatever sacred tradition.

In the midst of animated conversation and debate, when the minds of his companions are overheated, Ramakrishna bursts into song like a bird whose entire being transforms into melody. The atmosphere of the room is suddenly cooled and refreshed, plunged into the perpetual springtime of the Paramahamsa's own realization—spiritual completeness, here and now, without the slightest need for pressure or manipulation. Ramakrishna is an ocean of pure love without the slightest motive for personal gain. Into this shoreless sea our streams of limited desire flow and are released, without disturbing the perfect stillness of its depths. Yet the surface of this ocean continues to manifest gigantic waves of ecstasy, and brilliant teachings emerge from its silence. Often Ramakrishna sings:

> Dive deep, O mind,
> into the ocean of Divine Beauty.
> You will discover a new gem
> instant after instant.

Longing to plunge into this profundity, we now enter together the country fair of sheer delight which is Ramakrishna's room at Dakshineswar. Today the sage wears a yellow cloth, enhancing the golden color of his complexion. We prostrate ourselves at his feet or greet him with palms joined, whatever is most natural for us. The Paramahamsa accepts his visitors completely, even more so than a mother who loves her children no matter what they do. Gazing for just a moment into his serene face and shining eyes, our minds become calm and we experience an explosive sensation at the center of our chest.

We are enjoying simultaneously every powerful place of pilgrimage, right here in the Master's room. We are in Jerusalem, Mecca, Benares,

Lhasa. We are on every holy mountain: Kailash, Koyasan, Sinai, Tabor, Carmel, Hira. We are visiting the Virgin of Guadalupe in Mexico and other shrines to the Virgin Mother which proliferate throughout the world. We are also receiving blessings from every temple dedicated to the Goddess. Her Wisdom-energy flows through the strong feminine presence of Ramakrishna, who calls himself a child of the Mother but who often manifests during ecstasy as mysterious Mahakali, Great Mother of the Universe.

We are miraculously surrounded here by heavenly realms and transcendent Pure Lands, where illumined souls hear Divine Words and travel through mystic environments that far surpass in beauty and power the life-bearing planets scattered throughout space.

The illusory barrier to the past drops away in this wonderful room. We become the blessed earthly companions of Lord Buddha, Lord Kirshna, the noble Prophets Abraham, Moses, and Muhammad, the divinely transfigured Jesus of Nazareth. We are hearing with our own ears the electrifying discourses of the exalted saints and sages of human history.

A profound silence blossoms as we sit before the radiant figure of the Paramahamsa, the silence of total receptivity. To attain even a moment of this inner silence, practitioners persevere for years in their disciplines of prayer and meditation. We now receive this precious gift in abundance as Divine Grace, streaming through the presence of Ramakrishna. Although enfolded entirely within this embracing holy presence, we still hear birds calling from the flower gardens and the songs of boatmen drifting across the waters of the Ganges. Our senses are functioning with greater range, depth, and clarity. Even the murmuring of the sacred river can be discerned.

The communication that occurs in this mystic room of Divine Presence is intimate. Each question feels like our own. Every inspired response of the Paramahamsa enters into the very depth of our mind and heart, resolving our pressing problems, as well as those we have ignored or forgotten. Following this compassionate clearing away of our poisonous doubt, this skillful dissolution of our concealed skepticism concerning the infinite significance of human life, we experience indescribable peace. *Shanti, shanti, shanti.*

The sage suddenly leaps to his feet and sprinkles us with Ganges water from his blessed hands. He is laughing like a child. We are purified and sanctified. Our subtle nervous system becomes the holy sanctuary where

God manifests, appearing vividly on the twelve-petal lotus of the heart in whatever Divine Form attracts us most, or as formless radiance. The healing tone of the Paramahamsa's voice is more familiar than we could have imagined. Our comprehension of his unexpected words is instantaneous.

RAMAKRISHNA My dear friends, when you hear one of the glorious Divine Names—be it Allah, Tara, Krishna, or whichever revealed Name is closest to your heart—if tears of ecstasy come spontaneously to your eyes or if the sensation of weeping springs forth secretly in your heart, if your skin tingles and your breath catches, this is authentic confirmation that you are awakening. Then you no longer need to emphasize religious ceremonies or contemplative exercises, because what they exist to generate will remain constantly vibrant in the depth of your awareness. You will not have to renounce the formalities of religion. Formality of every kind will simply disappear from your being. The beautiful Divine Names will become your breath, heartbeat, sustenance, and joy—whether or not you are receiving sacraments or engaging in disciplines. Even the Divine Name most intimate to you will eventually disappear, and you will commune directly with the One Reality, which precedes and which emanates all names and forms. You will experience then only a subtle resonance or a delicate radiance. The world of conventional thought and perception will either disappear entirely or become transparent to Divine Light.

Beloved companions, consider how the process of awakening matures. During early phases, the practices one engages in are more elaborate, the passages one chants from the scriptures more extensive. Gradually yet inexorably, one is drawn into the living heart of worship. Simplification and intensification occur. Finally, the practice of religion merges into the source of religion. One abides blissfully in the supreme Source, even as this infinite fountain continues to flow with all the precious sacraments, all the powerful forms of worship and meditation ever revealed to humankind.

An entire afternoon has unaccountably disappeared enjoying discourses, hymns, and silence in the Master's holy company. The mystic thunder of conch shells, gongs, bells, drums, and cymbals now emerges from the Temple of the Great Mother, Mahakali, as the evening service to Her begins. A warm spring wind spreads fragrance everywhere. At the southern end of the Temple Garden, from a gracefully constructed circular music pavilion, crystalline melodic forms are arising from the *vina*, the many-stringed instrument of Goddess Saraswati, who embodies knowledge and harmony. The easy-flowing words of the Paramahamsa, steady and powerful as the Ganges, are simply Her Divine Words. Her tender speech, flowing through the honey-colored form of Ramakrishna, blends with the beauty of all manifest Being, pervading heart and mind like a musical wind. Ramakrishna's sweet voice is imbued with the spirit of universal worship, the integrity of complete consecration, the freedom of transcendent insight. We continue to listen and to become absorbed.

Here at Dakshineswar, the One Reality is honored and adored not only as the awesome Mother Kali, whose mysterious Divine Blackness illuminates the universe, as Ramakrishna often sings. Dakshineswar Garden also contains a temple dedicated to the incarnation of Divine Love as Radha and Krishna. These sublime lovers later manifested through a single body as Chaitanya, the ecstatic Krishna-dancer of Bengal, who ignited this entire land into flames of love. With Chaitanya, Ramakrishna experiences mystic identity. Joined with the Kali Temple and the Radha-Krishna Temple, there are also twelve Shiva shrines, which celebrate transcendent vision and absorption in the Absolute. This aspect of the Temple Garden invokes the spirit of renunciation that leaves behind every conventional social and religious context.

These three life-giving streams of spirituality at Dakshineswar can be perceived flowing from the living temple, the radiant body of the Paramahamsa—a body so tender that it can be cut by a sharp piece of bread, a body so sensitive that it manifests the pain of someone being beaten or even of new grass being trampled, a body so refined that it experiences a strange burning sensation at the touch of conventional objects such as coins or newspapers, a body so pure that it cannot even drink water drawn by someone of negative character, a body so beautiful that its intense amber color cannot be distinguished from the golden amulet that Ramakrishna wears around his upper arm.

Dakshineswar Temple Garden was founded by the revolutionary woman Rani Rasmani, who became a devoted disciple of Ramakrishna when he dedicated the Kali Temple as a young priest of nineteen. In this garden of Rani Rasmani, wandering practitioners representing every spiritual way, men and women of rare mystic attainment, are respectfully offered sanctuary and sustenance, their various other needs being generously met from the rich storehouses of the Temple.

As Divine Mother wills, these advanced practitioners meet the Paramahamsa—sharing with him their own initiatory streams and receiving in return mysterious blessings that accelerate their development, freeing them from subtle obstacles and attachments, including attachment to their own form of religious discipline or their own occult powers. The skillful sage simply steals away the powers of certain practitioners, explaining to them later: "If you manifest supernatural powers, people will consciously or unconsciously seek to exploit you and ruin your spiritual life."

During the thirty years of the Master's residence here, the Temple Garden has become an extended family of saints, sages, and aspirants. This is the Ramakrishna *mandala*, a model and seed for global spirituality—plurivalent and harmonious. Dakshineswar Garden is a greenhouse for the future evolution of humanity.

Early in this revelatory drama at Dakshineswar, Ramakrishna encountered his original woman teacher, Bhairavi Brahmani, who opened to him the full range of mystical relationships between the soul and its Lord—as Divine Friend, Divine Child, Divine Lover—and who led him as well through the intricate ceremonial practices of Tantra. Soon afterward, he encountered his principal male guide, Totapuri, who taught the Paramahamsa to wield the sword of unitive wisdom, which cuts away the veils called "soul" and "Lord" and which leaves esoteric ceremony behind. Both these advanced adepts, from opposite ends of the spiritual spectrum, received radical new awakening through companionship and communion with the blissful sage, who was then simply called the mad priest of Dakshineswar.

Ramakrishna moves spontaneously, like a young child. He never manifests as stern ascetic or respectable teacher, although his renunciation of self is flawless and his oral knowledge of scripture and tradition is encyclopedic. When the great woman practitioner, the Brahmani, convened the most highly regarded religious scholars and adepts of the day to consider the astounding realization of Ramakrishna, the childlike Paramahamsa sat naked among them on the sacred earth, chewing spices from his pouch and replying calmly to their affirmations about his unprecedented spiritual stature: "You may well be correct, respected mothers and fathers, but I know nothing about it."

These were disciplined, critical persons, not emotional disciples. They concluded unanimously that Ramakrishna is an *avatara*—a direct, fully conscious manifestation of Divine Reality in human form. One of the ·

pandits, who was also a tantric master, became absorbed in ecstasy while contemplating the variety and depth of Ramakrishna's realizations, including the nineteen modes of devotional ecstasy and the *siddhis*, or attainments, of the sixty-four Tantras. This pandit proclaimed Ramakrishna to be the distillation and manifestation within a single body of every holy being from sacred history, both earthly and heavenly. To this assertion, the Paramahamsa simply replied: "I am the dust on the feet of the servant of your servant."

The Great Swan now turns to us individually, as we sit with remarkable comfort on a thin palm mat that he tenderly spread for us on the stone floor. With great frankness, he questions us about our cultural and religious background, our marital status, our mode of livelihood. He even closely examines the features of our faces, the lines on our hands, the shape of our feet. He whispers to us with surprising intimacy.

> RAMAKRISHNA You see, there are some good signs about you. I know them by looking at the eyes and the forehead. Those persons who in previous incarnations passed their time in communion with God often appear to have just left their seat of contemplation. During the first intensity of falling in love, the meetings between the lovers come more frequently than at later times. You should now visit this place very often.

Throughout these inquiries, we can feel the Master's compassionate gaze probing and evaluating our previous experiences and clearly envisioning our destiny in this lifetime, extending his vision as well into the future, when we will reach the culmination, however we may understand this final goal in terms of the revelatory traditions most compelling for us.

During this process—our replies coming forth effortlessly, without the slightest sense of nervousness or embarassment, without feeling any need for hesitation or concealment—the Paramahamsa appears to be engaging in conversations on several planes of awareness as he briefly closes his eyes or gazes into the distance. But when the focus of his attention returns to us again after one of these mysterious journeys, which may take only a few seconds, his eyes are clear, sparkling, responsive—nothing of our interchange has been forgotten. The alertness and concentration of the sage are extremely sharp, like those of an experienced fisherman, craftsman, or athlete. Occasionally he becomes lost in ecstasy. He speaks to an invisible presence, stammering slightly in a charming manner, appearing like someone rather drunk on strong wine. These more extended moods also succeed one another with astonishing rapidity. We receive the impression of a secret inner richness of experience beyond our comprehension.

Sometimes, as if to propel himself toward the earthly plane of awareness, the God-drunken lover before us requests a glass of water or draws once or twice on a hubble-bubble, a water pipe that burns an aromatic mixture of tobacco. We wonder at first whether it contains some intoxicating herb, particularly since the Paramahamsa jokes that lovers of God are like hemp-smokers, who can always recognize one another. But we soon discover that the sage's radically purified and sensitized nervous system makes it difficult for him to digest plain food and that any use of intoxicating substances is impossible. When the blissful Paramahamsa sits, as he loves to do, in a circle of the esoteric worshipers of Goddess Kali, who pass around a skull cup filled with sanctified wine, he simply repeats the word for wine, which also means Great Cause, and immediately attains the sublime absorption which is the goal of this particular practice. The sacred wine bowl never even touches his lips. The same is true for sacramental sexual union, practiced among certain authentically initiated tantric adepts whom the Master never disdains, always insisting: "Divine Reality is infinite, and infinite are the ways to realize it." Ramakrishna needs simply to envision within his own subtle body the blissful union of Shiva and Shakti, the masculine and feminine energies of transcendence and immanence, in order to enter *samadhi*, the total absorption of body, mind, heart, soul, and spirit in the One Reality that he calls *akhanda satchidananda*—indivisible Being, Consciousness, and Bliss. When anyone asks Ramakrishna to become his or her religious guide, or guru, he invariably replies: "*Satchidananda* is the one and only guru."

Ramakrishna and his consecrated wife, Mother Sarada, have never engaged in the marital sacrament of sexual union, simply because of the intensity and fullness of their mystical union as Shiva and Shakti. When the young wife once playfully complained to her God-intoxicated husband about not bearing physical children, he laughed and replied: "Saradamani, you are the jewel of universal motherhood. You will have so many spiritual children that your ears will burn with the constant cry *Mother, Mother, Mother*." This prophecy has been fulfilled. Sarada is fervently addressed as Holy Mother by countless lovers of Truth who discover their eternal companionship with Ramakrishna—a relationship not definable in terms of social or religious structures, a relationship not contained within time or linear history, a relationship which is not characterized by any sense of duality.

Near midnight, we finally leave this miraculous room where conventional time disappears—where past, present and future manifest together as an indivisible transparency, clear in every direction. The sage addresses us warmly: "Come again! Come again!" This open invitation continues to vibrate with great initiatory power at the center of our consciousness, whether we are awake or sleeping. We experience intense restlessness, thirst, and longing until we do indeed return to the oasis of the Temple Garden—whether the journey appears as a carriage ride from Calcutta or a steamer trip up the Ganges, or whether it appears as an internal act of prayer or meditation. The laughing Paramahamsa likens this process of Divine Attraction to the practice of feeding small pills of opium to peacocks so that they will return every evening at the auspicious twilight hour to display their heavenly plumage. The plumage of the lovers is ecstasy.

Yet the desperate longing of the awakened human lover for the Divine Beloved is incomparably more powerful than the addictions of the egocentric world. Ramakrishna teaches that such true longing—cherished by the most refined saints of every tradition and beautifully expressed by the yearning of the milkmaid Radha for her beloved Lord Krishna—is more powerful than the combined forces of the miser's love for gold, the obsession of an illicit love affair, and the loyal attraction between consecrated husband and wife.

A few fortunate persons have experienced the very yearning of Radha, running several miles to the Temple Garden from the worldly metropolis of Calcutta, their eyes blinded with tears, their sandals abandoned somewhere along the way, their clothes covered with straw from scrambling through haystacks as they cut directly across open fields, not willing to follow the circuitous route of the ordinary road. Other elevated souls have experienced deep renunciation of limited goals and selfish desires, accompanied by nondiscriminating love for humanity and Divinity, arise within them—at home, at school, at places of business or service—simply when envisioning this miraculous Temple Garden and the Paramahamsa of Divine Love and Divine Knowledge waiting ardently and joyously for them within its innermost precincts.

Some aspirants shed tears so copiously that the words or numbers being inscribed by them with the ink of obsession on the ledger of convention are washed away, never to reappear.

"Come again! Come again!" The lilting tone, the unsuspected power, the infinite attractiveness of these simple words from the bearded lips of Ramakrishna Paramahamsa now pervade our entire being. We have come to the lotus feet of our Master. We have tasted intimacy with Divine Mystery. As the playful sage often remarks, smiling: "If you bite into a hot pepper, whether knowingly or unknowingly, your tongue will burn."

2
Face to Face
with the Divine Dancer

A s we enter the Paramahamsa's bare yet comfortable room today, the lovers are immersed in the joyful uproar of sacred dance, accompanied by singers and musicians playing expertly upon drums, cymbals, harmonium, violin, and other instruments from both East and West. Suddenly, the God-intoxicated sage—seated entranced within the circle of dancers, a smile playing across his sweet bearded countenance—leaps to his feet and moves with incredible vigor and grace, like a golden fish released from a bowl into the great waters of the Ganges. Sometimes he dances powerfully, like a whirling lion, at other times with the delicacy of a plume of incense in a windless place. He has unusually long arms and tapered fingers. Their movements are expressive beyond words. There seems to be no spatial or spiritual direction in which he cannot move at any given moment.

Ramakrishna is now improvising lines of mystic poetry, which he sings with flawless rhythm and perfect pitch—metaphors that further illuminate the traditional hymns about Radha and Krishna, lifting these teachings to an even higher level of purity and intensity. Tears of ecstasy stream from his half-closed eyes, literally soaking the white cloth he wears casually draped about his torso. Suddenly, his wearing-cloth falls away entirely, leaving him naked until a companion binds the cloth about the Master's waist again. His chest, wet with tears, is reddened by the uprush of spiritual emotion. His body appears to be floating and glowing.

The Divine Dancer is standing perfectly still now. The devotees, circling around him with enraptured minds like bees around a flower, are not able to contain their emotion and also begin to weep, singing for more than thirty minutes a single line: "Behold the Lord, bestower of infinite love!" The companions of Divine Love are now entering various states of ecstasy. One young man is lying on the floor in full trance, and all the participants have forgotten their limited selves and their limited worlds. Some are laughing and embracing each other with overflowing joy.

Our Master begins to attend to the beautiful young man, named Rakhal, with a mother's sense of tender concern, returning him to relative awareness by placing his right hand upon the heart *chakra* of the supine youth and softly repeating, *"Shanti, shanti, shanti."* Then the Great Swan plunges back into the circle of dancers.

The music falls from its crescendo and suddenly concludes, leaving the atmosphere throbbing and accentuating the stillness of the Temple Garden. These intimate companions—some of whom are leaders of society, bearing heavy practical responsibility—humbly serve each other with refreshments. The Paramahamsa, still in ecstasy, is speaking aloud with the Mother of the Universe. His words are living poetry. Her Presence is palpable.

RAMAKRISHNA *Ma, Ma, Ma*—Mother, Mother, Mother! Everyone foolishly assumes that his clock alone tells correct time. Christians claim to possess exclusive truth, and even modern liberal thinkers reiterate the same claim to exclusivity. Countless varieties of Hindus insist that their sect, no matter how small and insignificant, expresses the ultimate position. Devout Muslims maintain that Koranic revelation supersedes all others. The entire world is being driven insane by this single phrase: "My religion alone is true." O Mother, you have shown me that no clock is entirely accurate. Only the transcendent sun of knowledge remains on time. Who can make a system from Divine Mystery? But if any sincere practitioner, within whatever culture or religion, prays and meditates with great devotion and commitment to Truth alone, Your Grace will flood his mind and heart, O Mother. His particular sacred tradition will be opened and illuminated. He will reach the one goal of spiritual evolution. Mother, Mother, Mother! How I long to pray with sincere Christians in their churches and to bow and prostrate with devoted Muslims in their mosques! All religions are glorious! Yet if I display too much freedom, every religious community will become angry with me. I might even be forbidden to enter Your Temple again, O blissful Kali. Therefore take me secretly into the sanctuary of every tradition without exception, and I will worship ceaselessly with all humanity, night and day.

Following this conversation between the endearing divine child and his awesome Divine Mother—punctuated by silences, during which he listens attentively to Her voice in his secret heart—Ramakrishna bursts into a song from his most beloved poet, Ramprasad:

> Who in this world
> can understand what
> Mother Kali really is?
> The six systems of philosophy
> remain powerless to describe Her.
> She is the inmost awareness
> of the sage who realizes
> that Consciousness alone exists.
> She is the life blossoming within
> the creatures of the universe.
> Both macrocosm and microcosm
> are lost within Mother's Womb.
> Now can you sense
> how indescribable She is?
>
> The yogi meditates upon Her
> in the six subtle nerve centers
> as She sports with delight
> through the lotus wilderness
> of the pristine human body,
> playing with Her Consort,
> Shiva, the Great Swan.
>
> When anyone attempts to know Her,
> the singer of this song laughs.
> Can you swim across
> a shoreless ocean?
> Yet the child in me still
> reaches out to touch the moon.

As the verses flow on and on, the sweet tenor voice, the enthralling melody with its quarter tones, and the glowing eyes of the singer—dark embers of supreme devotion, direct acquaintance with Divine Mystery—bring the poetry of Ramprasad alive in every cell of our being. We are experiencing this small room as the entire universe, which has become a honeycomb of ecstasy.

The Paramahamsa often teaches: "When one awakens into the direct presence of Divine Mother, the revealed scriptures of the Vedas and the sublime philosophy of the Vedanta remain far below." No systematic treatment of spirituality—no theology, no theosophy, not even the dialectic of Shankara or Nagarjuna—can possibly match reality. Yet here is supreme Reality, openly manifested through and as Ramakrishna Paramahamsa. How blessed we are! How auspicious is this day in the drama of our accelerated awakening and the gradual spiritual evolution of all conscious beings!

The unpredictable sage suddenly flashes into crystal-clear awareness of this earthly plane. He gazes at us directly and speaks gently.

RAMAKRISHNA I borrow one-sixteenth of my mind back again from Mother to talk and laugh with all of you. Fifteen parts remain totally merged in meditation on Her Essence, which is *akhanda satchidananda*—indivisible Reality, Awareness, and Delight.

O beloved friends, please listen to my words! The sole purpose and goal for human life, the supreme ideal of which all other ideals are simply an expression, is to cultivate love—the most pure, passionate, intimate love that the milkmaids and cowherd boys in the green groves of Vrindavan cherished for the captivating, dark blue Krishna, the very incarnation of Divine Love. There is no boundary whatsoever to pure love—it embraces humanity and Divinity equally. In this most intense love, no sense of duality can remain. When Lord Krishna traveled to the city of Mathura to fulfill his administrative duty, his companions roamed the fragrant countryside, weeping with ecstatic love, their outward separation from Krishna's beloved form further intensifying their inward union with him as Divine Presence, as Love.

The dark eyes of the Paramahamsa turn upward as he directly enters those timeless glades of Pure Consciousness, where the mystic drama of separation and union is eternally displayed. This time, as our Master sings, his sweet voice trembles delicately in the ecstatic mood of *prema,* unalloyed love. The song depicts one of the young male companions of Lord Krishna, who stands beneath an ancient tree, holding a limb for support and attempting to call out the name of his Beloved. So lost in rapture, the lover remains unable to form words.

Upon hearing the special timbre of the sage's voice, tears instantly spring forth from the eyes and hearts of every companion in the room. Beneath the surface meaning of his words flow powerful currents of initiatory energy. The intensity of Ramprasad's hymn to Warrior Goddess Kali now melts into a river of clarified honey—the mystic union of Radha and Krishna, lover and Beloved. Our body and every atom in the universe have melted as well. As Ramkrishna often proclaims: "To someone who has actually perceived transcendent beauty, even the position of Lord Brahma, the ruler of existence, seems insignificant indeed."

3

Ancient Sage Meets Modern Pandit

Ramakrishna and Vidyasagar

THE RADIANT ATMOSPHERE of Ramakrishna's room and its alchemical power move with him, creating the spaciousness and tranquillity of the Dakshineswar Temple Garden wherever the Paramahamsa travels to meet with lovers of God and other persons of integrity, consecrated to Truth, wherever they may be. With all such persons, our Master feels intense affinity and solidarity.

Today we are delighted to be in his blissful company, riding in the cab of a horse-drawn carriage through the colorful streets of Calcutta—a city of cultural and intellectual ferment and creativity, where ancient and modern currents meet, colliding and blending. The Paramahamsa is seated cross-legged in the noisy, bouncing vehicle, immersed in the profound silence which arises as his mental and perceptual faculties become aligned and are drawn like iron filings to the powerful magnet of the Absolute.

Unexpectedly, the God-intoxicated sage enters another mood. He is now leaning dangerously far out of the carriage window, embracing with ecstasy every passing detail of the city, crying out drunkenly to the patrons of wine shops and perfume stalls: "Yes! You are experiencing a drop of Divine Bliss. But go further!" This admonition and encouragement to go further continuously along whatever path presents itself is the essential teaching of Ramakrishna. "There are an infinite number of perspectives," he passionately proclaims, "and each one of them is a path to God." He often tells the story of the woodcutter who, journeying further and further into a forest to find suitable trees, happens upon a precious grove of sandalwood. As the impoverished man stands in astonishment, contemplating his exceeding good fortune, a wandering sage appears and counsels him with the simple words: "Go further! Go further!" The woodcutter ponders this pithy instruction and ventures further into the wilderness, where he dicovers a rich vein of gold. The initiatory words of the sage spring up spontaneously in his mind and he continues his quest, eventually discovering a cave filled with diamonds. Some practitioners are still ordinary brushwood, others sandalwood, still others gold, while the mature of the mature have become clear diamond. Ramakrishna's only function is to accelerate this alchemical process. He often remarks: "I would sacrifice twenty thousand incarnations to encourage even a single seeker of Truth."

The morning is bright. We are traversing the six miles from the Kali Temple to the mansion of Pandit Vidyasagar, who lives at the fragrant spiritual level of the sandalwood grove but who has not yet reached the vein of gold. Though born in the pristine environment of a remote village, rather near the birthplace of Ramakrishna, this brilliant man chose to enter the Europeanized environment of Calcutta. Here he has become renowned as a scholar, educator, and philanthropist. He is at once well versed in classical Sanskrit and elegant modern Bengali. Far before the advent of Mahatma Gandhi, the morally sensitive Pandit Vidyasagar has given up drinking cow's milk in order to protest the lack of compassion toward these animals by dairy farmers. Nor will the Pandit even ride in a carriage because of the slavish conditions under which horses are kept. Uncompromising about ethical principle, Vidyasagar resigned his influential post as chancellor of the Calcutta Sanskrit College because he disagreed with its moral stance. His personal tenderness and loyalty are demonstrated by his profound affection for his mother. Once he swam a flood-swelled river, risking his life to fulfill his mother's wish that he should attend the wedding of his brother. Though wealthy, his mode of living is one of unpretentious simplicity, and his name—*vidyasagar,* "ocean of learning"—is richly confirmed by his careful studies in various ancient and modern fields of knowledge.

To such persons of unique spiritual, moral, and intellectual quality, Ramakrishna is drawn with the very fervor that attracts him to worship the One Reality in various temples and through diverse sacred traditions. The human being itself, to the illumined eyes of the Paramahamsa, is the most vivid and exalted manifestation of Divinity. Therefore he undertakes humble pilgrimage to persons of ecstatic love or encompassing knowledge, spontaneously accelerating their development by his very presence, crying out to them with his entire being: "Go further! Go further!"

Today's historic meeting on the fifth day of August has been arranged, at the repeated request of the God-intoxicated sage, by Mahendra, an intimate companion within the Paramahamsa's inner circle and the headmaster of a school founded by Pandit Vidyasagar. The Pandit initially inquired of the headmaster: "Is this sage of yours just another world-renouncing monk who escapes from responsibility by wearing an ocher cloth?"

Mahendra humbly replied: "No, no, my dear sir. This sage, as you call him, is far beyond all such categories. He wears the red-bordered cloth of a tantric practitioner and the polished black slippers of a gentleman. He lives in a beautiful room overlooking the Ganges in the palatial Temple Garden of Kali, built by the widow Rani Rasmani, who adores and protects him, allowing him complete freedom of experimentation and expression. Ramakrishna Paramahamsa keeps his lovely young wife and his ninety-year-old mother near him in the Temple Garden. He explains that the black basalt image of Goddess Kali, his venerable mother, and his radiant wife manifest the very same Divine Reality, and he makes no fundamental distinctions between these three holy forms. He went without sleep for twelve years during the period of his *sadhana,* his intense spiritual disciplines to generate evolutionary energy for all humanity, but now he displays no outward asceticism, sleeping instead on a comfortable bed and using mosquito netting. He walks in the rain with a distinguished English umbrella, yet his native-spun wearing-cloth falls from his body when he dances in ecstasy. Although a devout brahmin priest, he openly disregards various rules of caste and ritual purity. He vehemently repudiates the title of guru. Indeed, the Paramahamsa displays no recognizable, traditional forms of holiness, yet twenty-four hours a day he thinks, speaks, and sings only of the Divine, to the Divine, through the Divine, and from the Divine. He is so completely immersed in Divine Presence that no one can discover exactly who or what he is."

Vidyasagar's interest was piqued by these words, and his invitation to Ramakrishna Paramahamsa was strong, respectful, and sincere.

As our carriage gradually approaches the residence of this great man of learning and servant of humanity, the level of ecstasy radiating from the very pores of the Paramahamsa intensifies moment by moment. Someone in our party points to the historic home that belonged to one of India's most important modern cultural and religious leaders. Ramakrishna evinces total indifference, remarking with the sharpness of Kali's Sword of Wisdom: "How can precious attention be placed on something secondary? What do I care for famous men who have lived and acted in the external dimensions of history? We are now being drawn into the very core of timeless awareness."

Our carriage approaches elaborate gates, and the Master steps forth, reeling slightly with holy inebriation, gently and unobtrusively supported by his companion, Mahendra. The sage moves lightly and unpredictably, like a feather on a breeze. We stroll through a large courtyard filled with flowering plants, which obviously receive much tender care, perhaps from the hands of the Pandit himself. Ramakrishna enters a childlike mood as he nears the goal of his pilgrimage. His shirt is not properly buttoned, his wearing-cloth awry. He asks Mahendra repeatedly if this important man will be offended by his disheveled appearance. This disciple humbly reassures his Master: "Sir, there is absolutely nothing offensive about you." Ramakrishna accepts the words like an obedient child, comforted by his mother's voice.

Guided by a servant to the second floor, we see Pandit Vidyasagar seated at the far end of a reception hall in European fashion on a carved wooden chair behind a polished wooden table strewn with books and papers. Various friends and admirers are gathered around him on chairs and benches. This is an entirely different world from the Temple Garden, but the Paramahamsa is now completely relaxed and walks toward his noble host without the slightest awkwardness or hesitation. Vidyasagar rises to honor his unusual visitor, and the Paramahamsa stands perfectly still, right hand resting easily on the table, gazing deep into the eyes of the handsome, white-haired man as though they were the dearest of friends, meeting again after a long absence.

This vibrant moment is prolonged into several minutes of communion. The accepted form of polite interchange melts entirely. The Paramahamsa, attempting to keep his mind at least minimally engaged in the world of space and time, remarks, as he continues to gaze: "I think I would take a glass of cool water." At this point, various family members and even the servants of the household have gathered and are gazing in astonishment at the sage, sensing a spacious and peaceful presence, as if they were looking out over the sacred waters of the Ganges.

Suddenly, our Master takes his seat on a bench where a young man of seventeen is sitting, having come to the wealthy Vidyasagar to seek financial assistance for his education. Before any conventional conversation can begin, the Paramahamsa, still plunged in the ecstasy of communion with Truth, calls out to Goddess Kali: "O Great Mother of the Universe, You are clearly revealing that the young man beside me, earnest as he may appear on the surface, is narrowly focused on material gain and belongs entirely to Your projected realm of delusion." Although startled whispers spread like ripples through the gathering, Vidyasagar himself remains undisturbed and gracious, calling for cool water and courteously asking Mahendra whether the revered visitor would take some other refreshments. Without waiting for an answer, the dignified Pandit, a man in his middle sixties, eagerly rushes into another room and returns, carrying a round silver tray of sweets with his own hands, much to the amazement of everyone present. Servants bring more trays, and the atmosphere of shock, surprise, and power is somewhat lightened. The Great Swan sips delicately from a glass of water and enters a more accessible state of consciousness. He remarks jovially to Vidyasagar about another young man in the room: "That person is someone of excellence and purity. Very sound at his center. Yet his spiritual qualities remain somewhat hidden. He is a desert stream that appears to be merely a dry wash, but if one digs just below the surface, clear water will spring forth."

Ramakrishna now begins sampling sweets at random, just like a child. The large reception hall has gradually filled with interested observers, some sitting cross-legged on the floor, others standing with their backs against the walls. As Ramakrishna often remarks: "When the fragrant lotus blooms in the jungle, bees appear spontaneously, as if from nowhere, to sip its sweet nectar."

Exclaiming, "Ah, ah," the Paramahamsa finally addresses his host, crying out with enthusiasm: "Today, at long last, I have come to the *sagar*, the ocean. Up until now, I have only witnessed smaller bodies of water— mere canals or marshes, perhaps a river or two."

The Pandit responds playfully: "Then, sir, please take home some salt water from this bitter ocean so that it can be purified in the sunlight of your presence."

A warm wave of laughter spreads through the room at this humble and humorous reply. Discomfort and nervousness are released. Ramakrishna immediately cries out in response: "Oh no! Oh no! I can never regard you as a *sagar* of salt water, Pandit Vidyasagar. You are the ocean of *vidya*, spiritual knowledge, the ocean of milk. In fact, dear sir, you are an ocean of milk which has been boiled over the fire and richly concentrated." The beautiful, loving tones of the Paramahamsa and the subtle humor of his dismay causes delighted laughter to break forth, and this rather sedate room is transformed into the dynamic bazaar of joy that always surrounds Ramakrishna.

At this touching remark, Pandit Vidyasagar stops bantering and becomes mysteriously silent. The dignified, imposing figure, eyes shining with unshed tears, inclines his head before an eccentric, unlettered man twenty years his junior. Paying no heed to the presence of the Pandit's friends and household, our Master now launches into a frank evaluation of Vidyasagar's spiritual life. They are like intimate friends, seated together in solitude.

RAMAKRISHNA O noble Vidyasagar, your various activities in the fields of education, relief of human and animal suffering, literature and scholarship are authentically inspired by purity of mind and heart. These kinds of action are usually generated by ambition, but in your case there is genuinely selfless motivation. The primordial purity of selfless awareness is the only source of true compassion. Various good works can appear to be generous and compassionate on the surface, but very few, such as yours, actually spring from selflessness. Any action selflessly undertaken for the good of others is not harmful to spiritual development. However, public good works are usually a reinforcement of the conventional self and the conventional world, hence detrimental to spiritual progress.

The great sages have always been motivated by sheer compassion alone, but their action most often takes the form of ceaselessly transmitting spiritual teaching and initiatory energy to the people, rather than remaining satisfied with providing food and shelter. My dear Pandit, you are distributing material assistance as well as intellectual learning. This is good but not yet sufficient. Your generous actions will lead you—and others who are inspired by these actions—in the direction of the spiritual path, but can never bring about the awakening into God which is the true goal of human existence. Good works that spring from the motive to gain worldly renown or even to enter Paradise cannot lead in the correct direction, which is absolute selflessness. But why am I telling you all this? You are already complete, already a *siddha*.

The Pandit answers in a serious tone: "Revered sir, I cannot accept such an exalted title as *siddha*. I am far from being a perfected one."

"Of course you can," the Master replies, smiling brilliantly, "because *siddha* also means 'boiled.' When vegetables or potatoes are well cooked, they become tender and delicious. This is your compassionate nature, Panditji—tender and delicious." Fresh waves of laughter spread through the room, which has indeed become the ocean of love, always at play.

Once more deferential, but now with delicate self-irony, the Pandit replies: "Dear Paramahamsa, certain beans, when they are boiled, become all the harder." Both the ancient *paramahamsa* and the modern *pandit* are now laughing unrestrainedly.

Ramakrishna flashes again into a mood of serious penetration, decisively changing the atmosphere of the entire room.

RAMAKRISHNA Pandit Vidyasagar, you are definitely not a bean of that category. Self-interested scholars who use their learning—even their precious sacred learning—to accumulate fame, wealth, and power over the lives of others are like diseased fruit that remains hard and can never ripen. Such fruit possesses neither the fresh tartness of green fruit nor the sweetness of ripe fruit. Consider the vultures who soar to such astonishing altitude, yet whose sharp eyes are always scanning the ground for dead or dying creatures. Merely intellectual, egocentric scholars and philosophers engage in great flights of reasoning, pretending that the perennial wisdom is their own, but they remain fixated on selfish enjoyment and personal aggrandizement. The glorious qualities of true scholars and philosophers include the renunciation of conventional conceptuality and emotionality, selfless compassion, ecstatic love for God, and dispassionate insight into the nature of Reality.

Vidyasagar and the whole company now remain totally still, transfixed by the power of Truth tangibly flowing through the Master's words, as well as through his subtle expressions, the graceful movements of his hands, the musical tones of his voice.

Although very knowledgeable, the Pandit is a person of reticence, always reluctant to offer religious instruction, even to those who request it sincerely, much less to preach or lecture publicly about religion or philosophy. Once Vidyasagar remarked to Mahendra: "I think philosophers, even the most advanced religious thinkers, are incapable of really explaining what is in their minds." But the daily life of the Pandit is imbued with the sacred traditions and rhythms of Hinduism, permeated by the fragrance of an ancient ceremonial way. Whenever he is asked about knowledge of God, this good man invariably responds: "It is utterly impossible to know the Divine Essence; therefore we should abstain from speculation and put all our energy into living a life which, if everyone followed our example, would transform this earth into Paradise. Doing good is the only authentic religion."

Unerringly, the Paramahamsa now turns the conversation to precisely this issue—the knowledge of supreme Reality, or *brahman*—thus going to the root of Vidyasagar's thinking and indeed to the root of all possible thought.

RAMAKRISHNA O Vidyasagar, Reality is beyond *vidya*, or knowledge, no less than it is beyond *avidya*, or ignorance. Reality is beyond *maya*, beyond any appearance of duality or multiplicity. What conventional consciousness habitually regards as real—including both the complex social world and the religious world of creeds and visionary experiences—is simply the surface play of knowledge and ignorance. *Brahman* is not only beyond the drama of sexual attraction and the drive to possess, *brahman* is also beyond the most subtle philosophical knowledge and the most tender religious devotion. Reality is beyond ethical categories of right and wrong and beyond metaphysical categories of good and evil, no matter how important these considerations may be for our relative experience as responsible individuals.

Brahman is simply not touched by any considerations whatsoever. *Brahman* is the principle of illumination by which all phenomena without exception are made manifest. By the light of a lamp, one can read the sacred scripture of Hinduism that contains the noble words of Lord Krishna, or one can forge false documents by the very same light. The lamp, or principle of illumination, is not involved and is not affected either way. The great sun sheds its abundant, life-giving rays equally upon the righteous and upon the wicked. You may ask: "How, then, can we arrive at any explanation of naturally caused misery, human viciousness, pervasive unhappiness?" The answer is that these forms of suffering, which one sincerely struggles to overcome, are experienced by individual awareness but not by the very principle of awareness, which remains ever-free, ever-blissful. There is venom in the snake that may cause others to die or which may be used as a healing medicine, but this substance is neither poison nor medicine to the snake.

What Reality is can never be imagined or described in any way. Even the most exalted revelations and profound philosophies—including the Vedas, the Puranas, the Tantras, and the six traditional systems of reasoning—have become distorted and polluted by the limited mind of man. Only supreme Reality can never be grasped or even touched by the mind, and hence can never be defiled by those who are hungry for personal power. That is *brahman*—the inconceivable, the inexpressable, the indescribable. No being on any plane of being will ever be able to say what Reality is.

At this dramatic point in the conversation, Pandit Vidyasagar turns to his friends—his demeanor ecstatic, his eyes shining—and forcibly proclaims: "Now, that is a truly remarkable statement! Today I have received something completely new, completely revolutionary."

The expression of blissful freedom on the Pandit's face uncannily resembles the Paramahamsa's beaming countenance. A full transmission, or interchange of being, has miraculously accompanied Ramakrishna's words. The Great Swan responds, smiling: "Someone with direct acquaintance does not quote from even a single scripture or treatise. Mother's Wisdom is on the tip of his tongue."

4

From the God-man's Treasury of Secrets

THE PARAMAHAMSA IS seated in his pleasantly breezy room, open to the Ganges, communing with Kedar and other lovers of Truth. It is a warm, fragrant afternoon. Kedar, an important government official and an intimate companion of the Master, enjoys conversing with other companions about the depth and variety of Ramakrishna's experiences, which include living encounters and mystical union with Christ and Muhammad as well as with the great feminine figures of Hindu spirituality, such as Radha, Sita, and Kali. Kedar is convinced that these visionary experiences contain implications for future world civilization. He belongs to the contemporary liberal strand of Hindu thought, but by no means is Kedar dry, abstract, or merely intellectual. His passionate love for God is so intensely awakened, through close association with the Paramahamsa, that the slightest allusion to sacred themes brings tears to his eyes.

This entire day has been spent joyfully, listening to classical music and singing hymns of mystic union. Now that the sacred hour of twilight is approaching, Kedar is glowing with ecstasy. Suddenly the Great Swan, who has been swimming silently in the ocean of bliss for several hours, opens his eyes wide and begins to reveal rare gems from his treasury of secrets concerning the spiritual path—the path that not only leads to God but that unfolds entirely within God.

RAMAKRISHNA When one awakens into supreme Reality—which is at once Absolute Being, Absolute Consciousness, and Absolute Bliss— then all social and religious obligations disappear, not because one becomes insensitive or passive, but because all obligations are being spontaneously fulfilled by the living power of Truth, operating invisibly through the subtle body of the awakened person, who becomes the perfect Divine Instrument. Deep absorption, called *samadhi* in the yogic tradition, is then experienced ceaselessly by every cell of the body, every strand of the awareness. This total *samadhi* need not be expressed through any particular trance state. It is sheer awakeness.

Nor need this realization be expressed through words, songs, or ceremonial worship. Consider how we talked with such enthusiastic anticipation about the Muslim musician who was to perform for us today, the venerable Ustad. But the moment he arrived in this room, tuned his *sarod* and began to play a contemplative morning *raga,* our speculation and even our speech ceased entirely. Only music flowed throughout the universe. Everything else disappeared. The passionate artistry of the Ustad was beyond our expectation and imagination. Consider the honeybee, which at first buzzes loudly while circling a flower, but finally settles in silence deep within the core of the fragrant blossom. This is the portal to *samadhi.*

Yet the authentic practitioner never renounces prematurely the precious disciplines of his tradition—daily prayers, ceremonial worship, study and chanting of scriptures, silent meditation, and selfless service to fulfill the physical and spiritual needs of conscious beings. The genuine aspirant remains in a constant state of inward and outward pilgrimage until actually reaching the one goal of true pilgrims— complete God-consciousness, full awakening as Truth. After plunging irrevocably into that ocean of Being, Consciousness, and Bliss—that shoreless sea of *satchidananda*—the functions of clear philosophical reasoning and uncompromising spiritual discrimination do not disappear entirely. They become delight and compassion rather than doctrine or discipline. The honeybee sometimes hums faintly, even as it sits fully absorbed at the center of the lotus. Certain *paramahamsas* or *mahasiddhas,* beings who are completely free, still retain their external religious practices. Why? After successfully digging a well, some persons may throw away their spades and baskets, while others carefully keep these implements for the use of their neighbors. Some persons enjoy mangoes secretly, removing all traces of their pleasure by wiping their mouths with a damp towel, while others enjoy mangoes only when sharing them.

Ecstatic love for God—heart and mind melted by passionate longing for Truth—is the one essential factor in the process of awakening.

Divine Presence, however one may understand and experience it, exists in and through all conscious beings. And conscious beings exist solely in and through it. Who, then, deserves to be called a true lover? The one whose awareness dwells entirely upon God, awakens entirely within God. But such awakening is not possible so long as the mind is constantly distracted from Truth by remaining habitually egocentric, by instinctively seeking personal gratification. Divine Grace, the healing and illuminating energy that rains down ceaselessly upon the human mind, heart, and soul, cannot be absorbed or assimilated by the high, rocky hill of personal interest and personal importance. This precious, life-giving water runs off the high ground of ego, without ever penetrating its hard, barren soil. God is far, far away from the mind obsessed with conventionality. It is very difficult to gather the dispersed mind when it becomes identified with habitual egocentric structures.

Obsessive self-awareness, whether collective or individual, is a mere machine, an automatic function. God is the only living presence within us, our only true bliss and freedom. Divine Nature, which alone is our ultimate being, has nothing to do with narrow self-interest or limited self-consciousness. Divine Nature can be realized and fully actualized in daily life by sincerely following any number of revealed paths. All the integral transmissions of sacred wisdom and contemplative practice that survive the test of time are true—true in the sense that they function authentically and bear the sweet fruit of sanctity.

The goal is to reach the flat roof of the house, which affords an unobstructed view of the entire countryside. You can reach this highest point by climbing stone stairs, wooden steps, bamboo slats, or rope ladders. You can even scale a nearby tree and somehow clamber onto the roof along a large limb. Just get there! Then you will see clearly that the unimaginable variety of prayerful or meditative methods all lead to the same goal, to the same panoramic vision, to the same timeless awareness.

One certainly perceives errors of understanding and superstitious behavior in the various religious traditions as they are imperfectly practiced. So what? Every human approach inevitably contains error or partial understanding. Such distortions are, of course, most difficult to notice in your own approach, because each person stubbornly assumes that his own clock tells the correct time. There is no way to purge your personal, social, or religious context from every error, but if you persevere in sheer yearning for God, sheer love for Truth, these unavoidable limitations will gradually be dissolved. It will be sufficient simply to love for love's sake. Merged in motiveless love, one experiences every moment the tremendous natural attraction of Divine Presence. This Presence is the inner guidance that we feel flowing through us as conscience, intellect, intuition, sense perception, and longing. Divine Presence alone generates the yearning of our heart, the seeking of our mind, the ease of our body, the illumination of our soul. God sees everything because God constitutes everything, and therefore everything seeks God.

A tender-hearted father is intimate with all his children. The mature ones can greet him respectfully by his given name; others can at least address him distinctly as *Baba,* while the very youngest ones can only call out *Ba, Ba, Ba.* Is the father closer to the children who know his name and pronounce it correctly? Can he become angry or disappointed with the infants who cannot articulate at all and the young ones whose understanding is partial? Absolutely not! The children are loved equally by the father. This is even more true concerning Divine Love, which is not limited by any personality, however kind or open. All human beings who seek limitless love are addressing and approaching precisely the same Divine Reality. Each person proceeds on a different plane of knowledge or articulation, yet the intimacy of the divine embrace remains the same. There is no hierarchy among the children of God.

No one is a stranger to us in the human family or among living creatures. Why? Because it is God alone who dwells within all conscious beings. God recognizes God. God belongs to God. God alone enjoys when anyone enjoys, and God alone suffers when anyone suffers. God is all-embracing Oneness—although the names, facets, and appearances of this Oneness are beyond numbering.

Who are you? Who am I? It is the Great Mother who has become all this. Only so long as you fail to recognize Her Reality can you assert "I act" or "I am." Absolutely nothing exists within you except Her Power, Her Delight. She even manifests as the limited ego and its smallest desire.

The Master gazes at us, amused by our amazement, and laughs like a child.

RAMAKRISHNA The conventional mind is in a dangerous state of intoxication, constantly claiming: "It is I who own and control everything. All this—house, family, land—is mine." A drunken person must be given rice water as an antidote. For the aspirant, this sobering drink is companionship with a realized sage.

The Taste of Sugar

Boating on the Ganges with Keshab Sen

Today is an auspicious occasion on the sacred calendar for celebrating the Great Mother of the Universe. Keshab Sen, an eloquent religious leader who is the pride of Calcutta, has arranged a festive outing for his beloved Master, Ramakrishna, on the holy expanse of the Ganges. The elegant steam launch carrying Keshab, his devoted students, and socially important admirers arrives at Dakshineswar around four in the afternoon, casting anchor in the river beside the nine brilliant white domes of the Kali Temple. The central dome rises one hundred feet above green jungle and cultivated flower gardens that contain sweet-scented, milk-white *gulchi* trees, five-faced hibiscus, pendant hibiscus that resemble earrings of the Goddess, china rose, double-petaled jasmine, white and red oleander, and intoxicatingly fragrant gardenia.

As the small bark bearing the Great Swan and a few intimate companions comes alongside, the Calcutta passengers rush to the railing to catch a glimpse of the radiant upturned face of the sage, who has become absorbed in God-consciousness. Lost to the world, the man of God is brought aboard with difficulty. Finally regaining some relative awareness, Ramakrishna laughs and strikes his open palm forcibly on top of his head, again and again, crying out to the universal energy of consciousness: "Down, down, O Kundalini! Mother, please come down from way up there." Following this bizarre but humorous gesture, the focus of the Master's awareness does indeed descend from the thousand-petaled lotus at the crown of the subtle body into the twelve-petaled lotus center at the heart, which Ramakrishna calls "God's living room." At this fourth plane of awareness, he becomes cognizant of multiplicity again, although all phenomena still remain transparent to Divine Light. Here he can meet with lovers of God and knowers of Truth. These inspiring and convivial reunions, Ramakrishna often reminds us, are the only possible pastime for a person consciously immersed in God.

Still inebriated with holy ecstasy, the Paramahamsa reels as he walks to the cabin of the boat, leaning lightly for support and direction upon the shoulder of a trusted companion. He becomes so sensitive in these states of complete spiritual openness—during which all protective barriers drop between his physical body and his divinely infused subtle body—that he is unable to touch any person whose mind, heart, and motivation are not pure. This inability does not arise from any sense of separateness, aloofness, or superiority. Our Master's entire body simply experiences a stinging, burning sensation if he is touched by anyone of degenerate character during these moments of wide-open ecstasy. Once, when an outwardly respectable man, who secretly supplemented his income by forging false accounts, touched his feet in a gesture of apparent devotion, Ramakrishna cried out with pain.

As the vibrant figure of the God-man moves across the deck, the impressive Keshab Sen and other prominent gentlemen and ladies of Calcutta bow reverently before him. The Paramahamsa takes no notice whatsoever. Although he is now at least partially aware of the world of space, time, substantiality, individuality, and causality, he perceives it as none other than God. The river Ganges, the temples, the blue sky, the precious human beings—nothing but God. His shirt is unbuttoned, because he cannot tie knots, button clothes, bolt doors, close boxes, tuck the mosquito net under the mattress, or even bind his own cloth firmly about his waist. So released is the Paramahamsa that he can confine or manipulate nothing.

He now enters the large, wood-paneled cabin and is seated, Western style, on a chair. The major liberal religious leaders of Calcutta are seated on chairs to either side of him. His body, although strong, appears delicately constructed. Humility shines from his face. Beside him is a quaint basket of woven leaves containing puffed rice and sweets, which he requested his attendant to bring as a small gift for Keshab. The other guests sit comfortably on the floor, on the benches circling the room, or stand on the deck outside the cabin, looking in through open windows. The level of attention and expectation is intense, for the followers of Keshab Sen are well informed about the mysterious power that manifests through this simple, unlettered brahmin from the remote village of Kamarpukur.

The Paramahamsa responds to this attention by slipping again into total absorption. His consciousness and Universal Consciousness become one, leaving only a transparent bodily form seated in the chair like an empty picture frame. This can be disconcerting or even shocking to anyone who has never met our Master before. These modern seekers gaze with astonishment at the ancient sage, manifestation of the primeval roots of Indian civilization, who now gradually returns into relative awareness, blinks once or twice, looks around him, and cries plaintively to his Divine Mother: *"Ma, Ma, Ma!* Why have you brought me to this place? These persons are enslaved by rational and social forms. They are not experiencing even a drop of Your blissful freedom, Your ecstasy, O Goddess Kali. How can I liberate them if they continue to bind themselves, like caterpillars spinning their own cocoons?"

One of the gentlemen attempts to open a conversation by mentioning that a very advanced yogic practitioner, known to everyone in Calcutta, a certain Pavhari Baba, keeps a photograph of Ramakrishna in his place of permanent retreat. The Paramahamsa laughs aloud, points to his own body, and, stammering slightly, exclaims: "It is only a pillowcase! Only a pillowcase!" His holy laughter gradually spreads through the cabin, releasing nervous tension and mysteriously opening the floodgates of Divine Wisdom within Ramakrishna Paramahamsa. When he enters this mood of spiritual transmission, teachings can extend for hours on end.

RAMAKRISHNA Please remember. Although our conventional bodies are mere containers, the lotus heart of the lover is God's living room. A powerful sovereign may mercifully visit various regions of his vast kingdom at one time or another, but he remains directly accessible to his family and close advisors in the innermost chamber of the royal palace. This is the heart of humankind. God dwells and flows as consciousness in and through all conscious beings, no doubt, but Divine Reality manifests most vividly in the hearts of those who love only for the sake of pure love. O friends, I beg you to come. Come to the living room of God!

The voice of the Paramahamsa is so tender, so motherly, as he calls humanity to its own highest goal, that tears run down the cheeks or spring forth within the heart of everyone present. Ramakrishna can miraculously bring tears to the eyes of those who have never before wept for God. As a sailboat tacks into the wind, the Master now shifts moods.

RAMAKRISHNA The One Reality—called *atman* or *brahman* by Vedantic knowers of Truth—is called *purusha* by yogic practitioners, who experience conscious states of limitless, formless radiance. Precisely this Reality is encountered by devotional practitioners as *bhagavan*, the glorious Lord of Love. The situation is like the very same person being known as "priest" when dressed in ceremonial robes, performing elaborate rituals in the temple, and as "cook" when preparing a humble meal in the kitchen. One should never become fixated upon these or any other roles.

For instance, the *jñani*, the adept of transcendent knowledge, can become confined in the process of philosophical reasoning and spiritual discrimination, staunchly proclaiming *neti, neti*—"Reality is neither this nor that"—and stubbornly rejecting the vast universe and its countless living beings as illusory. This approach does indeed steady the mind, which no longer encounters anything finite to hold on to and therefore gradually disappears in the blaze of the Only Reality. Such is the authentic function of the radical Vedanta, which teaches: "*Brahman* alone is real and all else is illusory." According to this venerable approach, the countless names and forms that now appear so vividly and tangibly before us are like vivid and tangible experiences in a dream. One eventually wakens from a dream. *Brahman*, the ground of name and form, is not a distinct existence that admits of any description whatsoever. Much less is Reality some Divine Personhood, tenderly responsive to its own created universe.

But ecstatic lovers do not get caught within the perspective of knowledge, no matter how universal or how exalted it may be. Nor are they engaged in blindly following one-sided devotional scriptures. These liberated lovers accept all possible states of consciousness as transparent manifestations of the astonishing power and radiance of the Lord of Love. They accept the entire universe, in its magnificent and confusing detail, as sheer Divine Manifestation—sky, stars, moon, sun, snow mountains, vast ocean, the intricate human being, and all the other marvelous forms of life.

The mature ones among these ecstatic lovers know for certain that the Divine Mother has displayed Her own Heart as this entire living, conscious creation and as the cosmic principles and laws by which it manifests coherently. These souls fall in love with immanence, not with transcendence. The lover of God wants to taste the ineffable sweetness of sugar, not to become a transparent crystal of sugar.

The Paramahamsa bursts into laughter at the mere thought of strict Vedantic practitioners becoming immobile crystals, and the entire gathering responds to his prolonged laughter with wholehearted mirth. A joyous uproar now arises from the center of the Ganges, attracting surprised attention from various boatmen plying the sacred waters. It is a relaxed laughter of acceptance, a wisdom-laughter that brings down every philosophical, religious, and cultural barrier. Everyone present is receiving subtle healing and illumination from this miraculous, spontaneously manifesting laughter—the words of the Paramahamsa acting as circuits through which energy is flowing. Barriers between personalities are the last to fall. Subtle personal rivalries among those present are being replaced by a comradeship and harmony rooted in Divine Reality—a delicious experience that many here have never known before. This is indeed the taste of sugar—Divine Love, manifesting as the universe, blissfully sensing and knowing itself through itself. Everyone on board this mystically transformed vessel looks at each other and recognizes Truth.

The Paramahamsa, who has been speaking for several hours, is vigorously sprinkling Ganges water over the elaborate refreshments now being served. A prominent Calcutta lawyer asks the sage if he would like to step out on deck and peer through a telescope mounted there. With courteous and loving tones, Ramakrishna replies: "My mind is ceaselessly gazing into God. How can I remove my attention from the blissful Mother of the Universe and confine it within a telescope? Let Mother do whatever She wills with you. Give Her your power of attorney."

6

One Hemp-Smoker
Recognizes Another

Today is Saturday, auspicious to the Goddess. The most prominent liberal religious society in Calcutta, the Brahmo Samaj, is
holding its major yearly festival—not to celebrate the feast day of any
particular Hindu Divinity or Divine Incarnation but to express its own
rational, universal, unitarian attitude. This is a rather courageous and
fresh approach to spirituality in an ancient land of intractible traditions
that exist in constant subtle tension with one another. The Paramahamsa's
embracing openness does not exclude the Brahmo Samaj, however modern
and composite its views may be. And the Master loves Shivanath, one of
the leaders of this movement, with a *paramahamsa's* instinctive love for
freedom, intensity, and generosity of spirit, wherever it may manifest.
This great current of love flowing from Ramakrishna—who is a boundless
ocean of love, without finite motivation or limiting rationality—is deeply
reciprocated by Shivanath, who is now eagerly awaiting the arrival of the
God-intoxicated sage.

This festive gathering of the modern knowers of Reality, as Ramakrishna playfully calls them, has been convened at the garden house of a
wealthy Brahmo devotee, located on the Ganges about three miles north
of Calcutta, the major metropolis of Asia, where Western and Eastern
cultures are fruitfully mingling. This historic confluence of the ancient
and the modern is precisely where Ramakrishna chooses to manifest.

We are delighted to see the carriage bearing the God-man arrive around
sunset, moving slowly through golden light among flowering trees and
playing fountains. This scene unveils a sudden glimpse of Paradise or Pure
Land. Wherever the Great Swan happens to touch this world, it ceases to

appear as the heavy realm of reason and convention, anxiety and suffering. As Ramakrishna steps lightly from the carriage and approaches, the august assembly rises respectfully to welcome its honored visitor. The sage is immersed in a timeless experience which has no apparent relationship with the timeliness of the Brahmo Samaj, its commitment to religious and social reform. Yet the fascination generated by this timeless man, this transparent presence, sweeps through these brilliant cultural leaders and social pioneers, so conscious of their important place in history near the turn of the European nineteenth century. Conversation stops. All eyes are focused on the serene, smiling face which now rises over the Brahmo festival like a full moon.

Ramakrishna—somewhat stout, with an astonishingly golden complexion—moves through the ranks of gentlemen and ladies like a flame through dry grass. Hearts are being ignited, spirits elevated. He seeks out his beloved Shivanath and cries ecstatically, in a high tenor voice: "Shivanath! Shivanath! At last we are together again. I cannot bear separation from you, because you are truly a lover of God. Your companionship is ineffably sweet. The very sight of your luminous face and tender eyes sends a thrill through my entire body." After the two God-drunken lovers greet with reverent salute—palms together, both heads bowed low—our Master loudly exclaims, to the consternation of conservatives and to the delight of the rest of us: "You see, my dearest Shivanath, one hemp-smoker is always very exuberant when encountering a fellow hemp-smoker. They recognize in each other instantly the same blissful, carefree, intoxicated state of mind. They embrace each other and begin to dance with joy." Laughter spreads in concentric waves, beginning with the Paramahamsa. Even the most prim and proper among those present cannot resist joining. One minute after the arrival of the sage, this rather polite gathering is liberated into mirth and merriment.

These modern seekers now sit eagerly around the ageless Master beneath a large tree in the garden, as though they were renunciates, retired to the forest life, gathered around a sage from the ancient wisdom tradition of India. Teachings begin to flow from the faintly smiling, bearded lips.

RAMAKRISHNA Calcutta people who visit the Temple of Mother Kali at Dakshineswar these days act more like sightseers than pilgrims. When these persons enter the room where the companions of Divine Love are conversing, I notice instantly that they lack the burning attraction for God which alone opens the spiritual way. Gently, I suggest to them: "Please go and enjoy the architecture of the Temple."

The playfulness in the voice and bearing of the Great Swan, as he theatrically makes this request, again causes laughter to spring forth like clear, refreshing water in the somewhat arid minds of those assembled.

RAMAKRISHNA I have observed that genuine seekers of God, on fire with love for God, are often accompanied in their pilgrimage by associates who are lukewarm or even indifferent to the sacred quest. These conventional friends have become accustomed to unrefined thoughts and perceptions, and have therefore lost all taste for spiritual delicacies. They become noticeably restless, progressively distracted as our blissful conversations about Divine Reality unfold, hour after hour. It becomes physically impossible for them to continue sitting with the ecstatic lovers. They begin shifting and whispering, and finally, as if overcome by an allergic reaction, they leap to their feet and abruptly leave the room, with the remark: "We will wait for you in the boat. Please hurry!"

These minutely accurate observations charm everyone. The entire assembly is breathing, laughing, and listening as one single conscious being. Our Master now draws forth the uncompromising sword of wisdom— without hurting anyone, without allowing anyone even to notice the surgical skillfulness of its liberating strokes. His words bear the subtle energy of spiritual renewal.

RAMAKRISHNA Persons who are bound by conventional, egocentric perspectives will never be able to listen to true teaching, which always calls one to renounce convention of every kind and to consecrate each breath and every uniquely precious moment of experience to Divine Reality alone. Lord Chaitanya—the Krishna-dancer of Bengal, Divine Love incarnate, whose sanctifying waves of devotion still sweep across this land after three hundred years—used skillful means to attract persons hopelessly enmeshed in the habit of selfish desire. He would promise such individuals: "If you repeat the beautiful Divine Names with even a modicum of intensity, you will receive a bowl of rich fish soup and the delightful embrace of a pure young woman." Beguiled by this surprising promise from the lips of a holy sage, conventional persons were transformed into ecstatic lovers by chanting *Radha-*

Krishna, Radha-Krishna, which is like drinking inebriating nectar. These awakening souls would then realize that the *fish soup* was the copious stream of tears they shed at the sound of the Holy Names. The *delightful embrace* was the pure touch of the sacred earth, as they fell upon their knees and then rolled on the ground in the delirious rapture of Divine Love. They felt not cheated but magnificently rewarded.

The inspired Chaitanya and the companions in his Divine Play would go to any length to encourage people to sing with their entire being the powerful names of the supreme Lover, Radha, and the supreme Beloved, Krishna. This is the *mahamantra,* the master key to mystic union. The healing and illuminating energy of the glorious Divine Names will eventually open every conscious being in creation to the ineffable experience of infinite love. As Chaitanya used to teach in his gentle, heart-melting way, each and every revealed Name of the One Reality possesses irresistably sanctifying power. Even if the energy of the Divine Name does not produce immediate results, its repetition will eventually be fruitful—like a seed fallen on the roof of a deserted house which crumbles over decades, finally enabling the germinated seed to take root. The conventional world and the conventional self are this disintegrating old structure.

Devotion to God, like every tendency of heart and mind, can be expressed through one of three modes: *sattva,* or tranquillity; *rajas,* or ambition; *tamas,* or resistance. These are three strands of energy that extend throughout manifest Being, intertwining in subtle patterns. Consider three persons, the first dominantly rooted in *sattva,* the second in *rajas,* the third in *tamas.*

Even a person who accepts and serves the limited assumptions of society becomes purified if he is endowed with a preponderance of *sattva.* He permits the family residence to become somewhat dilapidated and does not particularly care. There are pigeon droppings around the courtyard shrine where he offers daily worship. The stone steps to the altar become gradually covered with moss. He pays no special attention to external appearances, such as furnishings or personal attire. He becomes more and more quiet and humble in his movements, more and more kind and gentle in his dealings with everyone. Violence of any description disappears from his being.

The person who is predominantly endowed with the energy of *rajas,* by contrast, always carries a silver watch with a golden chain and wears two or three rings, the larger the better. The furnishings of his home are expensive and kept shiny by constant polishing. The walls are crowded with large portraits of the Queen, the Prince of Wales, and other prominent people in the modern world. His house is regularly whitewashed, whether it needs it or not. His large closets are filled with elaborate costumes. The servants are required to wear matching uniforms.

The situation of the individual who is drawn down entirely into *tamas* is bleak. He is addicted to external intoxicants and to the expression of impatience and anger, even concerning the smallest details of his life. He never entertains a single thought or feels a single emotion that does not relate directly, and often exclusively, to his own narrow self-interest.

How is *bhakti,* the impulse to love God, expressed through the blessed mode of *sattva?* The sattvic lover meditates on the beautiful Lord of Love in solitude and in secret, without any dramatic outer display of piety. Such a pure soul may complete his prayers surrounded by the mosquito netting on his bed—late at night or very early in the morning—rather than going to the shrine to make formal prostrations and outward offerings. Even close family members assume that he is sound asleep all night or is getting up late because he did not sleep well. His care for the continued existence of his own physical form is just strong enough to appease hunger, and that only with the plainest food which causes the least trouble to obtain and prepare. There are no elaborate arrangements about any aspect of his life. Such a sattvic lover, who belongs only to God, is immune from feverish desire for money, power, or respect, and therefore he never needs to flatter or to act in a servile manner toward anyone. Least of all does the sattvic lover seek any results or rewards from Divine Reality.

The aspirant whose *bhakti* is touched by the flames of *rajas* places a brightly colored mark on his forehead every morning, wishing to display to the whole world his state of consecration. He wears his rosary of holy *rudraksha* beads outside his robe as a kind of necklace, even linking the beads with silver chain, perhaps interspersing a few golden beads among these rough seeds sacred to the all-renouncing Lord Shiva. He points out the impeccable white marble floor in his shrine room to all those who visit his house. He gives in charity to attain honor among men and a high rank in Paradise. When this person strides proudly to his place of worship—preferably at the most popular temple—he wears an expensive silk meditation shawl.

The Paramahamsa is engaging in these descriptions with such humorous lightness that no one feels the slightest sting from his words, although everyone can now recognize his or her own limited tendencies playfully portrayed. Our healing laughter is directed at ourselves and at the foolishness that can masquerade as religion.

RAMAKRISHNA Finally, a person whose *bhakti* is profoundly tainted with *tamas* may actually possess an intense faith in God, but he is narrow-minded, fanatical, and even vicious toward members of other religious communities. He seeks to extort favors or salvation from God and attempts to impose religious conformity upon others, including his own family, with the same ferocity displayed by a highwayman— binding, beating, and even murdering his innocent victims.

Passing quickly from this indictment of tamasic religion, the Paramahamsa enters a delicate state of ecstasy. His tear-filled eyes are turned upward. Pure love—beyond all influence of *tamas, rajas,* or even *sattva*— streams from his very pores. We are mysteriously lifted into his spiritual mood. Personal motivations dissolve. As dusk descends, the Master now sings, with deep rapture, a mystic hymn to the Goddess of Wisdom, plunging the entire gathering into communion with Her infinite Love, Her infinite Freedom.

> O Kali, why should we make
> the arduous journey
> to distant sites of pilgrimage?
> Simply permit this child, O Mother,
> to breath Your Name with every breath
> as though each breath were the last.
> What need will then exist
> for external rites
> or study of scriptures?
>
> Blissfully repeating KALI KALI KALI
> at dawn, noon, sunset, and midnight
> will be entirely sufficient.
> The conventional forms of religion
> may chase after this ecstatic lover,
> but they will never apprehend him.
> Conventional giving in charity

and conventional ascetic vows
no longer appeal to my heart,
since the delicate Lotus Feet
of Your Presence, O Mother,
have become my only study,
only prayer, only delight.

The Great Swan is now visibly on fire with Divine Love. Even in the dim twilight, he is shining like a golden morning sun, balanced perpetually on the horizon of finite existence. As night falls, he is still singing hymns from the vast treasury of his many initiations. The gathering is electrified. Habitual conventionality and egocentricity have been entirely stripped away.

7

The Sage Opens a Gap
in the Net of Convention

THE PARAMAHAMSA IS lying on his simple bed, enjoying an afternoon rest. His lithe limbs are so relaxed they seem hardly animated, more like hollow bamboos, yet such intense energy is flowing from his body that he also barely seems to be sleeping. Various companions are seated in the fresh, breezy room, communicating in whispers or lost in contemplation. There is a sense of family intimacy. We sit cross-legged on the floor, facing west, gazing at the peaceful waters of the Ganges glinting in the afternoon sunlight through the open door. Suddenly, the Paramahamsa arises from his ecstatic repose—exclaiming, "Did I sleep?"—and sits on his bed facing east. His movement is easy and natural, without the slightest strain or effort. The sage's eyes are clear and shining. He is obviously far beyond the states we experience as sleeping and waking.

As we shift our attention swiftly to his mysterious form, we briefly perceive it as an open door into infinite consciousness. Ramakrishna often speaks of Divine Reality as a boundless golden meadow, blocked from view by the apparent wall of space and time, substantiality and separation. The awakened person, he explains, is an opening in that wall, through which a certain segment of the dimensionless expanse of God can actually be perceived. The God-man, or *avatara,* is like a vast opening in that wall, through which millions of sincere human beings can pass without need of the superhuman efforts at contemplation exerted by the saints.

As he speaks, our Master's voice expresses the same *paramahamsa* quality as his bodily movements—freedom, ease, cheerfulness, naturalness. The subject of conversation, however, is a very heavy one: the recent death of a beloved young friend.

RAMAKRISHNA I felt extremely unhappy when I heard of his passing away from the surface of existence, for I will never encounter him again in precisely the same charming form. My heart was actually wrung like a wet towel, and as a result, tears streamed from my eyes for an entire hour. This young man was truly unusual. He chose to live with poor relatives in a distant village so he could enjoy solitude, wandering through wild meadows and hills. He practiced meditation beside streams in forest glades like the ancient sages. Then he decided to take up social responsibility and moved to Calcutta to study. He often visited this room, where he would relate visions of Divine Forms experienced during his solitary practice. He used to remark that it was difficult if not impossible for him to take any pleasure in the ambitious life of the city. Evidently, this was the final incarnation in his long process of evolution. His blessed soul is now free to manifest or not—whatever its ideal may be for communing with Divine Reality and expressing Divine Love. Most of his contemplative exercises, and certainly his disciplines of family life and social responsibility, were fulfilled in previous incarnations. The last few visions and insights came to him spontaneously during this lifetime, and then he was led to Dakshineswar Garden for the experience of culmination.

Consider the case of a tantric practitioner who has the good fortune to discover a fresh dead body in an uninhabited jungle. He begins to prepare for the special worship of the Wisdom Goddess in which the worshipper, aspiring to total liberation, uses a human corpse as his sacred meditation seat. Just as the advanced practitioner finishes the complicated external and internal preparations for this esoteric ceremony, he is killed by a hunting tigress and dragged away to feed her hungry cubs. Another man happens to be wandering through that remote wilderness. He holds no high tantric initiations but is pondering most profoundly the true nature of the human being and the universe. He is a pure-minded, pure-hearted seeker. Hearing the life-and-death struggle, he comes there and discovers the altar, the array of offerings, and the macabre meditation seat. He also glimpses the wild beast retreating with the limp form of the adept in her jaws. Sitting down at once on the sacred *asana,* he prays intensely to realize Truth. The blissful Goddess appears in Her full splendor before his inner eye, granting him the complete realization for which he yearns. He now knows clearly that Mother Reality alone exists and that the world is simply Her Theater of Wisdom, where souls are educated and refined. The Goddess of Transcendent Insight transmits this teaching directly to his heart and mind from Her own captivating lips, which resemble fragrant red blossoms. This divine communication is a stream of energy, not human words arranged in conventional phrases. The seeker is immediately transformed into an illumined sage.

Astonished, he asks the Wisdom Goddess, Who is now his intimate companion: "Why has Your transforming Grace not descended upon the knowledgeable person who made these arrangements for worship? Why have You blessed instead someone of no esoteric training, who has made no disciplined efforts to know Reality?" The blissful Mother fills the universe with Her ecstatic laughter, responding: "My dear child, with your gnostic eye now fully open, gaze upon your previous incarnations. The most austere, advanced disciplines have already been performed by you and have opened the way for this auspicious consummation."

"But your young friend committed suicide," a companion cries out to the Master in genuine dismay. The eternally awakened sage, who was born with full illumination, slowly turns his compassionate glance upon the one who has voiced the painful question that bursts forth from all our hearts. His tender smile miraculously heals our pain even before he speaks.

RAMAKRISHNA Undoubtedly, an ego-driven act of suicide brings disastrous consequences for the after-death experience of the soul if there is no immediate intercession for this soul by a realized saint or at least by a sincere lover of God. Such a desperate act can certainly initiate a degenerative cycle of reincarnations. But divesting oneself of the physical body after the full gnostic vision of Truth—simply dropping the body, whether by yogic or other means—cannot properly be called suicide. Perhaps the tantric practitioner who died violently in the jungle received the liberating vision of Goddess Kali at the moment of death through the auspicious form of the mother tiger. There is spiritual confidence and even sheer delight when giving up one's limited physical form after realization has dawned. One should only mourn the death of immature or faithless persons who have no one to pray for them.

Depending upon the unique predilection of each soul, some sages choose to cast away the physical form, just like spitting out mucus, soon after they have attained perfect knowledge of Reality. After molten gold has been poured into the clay form and has sufficiently cooled, this earthenware mold can be broken away, although some craftsmen carefully disengage the clay form to be used as a model for their apprentices. Some awakened sages preserve their physical bodies with great care in order to serve humankind—offering instruction, initiation, inspiration. Most of my intimate companions will take this second approach, and will incarnate with me whenever I return into embodiment in order to serve living beings. But gold remains gold, nevertheless.

Several years ago, another of these rare young persons who complete their evolution early in life came to visit this place to attain final perfection. He received some powerful vision whenever he gazed at the form you see now seated before you. His ecstasy and absorption were so intense that my nephew, Hriday, had to support him with both arms in order to protect the boy from falling to the floor or colliding with the walls. This drama manifested every time the highly evolved youth visited Dakshineswar. One morning, he arrived totally calm and contained, placed his forehead upon these feet, and took leave in the most dignified manner, proclaiming tenderly: "Blessed Paramahamsa, I will not be able to meet you anymore on this earthly plane. I bid you most loving and grateful farewell." A few days later, I heard that he had consciously and voluntarily given up his body during meditation.

You see, beloved friends, there are four possible modes of experience. Some persons are expressing the illusion of being bound or limited by ignorance or finitude. Others express, during every moment and with every movement, the longing to be liberated from all possible limits. Then there are the totally transformed human beings who have become liberated while still living upon this earth. Finally, there is the sublimely mysterious manifestation of those who are ever-free, ever-perfect. They are simply rays of light from the Source of Light, rather than souls in various stages of spiritual evolution—whether bound, aspiring, or liberated. These are the four basic roles in the Theater of Wisdom. The lines are composed by the Wisdom Mother. The characters and scenes are simply Her Reality.

O intimate companions, this world is a vast fishing net. Souls are brightly colored fish. Divine Reality, whose dream power projects the entire drama, is the sublime fisherman. Certain powerful oceangoing fish, when they become tangled in this inevitable net of *maya,* try to tear its transparent strands. These are the souls striving after liberation. But the net is Mother's Reality, which can never be torn. Only a few such fish who long to return to the open ocean actually escape, heroically leaping over the net and landing with a great splash. The Divine Fisherman exclaims: "Ah, there goes a big one." Only a few saints of love or gnostic sages attain such liberation in any generation within any culture. Other sincere seekers must rely upon various Divine Manifestations—saints, prophets, emanations, *avataras*—to open a gap in the net right before their eyes. This occurs only through Mother's ineluctible Permission.

Certain rare beings of pure consciousness live so deep in the ocean of Reality that they simply never encounter the net, which is cast in shallower waters. These are the ever-perfect souls, such as the ancient Narada, the adept of pure love who first brought humankind the Path of Love. These ever-free beings never encounter the tangled meshes of the conventional, egocentric world, because, from birth, they clearly perceive that God alone exists.

The majority of fish are easily trapped in the shallow waters of family and society by the net of cosmic dream projection. They are not even conscious of the fact that they are bound. They grasp the net in their mouths and bury themselves comfortably in weeds and mud, feeling perfectly secure until the Divine Fisherman, at the destined moment of their death, suddenly pulls them in, rudely awakening them from complacency and delusion. These secular persons who reject sacred teachings, as well as superficially religious persons who accept such teachings but fail to act upon them profoundly, always imagine themselves to be quite safe. They may even feel comfortable in their limited world—plunging deeper and deeper into the weeds and mud of self-justification, ambition, and autostimulation, mistaking states of passivity or degradation for states of enjoyment or even enlightenment.

Other fish, not so easily domesticated, are constantly swimming, searching for a gap in the net. They regard the habitual, egocentric network of the world as dangerous, as life-threatening. They cannot naively enjoy bondage, even if it seems comfortable or justifiable, but yearn instead for the bliss of authentic freedom. Some of these beings actually make the brilliant leap of liberation. Such rare persons, who actually attain full realization during earthly life, can give up their physical embodiment at any time, as in the case of the two young men whom we have been discussing.

Many men and women, who consider themselves intellectually sophisticated or even religiously devout, are not aware of being entangled in this magical net. Such persons are undergoing countless forms of obvious or subtle suffering during their daily lives and are threatened by even more severe spiritual dangers, yet they simply fail to open their eyes. They refuse to awaken from the meshes of self-orientation and self-obsession. They even grasp the sharp strands of the net in their mouths.

This is the behavior of the camel. It becomes attached to the peculiar taste of thorny bushes, although it bleeds profusely while eating them. Similarly, the egocentric person, eyes stubbornly closed to the dimension of transcendence, imposes unnecessary sorrow and affliction upon himself and upon other conscious beings as well. Some particularly intense moment of suffering may cause this person to doubt the value of his limited mode of existence, but he forgets his physical agony or emotional anguish after a few hours or a few days, and begins to eat thorny bushes again.

Listening to these uncompromising words of the Paramahamsa, delivered with disarming humility and grace, we experience the distinct sense of awakening from a dream. There is a spiritual energy flowing through these parables which makes them more powerful than reasoned discourse or religious instruction. Our well-meaning yet conventional sense of shock and moral outrage at an act of apparent suicide has been transformed. We have been taken backstage in the Theater of Wisdom. We have been awakened to the wider drama of spiritual life and spiritual death by this wonderful Paramahamsa, this mother-tiger emanation of Goddess Kali.

Beyond the western door stretches the holy expanse of the Ganges, glistening brilliantly in the late afternoon sun. Our souls leap courageously toward the lip of the magical net, but encounter no obstruction. Ramakrishna has opened a vast gap. We are swimming freely into boundless light.

8

The Bliss of Ramakrishna's Birthday

TODAY IS THE birthday of Ramakrishna Paramahamsa. The small circle of those who love him above all and who perceive his beautiful human form as sheer Divine Manifestation are gathering to celebrate. From early morning, the lovers begin to stream into the sanctuary of his room, some pausing along the way to worship at various sacred sites and shrines or to enjoy the classical Indian melodies streaming from the southern music pavilion.

It is full springtime. The chamber of our Master, open in all directions, is inundated with the fragrance of the green earth. This renewal of nature leads the devotees to consider the radical renewal of humanity by the perfectly pure body, senses, mind, heart, soul, and spirit of the Paramahamsa. Ramakrishna always makes it clear that the contemplative practices of every variety in which he engaged during the vertiginous sixteen years of his *sadhana* were undertaken solely in order to generate evolutionary energy for his intimate companions throughout time and for all conscious beings. As he often remarks: "I have kindled the fire. Now please come enjoy its warmth." In this sanctifying flame called Ramakrishna Paramahamsa, all limits falsely imposed by the narrow ego and conventional society have been consumed. His transparency and openness of spirit belong to all who are linked with him through outer or inner initiation and who will eventually merge with him and awaken as pure love. Today, therefore, is our own birthday as well.

Mahendranath Gupta, one of the more conservative and reserved of the companions, arrives at midmorning, having walked barefoot from Calcutta bearing fruits for offering. He places his forehead at the Paramahamsa's feet in the traditional gesture of loving respect and receptivity offered by the disciple to the guru. Timeless silence pervades the room as a field of Divine Light subtly engulfs the two figures.

Our Master never regards anyone as his disciple but sees all as messengers or manifestations of his Divine Beloved. *"Akhanda satchidananda—* indivisible Being, Consciousness, and Bliss—is the one and only guru," the Great Swan reminds his friends constantly. If anyone asks him for blessing, healing, initiation, or even just words of wisdom, Ramakrishna immediately directs the seeker to commune with the mysterious Presence manifest in the Kali Temple, proclaiming fervently: "My blissful Mother knows everything. I know absolutely nothing. I am simply Her child." He often cries out in genuine pain and distress: "These conventional words you apply to me—master, spiritual father, guide, guru—are like sharp thorns. Please desist, I beg you."

As Mahendra arises from his prostration, eyes shining, Ramakrishna warmly greets this reticent companion, who hesitates even to sing the Divine Names aloud, much less to dance freely in ecstasy.

RAMAKRISHNA My dear, one cannot experience profound awakening—the conscious arising of Mother Kundalini's energy through the six lotus centers of the subtle body—as long as one retains the slightest sense of shame, shyness, inhibition, or hesitation. These are really just forms of fear. Fearfulness, in turn, is the environment in which suspicion and even hatred can grow. Mahendra, today Mother Kali will provide a precious opportunity to experience Her Great Bliss. Please drop conventional barriers between persons and cross over artificial boundaries between human reality and Divine Reality. Those whose self-consciousness is so strong that they cannot dance and sing with abandon, tasting at least a drop of the sweet madness generated by the glorious Divine Names, will not be able to awaken into God and eventually as God. How can one become embarrassed or remain hesitant if God alone exists? God is dancing for God. Now sing, sing, all of you, sing!

Our spiritual sense is immediately intensified by this softly spoken yet immensely powerful command. We begin to sing a familiar mystic hymn with surprising new fervor, each companion more fully immersed in Divine Reality than ever before, thanks to the palpable inspiration of this auspicious birthday. Our voices rise into one universal crescendo of human longing.

Blessed with inconceivable blessings
is this day of total joy,
this conscious union of all souls
in the religion of limitless love.
O glorious Lord of Love,
You alone dwell within the heart,
making every land a sacred India.
Your self-revealing Names resound
through the breath and heartbeat
of every being in the universe.

Your ecstatic lovers humbly praise
the majesty and mystery of Love.
We have no desire for wealth or power.
Our only hope is the hope of all lovers—
blissful meeting with the Beloved.

For mystic union with You
we cry without tiring,
intimately embracing Your Feet,
divested of all opinions, all fear.
What can we gain or lose?
We have discovered the fountain
of timeless awareness.

O supreme Love,
our victory is Yours alone.
Victory unto Thee!

The God-intoxicated sage listens with eyes closed, palms joined at his heart, his consciousness soaring to inconceivable heights of rapture, his body as still as open space. For an entire hour after the hymn concludes, he remains lost in meditation, drawing our minds and hearts along with him somewhere far above and beyond this lovely spring morning.

Ramakrishna is wearing a yellow cloth that blends with the amber color of his skin, now suffused with radiance. While the Great Swan is still immersed in ecstasy, some companions place a flower garland around his shoulders and apply streaks of white sandalwood paste upon his forehead. His mysterious body radiates Divinity, shining more powerfully than the morning sun. We gaze in awe at this vision of Paradise right here on earth.

Regaining awareness of the relative world, the liberated sage laughs aloud, removes the garland, and vehemently casts it aside, vigorously rubbing the traditional marks of sanctity from his forehead.

> RAMAKRISHNA What is my connection with all this? I cannot bear these trappings. Why do people experience so much attraction for this form? O Mother, this mind is nothing other than You. Here, all the doors are open. I feel only like laughing.

He bursts into rich laughter, standing suddenly and shouting: "Drunk! Totally drunk with the wine of Love!" We are on our feet instantly in ecstasy, experiencing an upward-flowing bolt of lightning within us, like the floodtide rushing up the Ganges from the sea. Many of us begin to dance. Others weep like children, sobbing MA MA MA—Mother, Mother, Mother. We become the sacred playground of Lord Krishna, who is now moving mystically through our bodies, freeing them from the slightest sense of gravity. We have become Krishna's sacred playmate, the passionate and illumined Radha.

As he whirls, the God-drunken lover sings one line over and again, each time with unique melodic development: "Every structure is swept away by the flood of love." The verandas surrounding the room are now crowded with persons attracted to this heavenly dance. Several passenger boats have pulled over to the eastern bank of the Ganges to enjoy the sweet uproar.

An unexpected wave of silence suddenly washes over the gathering. The beautiful tenor voice of the Paramahamsa rises high and clear.

> Sisters and brothers, please come
> to taste Radha's own love.
> The floodtide of ecstasy
> flows through her holy body
> in countless streams.
> As much as you can contain
> is yours to receive.
> Radha is composed of Divine Love,
> so she pours forth only love,
> intoxicating hearts, here and now,
> with the bliss of Paradise.
> Consumed with longing for Krishna,

> come sing the sacred Name
> of Radha's ineffable Beloved.

The entire scene becomes golden—a divine dream tangibly unfolding beneath the brilliant blue sky of Bengal. What meditation or vision could compare to this beauty, this intensity? We dance for hours, perspiring profusely. After soaring with the Great Swan into this perpetual spring-time, none of us will ever be the same again.

The New Dispensation
Harmony of All Religions

RAMAKRISHNA HAS COME today, drunk with longing, to visit his beloved friend Balaram at his spacious Calcutta mansion. The head of the household meets the Master in the formal entrance hall. Dressed more like a Sufi than the Bengali Hindu that he is, Balaram is wearing a turban and a robe. He keeps his beard long and walks with a tall wooden staff. This intimate companion was with Lord Chaitanya some three hundred years ago, as revealed to the Paramahamsa in transcendental vision. Balaram sleeps in a narrow bed and economizes in every way, concealing his substantial wealth and disbursing it among wandering holy men and holy women to meet their basic needs. He has devotedly received and graciously served Ramakrishna in this elegant residence on hundreds of occasions. Sometimes he hires a country boat and, early in the morning, walks humbly to the houses of the various companions in Calcutta, inviting them to share his pilgrimage up the river to Dakshineswar.

A large painting was recently commissioned. Entitled *New Dispensation*, it depicts our Master standing before church, mosque, and temple as an embodiment of all the saints, sages, prophets, and divine manifestations from every noble wisdom tradition, graciously leading various religious communities into the harmonious light of the New Day. Gazing at the painting, Ramakrishna remarked with great fervor: "Yes, this contains everything. This expresses the spiritual ideal for modern times."

The Paramahamsa smiles radiantly as he moves toward the circle of young aspirants who are waiting to share a meal. Often Ramakrishna reiterates to Balaram: "You will sanctify your considerable wealth only by feeding persons in whom the current of holy power is awake and flowing upward. Otherwise your mind will become imperceptibly covered by the dust of worldly pragmatism."

The God-intoxicated sage perceives his intimate companions—particularly the youngest, most precocious ones—as actual embodiments of Divinity. With us today is the most amazing of these young persons, Narendra, whom the Master refers to as "the Unsheathed Sword." Narendra uses the sword of wisdom with great intensity to cut away all sense of limitation, all superimposed conceptuality, leaving naked Truth alone shining in the hearts of those around him. This demonstration of transcendent insight by a young man just twenty years old is startling. Narendra's presence is more than his verbal facility, his philosophical gift, the nobility of his features, his high moral ideals and strong conscience, his athletic prowess, his beautiful singing voice. He demonstrates Truth by his very being. The Paramahamsa ecstatically drinks in the atmosphere around this fiery young man, tasting the nectar of timelessness, feeling extremely restless if he cannot meet with his beloved Naren even for a period of a few days.

When Ramakrishna has Narendra at his side, an aura of completeness, a sense of mystic union, surrounds and pervades the gathering. Such is the case today. The blissful sage turns tenderly toward the young man and requests him to sing. Narendra is slightly indisposed, but the child of the Divine Mother continues to importune him in the sweetest manner. Now the Paramahamsa begins to praise the spiritual qualities of this youth, who is destined to become the world-transforming Swami Vivekananda, exalting him above Keshab Sen and other mature religious leaders of Calcutta. The sage places his right hand at his heart center, palm open as if bearing an invisible offering: "When you sing, Naren, the One who dwells here rises up like a beautiful black cobra, hisses faintly, spreads its hood, holds itself perfectly still, and listens to your music."

Finally, and rather brusquely, Narendra picks up the many-stringed drone instrument, as if to silence this flood of adulation. After he has tuned for what seems an inordinately long time to the expectant companions, Narendra's tumultuous spirit melts into the rhythmic waves of the *tanpura.* His sensitive and expressive lips begin to form the words of sacred hymns, face serene as a golden Buddha image, heart on fire with the most intense Divine Love.

The music sweeps like a wind through the spacious, marble-floored rooms of the mansion and out into the lush green garden. Ramakrishna enters a state of exultation and receptivity. The companions are carried to unaccustomed heights by the tender yet thunderous voice of this youth, who is almost too beautiful to gaze upon. The familiar verses are transformed by his intelligence and penetration, revealing new depths. New levels of aspiration are opened by the emotion that permeates his strong tenor voice. Refreshments sit untouched and unnoticed on low tables before us. We are transported, our breath almost in suspension.

Sing with selfless abandon,
O rare bird of Paradise,
hiding deep in the heart's realm,
high in the tree of Reality.
Sing infinite praises
where no one can overhear.

O spaceless, timeless One.
O boundless bliss of Knowledge,
a drop of which intoxicates
the manifest universe.
O Radiance without beginning.
O ecstatic Lord of Love.
O King of kings, Life of my life,
unveil Your Countenance
as clear light within my heart.

I long for a single glance
from Your Eyes of pure love.
To You alone I consecrate
my entire existence without ceasing.
I am tortured in the fiery furnace
of the selfish, conventional world.
My heart and mind are stained
by its egocentric obsession.
I am suffocating, O Lord,
in the embrace of delusion.
You alone are infinite compassion.
I supplicate You, heal me now
with the life-giving nectar of wisdom.

Sun and moon blaze in one vast sky
as lights offered on a sacred shrine.
Stars are diamonds adorning
the black image of Divinity.
The sweet evening breeze
is sandalwood incense,
moving the leaves like ceremonial fans
before Your holy Presence.
Flowering groves are garlands,
still ponds are mirrors.

How awesome this natural worship,
this perpetual praise of You,
O Dissolver of birth and death.
The primordial sound of OM,
arising like thunder from the void,
is the great temple drum.
"Nectar, nectar, more nectar!"
cries thirsty Nanak,
ecstatic singer of this song.
"May Your glorious Name alone,
its resonance and illumination,
become my breath and my abode!"

Narendra completes this medley of sacred hymns with the Master's favorite—a song about the New Dispensation, the New Day envisioned by radical lovers of Truth. One intoxicating verse follows another, with gradually intensifying rhythm which becomes the very heartbeat of humanity. Finally Narendra sings the first verse again—slowly, arhythmically, with charming melodic improvisation.

Within the black sky of Wisdom,
the full moon of Love is rising,
creating a floodtide of ecstasy.
Waves of Divine Bliss are surging
up the river of relativity.
The victory is Yours alone,
O blissful Mother Kali.
Victory unto Thee!

Setting aside his instrument, the vibrant young man absorbs this exalted mood into the secret dimensions of his being. At once, he begins to joke. Pointing to one of the most earnest companions, Narendra proclaims with mock seriousness: "Bavanath has firmly renounced eating fish and chewing betel leaf."

Ramakrishna responds humorously, with mock dismay: "Why so? Does eating fish diminish his power of concentration? Does chewing a slightly intoxicating leaf steal his mind away from the beautiful Lotus Feet of Mother Kali?"

Everyone laughs at the Master's playful tone. Suddenly shifting emphasis, the sage continues with great seriousness: "The only true sacrifice to offer God, O lovers of God, the only authentic renunciation that can clear away obstacles to spiritual progress, is to abandon once and for all this constant drive for self-perpetuation, this instinctive urge to survive and dominate which manifests in so many subtle and obvious forms—including the obsession with becoming holy or elevated." The Paramahamsa's remarks are powerful and uncompromising yet not heavy. Somehow these words awaken in us the very sense of spontaneity and lightness which is freedom from self.

The brilliant storm of music has passed as swiftly and mysteriously as it came. We begin to partake of refreshments together with childlike joy. Narendra continues to joke with the Paramahamsa in hilarious ways. The playful companionship of this lion and lion cub is a living demonstration of mystic union. We feel embraced and absorbed within the effulgent, indivisible reality called Ramakrishna-Narendra, this fusion of lover and Beloved, in which each is lover, each Beloved.

Tears in his eyes, Ramakrishna turns to the youth and cries out in ecstasy: "You are Nara, the ancient sage, emanation of the Divinity Narayana, come back to earth to relieve suffering and to pour forth the nectar of wisdom."

Laughing, Narendra replies: "After you touched me when I sat casually conversing on the porch of your room at Dakshineswar, I returned home divinely inebriated. Sitting down to eat, I clearly perceived that every-thing—the plate, the food, my mother who was serving, and I myself—that everything is God and nothing but God."

Shoulder to shoulder they sit, this wonderful New Dispensation, for which the relative disappears into the Absolute, and the Absolute into the relative. They laugh and radiate delight throughout the afternoon and well into the evening. How delicate and special the hospitality here! As Ramakrishna so often proclaims: "Balaram's house is my spiritual stronghold in the modern world of Calcutta. Its food and atmosphere are very pure."

10

Cry with an Infinite Cry

The Master Responds to Burning Questions

SURROUNDED BY contemplative practitioners on every level of devel-opment, the Paramahamsa is an inexhaustible fountain, overflowing with Divine Love and Divine Wisdom. Each person finds his own vessel inexplicably filled, her own capacity spontaneously fulfilled. This powerful transmission is now occurring through silence, as our Master sits on his bed, gazing peacefully across the brilliant flower gardens and the sacred river.

Suddenly he remarks: "Mother Ganga is a living Goddess. One should devoutly worship Her." Several persons in the room who have adopted European modes of thinking are taken aback. We realize that no veil of any ordinary world, Eastern or Western, covers Ramakrishna's perception. His remark about the Goddess mysteriously stimulates one of the lengthy, multileveled discussions that help the companions to appreciate and assimilate the Master's mode of silent transmission. Sincere and heartfelt questions begin to arise within everyone. They are not merely conversa-tional or intellectual. Some of these queries are voiced—coming into full fruition within these particular persons at this particular moment and receiving a miraculous response from the sage. His inspired, compassion-ate replies satisfy the precise needs of the questioner as well as everyone present in this room of mystery, whether intimate companion or casual visitor.

VISITOR Revered sir, what is the essence of the path?

RAMAKRISHNA The secret of the mystic way—including both path and goal, for they cannot be separated—is total, passionate love for God alone, for sheer Divine Reality, however you may envision or experience it in the depth of your being. This all-embracing, all-transcending love comes first. Formal disciplines of prayer and meditation are of secondary importance, although they do arise spontaneously out of authentic love.

Existentially manifesting his own teaching, the Great Swan is swept into song by the consuming fire of ecstatic love, which, he often explains, is not a hot flame but a cool, gemlike radiance, much more powerful than earthly fire. Into this luminous love, the ordinary surface world instantly dissolves. In the charming cadences and alliterations of the Bengali tongue, the God-drunken lover sings with abandon, eyes glistening.

> O ceaselessly searching mind,
> if your longing for Truth is real,
> let me hear you cry out
> to the beautiful Black Goddess
> with an infinite cry.
> Could the Mother of the Universe
> then sustain the playful illusion
> that She is separate from you?

Returning with startling facility from this state of rapture, our Master continues to reply to the question concerning the spiritual path.

RAMAKRISHNA When all-victorious love actually dawns, the lover's mind, heartbeat, breath, lips, and even limbs are constantly repeating and celebrating the beautiful Divine Names. This ceaseless remembrance fills the entire atmosphere of the person with the glorious radiance of Truth. This is the life of immersion in God—whether waking or sleeping, in company or in solitude, in the workplace or in the shrine room. This is both path and goal.

In the humid climate of Bengal, the brass vessels for sacred offerings in the Temple must be shined vigorously every day, not just once or twice a week. So in the humid environment of egocentric ambition called the world, one must pray fervently—not only every day but every moment—in order to keep the sacred vessel of the mind clean and bright. This prayer is not simply petition, but the silent fullness of adoration. Through this total life of prayer, one develops the swordlike wisdom that discriminates between cultural and personal projections and the single stainless Divine Reality. Only the constant practice of this total prayer will enable you to renounce habitual, conventional projections, moment by moment, by becoming calmly aware of their intrinsic unreality. You will move from the surface of existence into its very depths.

VISITOR Honored sage, should we take the way of monastic renunciation after our social and family responsibilities are completed?

RAMAKRISHNA The path of monastic discipline is not necessary for everyone who longs to awaken. The passion for external renunciation is like a bolt of lightning. It may strike at any time. It is not a reasoned choice. But why not renounce all sense of limitation, even the limitation of monastic forms? Why not enjoy all possible dimensions of human experience as already merged in God? Can one get completely inebriated on just a few pennies' worth of wine? Fill up the whole pitcher!

This radical response surprises the questioner, who had already tacitly assumed a traditional, pious answer. He gazes, speechless, at the laughing sage, and then asks with astonishment: "A spiritual practitioner should lead a worldly life?"

RAMAKRISHNA Why not? What is there to fear or avoid when Divine Reality is known to be all-embracing? The realized adept can engage in fulfilling communal and personal responsibilities with a clarified and illumined mind—a mind so transparent that nothing can reflect from it to create any illusory surface. Before breaking open a jackfruit, you carefully rub your hands and forearms with clear oil so that the sticky milk of the fruit cannot adhere. Apply the oil of limitless awareness, and nothing will stick. The servant who lives temporarily in a grand Calcutta mansion to supplement the income of his village family is always thinking fondly of the thatched huts, clear streams, open meadows, and mango orchards at home, although outwardly carrying on the complex rituals of city life. Similarly, the mind's true home is the natural purity and simplicity of Reality. This primordial abode must never for a moment be forgotten as we carry out our multileveled responsibilities for humankind.

Allow your mind to dwell in the most rarified Himalayan retreat, the unity of Reality. Remain joyous and undistracted among the trials and purifications of daily life—in the family, in the fields, in the marketplace. Relatively few persons have the destiny to drop social and personal connections entirely in order to enter the external state of *sannyasa*—wandering aimlessly in the ecstasy of knowledge and love, taking no direct responsibility for educating or serving society in pragmatic ways. In the case of the wandering *sannyasi*, it is God alone who subtly fulfills the responsibility of this man or woman to serve, using the inspiring outward form, the powerful inward mind and the secret heart of the renunciate as sacred instruments.

VISITOR Master, what does it mean to say that a person has reached the end of worldly enjoyments?

RAMAKRISHNA Conventional enjoyments are the mere surface of true enjoyment—a rough surface, which consists of egocentric gratification and personal aggrandizement. The limited ego is like a typhoid patient who cannot drink water without suffering a painful and dangerous relapse. What torture to keep this recovering patient in a room containing large jars of pickled tamarind—which vastly increases thirst—along with clay jugs of temptingly cool water! Selfish enjoyments are this pickled tamarind. It has absolutely no nutritional value, and it threatens one's genuine recovery from the deadly typhoid of egocentricity.

Many people cannot begin to feel the life-giving attraction for Divine Reality until they pass through the painful experiences associated with grasping at habitual enjoyment. This desperate grasping includes selfishly accumulating material wealth, arrogantly cultivating power over others, and welcoming flattery as well as enjoying absurdly refined comforts and ever more bizarre diversions. We must unequivocally see through this deceptive surface in order to enter the depth of ecstatic Divine Enjoyment. To come to the end of worldly enjoyment is to experience Divine Bliss flowing through every action, every perception.

VISITOR Beloved Paramahamsa, who is really to blame for sexual obsession and its bondage? Men or women?

RAMAKRISHNA You are male, so I will speak to you about women. To women, I give the same teachings about the spiritual danger and the spiritual potential of men. A woman who has awakened in her body and mind the energy of transcendent wisdom, which is the brilliant healing and enlightening presence of the Goddess, can be a tremendous blessing for a male practitioner—as tantric consort, as consecrated wife, or simply as the inspiring friend of his soul. But a woman who has developed exclusively her biological and social drives is filled with a subtle energy that can be detrimental to the progress of a male aspirant. Eventually—without either person recognizing any danger—she can stifle his aspiration by drowning him in the forces of the limited ego world. Precisely the same facts must be explained to women concerning men.

But this whole universe is miraculously projected by the dream power of the Absolute. It is the coherent, magical display of *mahamaya,* the Great Goddess in Her role as cosmic manifestation. The energy of limitation is just as much an organic part of this universal magical display as the energy of liberation. Mother plays as knowledge and as ignorance, so I bow respectfully before both with palms joined, though I salute Her tiger-manifestation from a safe distance. Both worldly bondage and spiritual freedom are simply aspects of Mother's Theater, *mahamaya,* which exists for no reason—not even for the education of souls, because this, too, is simply part of the play. Nonetheless, this Divine Drama is significant, meaningful, and complete beyond any human conception or imagination.

The brilliant feminine energy of wisdom, which incarnates through the bodies and minds of both men and women, cultivates the refined taste for sweet spiritual companionship, for knowledge of oneness, for tears of pure love, for ecstatic union with various revealed forms of Divinity, and for refreshing renunciation of all deceptive, habitual expectations. By contrast, the energy of limitation consists of the random, compulsive play of the mind and senses with their objects— an instinctual drive for experience that lacks subtlety and harmony and causes the heart to forget the delight of Divine Reality, the communion that is natural to the human soul. But both currents—the energy of wisdom and the energy of limitation—are simply Mother's Energy. When only God exists, who is there to praise and whom to blame?

VISITOR How can I get rid of sexual passion?

RAMAKRISHNA Why get rid of it? Turn its powerful energy in another direction. Lust is blind, but the Great Delight conferred by the Goddess is ever-pure and resplendent.

The new questioner is also disconcerted by such a radical response, delivered with such wonderful laughter. This seeker has been conditioned by the teaching that cultivates liberation by categorically rejecting whatever appears as ignorance, limitation, or bondage. Intrigued by the relaxed, all-embracing tantric attitude of the Goddess-worshiping sage, drawn deep into inquiry by this magnet of Divine Mother's Knowledge and Love, this visible form of the dancing Kali—the seeker cries in consternation: "Please, most revered Master, why would a benign Deity project the power of ignorance and limitation?"

Ramakrishna melts into laughter, his eyes swimming in ecstasy, his body, like burnished gold, glowing with heavenly light. This response emanates directly from Mother Mahamaya, beyond reason, religion, philosophy. Now our Master is weeping tears of pure love: "It is all Her Play, Her delirious Play. OM KALI, OM KALI, OM KALI!"

For a moment, we expect the Great Swan to disappear into one of the many dimensions of Divine Ecstasy. Sometimes he enters formless absorption, which may extend for several hours—breath completely stilled, heartbeat suspended. At other times Ramakrishna enjoys direct conversation with the Source of the Universe, speaking to his blissful Mother intimately, with phrases sometimes barely audible or entirely unintelligible. Sometimes he utters eloquent teachings directly from the Wisdom Goddess or bursts into song, words and melody entirely improvised, descending afresh from Her mysterious Abode. At other times our Master manifests Kali's Divine Dance through his lithe body, modulating freely between movements of stately magnificence and thunderous storm, like the lashing wind that signals the monsoon rain.

Now the Paramahamsa surprises everyone by regaining crystal clarity on the plane of human conversation.

RAMAKRISHNA These apparently opposite energies—knowledge and ignorance, positive and negative—are simply God's unitary play. I clearly see that Mother has become the sword, the wielder of the sword, and the sacrificial animal. There is no duality. We appreciate glorious light as well as dense darkness. They enhance one another. When spiritually mature, one can appreciate as sheer divine manifestation both happiness and misery, which depend upon one another to be fully experienced. Some suffering is good. It helps one find the path to Truth and make actual progress. If there were no suffering, how many persons would intensely chant the Divine Names? The cosmic conflict between good and evil is an integral part of Mother's Drama, Her testing of souls. Could you enjoy the sweet golden mango pulp if the bitter green skin did not also play its role? The skin is not only inedible but mildly poisonous, causing pain to some sensitive lips. It must be separated from the fruit with a sharp instrument and discarded, but it is an integral part of the mango, permitting the process of ripening. The green skin called ignorance, the instinctive grasping of the life force, enables the delicious fruit of awakened mind to grow and ripen. Appreciate the bitter skin of ignorance as *maya*, Mother's magical projection. But do not bite into it. The golden pulp of knowledge is also Her magical projection. There is the *maya* of ignorance and the *maya* of knowledge. Each is integral to the functioning of the other in this theater of *mahamaya*. As timeless awareness, *nitya*, Mother abides far above, while incarnating fully as *lila*, Her cosmic Play.

An unusual silence follows these words, at once simple and utterly profound. What is forever untouched by mind and speech is being palpably presented here, like a ripe mango placed on the palm of the hand. The blissful sage is now gazing into the eyes of the seekers of Truth, probing for resistance or avoidance, and dispelling these obstacles wordlessly. We intuit that he is actually leading us across an uncrossable threshold.

The mood of the room changes again as, through Mother's Grace, another burning question arises, this time in the heart of a modern intellectual. This dignified man is attracted to the vastness of Indian philosophy but is shocked and even repelled by the traditional image of Goddess Kali wielding unitive wisdom as a bloodstained sword and holding the human ego as a gruesome, freshly severed head.

VISITOR Listen here, Paramahamsa. I cannot believe it necessary to adore bizarre images of Divinity—mere fanciful forms, shaped by the primeval human imagination.

Some of the companions raise their eyebrows at this ferocious query, with its pointed hostility toward Ramakrishna's own beloved Goddess, his blissful Mother. But not a trace of reactivity exists in the empty, God-pervaded form of the Paramahamsa. He responds cordially and jovially.

RAMAKRISHNA Excellent! You do not accept the manifestation of Divine Forms. You do not wish to impose any personal or cultural limits upon Reality, which is intrinsically limitless. And you feel strongly about it. Admirable, indeed! Such traditional images will not be necessary for your particular advancement. There are infinite paths to God-realization—each one unique, each one authentic. But please become more radical and uncompromising about your spiritual ideal. Do not accept even your own form or your own ideas as independent, solid realities apart from the One Reality.

There is a way, however, that you can receive inspiration from practitioners who worship through traditional images. Consider the intensity of their yearning. It is like the powerful attraction between lovers who long to meet and merge, free at last from the strictures of convention. Much more intense than ordinary lovers, however, whose mutual attraction is strong but finite, these devout worshipers are like the divinely human lovers Radha and Krishna, for whom this burning attraction is actually infinite. The advanced practitioners who commune with Divine Reality through various sacred icons shed tears of longing to be able to penetrate beyond the outer form of wood, stone, or clay— no matter how beautifully they may adorn these icons, no matter how concrete their devotion may be. These blessed lovers long only to experience Divine Reality directly—dancing within the lotus of their secret hearts, composed of Pure Consciousness alone. Emulate their infinite cry, which emerges from the very foundation of their being: "Mother, Mother, O blissful Mother!" Generate within yourself the intensity of their purified emotion, and simply ignore whatever external image they may be worshiping.

Ramakrishna suddenly enters ecstasy. He tries to speak but no words come. He rubs his face vigorously with both hands, attempting to regain enough objective awareness to continue the conversation, but to no avail. Instead, he bursts into musical worship. Every cell in his body is singing. The rhythm of his song is the heartbeat of the entire universe. The Master's unique version of this traditional hymn is impregnated with every drop from his vast reservoir of initiatory energy.

> O ceaselessly searching mind,
> if your longing for Truth is real,
> then let me hear you cry out
> to the beautiful Black Goddess
> with an infinite cry.
> Could the Mother of the Universe
> then sustain the playful illusion
> that She is separate from you?

Timeless Man
Meets Contemporary Man
Ramakrishna and Bankim Chandra

TODAY THE GREAT SWAN is visiting the residence of his beloved
friend Adhar, a place of warm hospitality that Ramakrishna calls
"my intimate Calcutta living room." Adhar meets often with the Paramahamsa at the Temple Garden after an exhausting day of legal and administrative work. The tender sage always requests a mat to be spread on the
floor of his room, and Adhar sleeps peacefully at the holy feet of his guide,
missing the oral teachings but receiving a strong infusion of Divine
Presence.

The dignified, well-dressed Adhar now welcomes the ecstatic, disheveled
God-man with great devotion and enthusiasm, openly adoring this perfect
union of Divinity and humanity, even before the critical gaze of other
deputy magistrates, colleagues whom he has invited to his home for this
festive occasion.

> ADHAR Reverend sir, you have not graced our residence with the dust
> of your holy feet for much too long. The very rooms seem dim and
> depressing without your heavenly radiance. There is a faint musty smell
> of worldliness here when you are physically absent, no matter how
> much we may chant or burn incense. But now the fragrance of your
> love for God pervades the entire house. Everyone is cheerful. This
> morning, I even wept during prayer and meditation, contemplating
> your arrival.

The Master smiles like a delighted child, gazes intently into the eyes of
his companion for a single moment, and steps into the reception hall,

stammering with rapturous joy: "Is that so? Tears of love. How wonderful! How wonderful!"

Several important Calcutta intellectuals have also been invited today to meet the Paramahamsa, who is, for most of them, a quaint survival from the ancient Indian past. Certain of these guests regard Adhar as eccentric for retaining such deep contact with primitive forms of knowledge, rather than fully embracing the British cultural and educational model, as they have had the foresight to do. Others among the sophisticated visitors are open-minded enough to observe the Master objectively and test the authenticity of his teaching in the crucible of their Eastern sensibility and Western predilection.

Ramakrishna passes among these impressive gentlemen and ladies without even a sidelong glance, and unites with a small circle of ecstatic lovers gathered on one side of the elegant drawing room, which is filled with flowers and sumptuous refreshments. We begin to play and laugh, as if we were sitting together at the Temple Garden.

Attempting to integrate the gathering, Adhar brings forward the most prominent guest and introduces him to Ramakrishna. "Revered sir, may I present the renowned Bankim Chandra Chatterji. He is a great scholar and the author of books that develop new interpretations of ancient scriptures. He eloquently advocates social reform."

Manifesting precisely the same delightful smile with which he greeted his beloved Adhar, the blissful sage turns to welcome this great Bengali literary figure of the day, bowing respectfully and inquiring: "What has caused you to become so bent, so *bankim?*"

Some conservative guests are disconcerted by this strange play on the meaning of Bankim's name, but Bankim Chandra himself obviously enjoys the Paramahamsa's wry humor and unconventional air. Seating himself on the Persian carpet with the sage, he answers back immediately, with humorous irony: "Good sir, your perception is completely accurate. I have been bent by kicks from the boots of our British colonial masters." The nervousness in the room subsides as everyone senses that a most interesting conversation is about to ensue.

RAMAKRISHNA No, no, my dear sir. You must not underestimate yourself this way. The sublime Lord Krishna was also bent in three places—knees, waist, and neck—bent by ecstatic love for his exquisitely beautiful consort, the passionate Radha. This is how the ancient commentators interpret the traditional icons of Krishna, the incarnation of Divine Love. Do you know how they explain his dark blue complexion?

Bankim is now the one who is slightly disconcerted, taken aback by the resonant energy of the Paramahamsa's voice, his effortlessly flowing speech, the unearthly grace of his gestures. The literary man responds to the Master's question in the negative, with a slight movement of his head, a charmed look of surprise playing across his handsome features.

RAMAKRISHNA Then perhaps you are also unaware of the profound interpretation offered by realized sages concerning the small physical stature of Krishna? Does it not strike you as strange that the Lord of the Universe appears as only three and a half cubits tall, measured by the span of his own delicate Divine Hand?

Bankim shakes his head in amazement, obviously no longer functioning from his habitual center of gravity.

RAMAKRISHNA Then please permit me, dear sir, to elucidate these venerable ancient teachings. Like the deep waters of the open ocean, so Divine Reality appears dark blue when seen from a distance. If we draw near to the ocean and take the water directly into our own hands, we discover it to be brilliantly clear, perfectly transparent. The same holds true if one is courageous enough to come close to that ocean of Being, Consciousness, and Bliss that appears from a certain distance as the dark blue Krishna.

The sun appears to a child like a radiant golden disk precisely the size of a human face. Why? Because it is so far away, and the child has no notion of such vast distances. If we were to come close to the sun, we would no longer find the sky or even ourselves—only the sun in all its inconceivable intensity. We must cultivate this direct acquaintance with the true nature of God. Then Divine Reality will no longer be experienced as bent in three places, dark blue, small in stature. But, my noble friend, what an extraordinary attainment it is to make this direct acquaintance! This intimacy with supreme Reality is not possible through ordinary modes of perception, knowledge, or belief. Only the total concentration of our conscious being, called *samadhi*, can actually take us to the shore of the ocean or to the surface of the sun. Beyond that, no words apply.

As long as "I-ness" and "my-ness" remain habitual, we will continue to experience each other as names and forms, and will therefore most appropriately relate to God through Divine Names and Divine Forms. But this situation need not be experienced as a depressing separation from God. The dynamic universe of name and form is not a dim, miserable, musty place. It is the magnificent *lila,* the Divine Play—filled to the brim with the delight of tasting God, serving God, and wondering ceaselessly at the awesome Divine Mystery.

The heart-melting Krishna is actually Pure Consciousness. His captivating consort, Radha, is the primordial power of Pure Consciousness that projects complex worlds of name and form. What is the meaning of their ecstatic union, depicted by the traditional icon of Radha and Krishna dancing side by side, merged into a single current of Divine Delight? The interpretation is simply this. Pure Consciousness and its own Primordial Power are one Reality, not two. You cannot realize the Absolute without participating in the dance of the relative. You cannot understand the play of relativity without being immersed in the radiant stillness of the Absolute. Wherever there is butter, there is buttermilk. The two are not two. They are called *purusha* and *prakriti* in the technical language of the yogis, Krishna and Radha in the ecstatic parlance of the lovers.

Krishna's entire attention is focused upon the flashing dark eyes of Radha. Radha's entire being is plunged into the shoreless ocean of Krishna's gaze. The complexion of Radha, the Primordial Power, resembles a continuous golden flash of lightning; therefore Krishna wears a gold-colored cloth, indicating that cosmic creativity emerges from Pure Consciousness alone. Krishna, the Absolute, is depicted as dark blue, like the awesome thunderhead within which golden lightning flashes. Therefore the golden-complexioned Radha wears a royal blue sari, with rings, bracelets, and necklaces of dark blue sapphire, indicating that the Absolute alone is being expressed through its Primordial Power, the relative. There exists both inward and outward harmony between these two poles of Reality—Absolute and relative.

A profound silence comes over this drawing room, decorated and furnished both in British and traditional Indian fashion. Our instinctive attachment to duality evaporates for just a moment. Bankim Chandra and his admirers, who have been educated in European and Indian modes of thought, are experiencing the profound impact of the perennial tantric teaching just unveiled with such power by the Paramahamsa. Their composite modern worldview is being nonviolently challenged at its very foundation. They begin whispering excitedly together in English. We overhear certain phrases expressing astonishment at the Master's dialectical brilliance.

Ramakrishna calls out to them in his idiomatic village Bengali: "What is so important that you are discussing it in English?"

Laughing, Adhar replies: "Beloved Paramahamsa, we were simply commenting on the excellence of your discourse."

The God-intoxicated sage bursts into laughter. This cascade of heavenly sound brings the entire room once again to stunned silence. Completely unselfconsciously, the Master now launches into a hilarious story about an anglicized Hindu who shouts the English word *damn* at a barber who has nicked him while shaving. The burly barber puts down the razor and rolls up his sleeves, even though it is a chilly winter day. His voice is deep and powerful: "You attributed that word to me. Now what does it mean?" The sophisticated gentleman replies in superior tones, which the sage mimics unerringly: "You do not have to worry about what the word means. Just concentrate better on your task." The barber stands his ground and replies in a booming voice, also well rendered by the Paramahamsa: "If *damn* has a good meaning, then I am a *damn,* my venerable mother is a *damn,* my revered relatives for seven generations in both directions are *damns.* But if the meaning is insulting, then you are a *damn* and all of your ancestors without exception are *damns.* They are *damn, damn damns.*" The sage utters these three words with a most peculiar, approximately British accent. Laughter explodes from everyone in the room. The uproar must be audible throughout the entire neighborhood.

After the waves of mirth gradually subside, Bankim Chandra clears his throat and proposes: "Revered Paramahamsa, with your evident gift for language and your brilliance, why not preach from the various pulpits and podiums of Calcutta? It would far surpass what we are hearing from contemporary *pandits.*"

RAMAKRISHNA The very word *preach* is utterly distasteful. It suggests that someone can dispense Truth as if it were a commodity rather than the supreme and only Reality. It is chronic human vanity alone that assumes anyone can preach, that anyone can stand in front of an audience or a congregation and present Truth. Human egos are flimsy, insignificant structures. They cannot withstand the slightest impact of genuine Truth-force. Divine Reality alone is capable of transmitting

Truth, and the timeless essence of the soul alone can receive this powerful transmission.

Through the mysterious activity of its primordial Power, consciousness crystallizes the structures within which the human form exists—broad earth, life-giving sun, infinitude of stars. Divine Light alone illuminates and eventually enlightens all manifest Being. To be a spiritual teacher, one must become transparent to boundless radiance. Is this an easy attainment? Can this transparency be brought about by study, by willpower, by public acclaim? No one can transmit Truth unless the Divine Light consciously shines through this person, not just partially but entirely. The initiative must come from God, not from individual ambition of any kind. Of course, no one can stop popular preachers from shouting slogans and creating an emotional response among their blind followers. People will listen to them for a few moments or a few years, and then forget all about it again, just like any novel sensation that eventually becomes tiresome.

Consider carefully, Bankim Babu. Even if intelligent readers and audiences congratulate you enthusiastically on your eloquent words, they will certainly forget your intended meaning. You will have to write more books and give more lectures to remind them. Afterward, your teaching once more slips away from their busy minds. Thus you become caught in a negative cycle. And when you die, all your work will disappear, instantly or gradually. Boiling milk foams up and appears to fill the entire pot, but the moment one removes it from the flame, the level drops way down. You must gradually increase your capacity to bear and transmit Truth-force. How? Through intensive *sadhana*, through sincerely and selflessly practicing spiritual discipline. You Calcutta people try to teach without realization. As the wise proverb indicates, "The one who has no room to sleep always invites a friend to sleep with him."

Once in my native village of Kamarpukur, some thoughtless, unrefined people used to urinate and defecate on the bank of the reservoir which held precious water for everyone. The villagers were incensed, but their shouts and threats had no effect on the barbaric offenders. Then a government official came to the village and posted a printed warning that pollutors would be subject to legal prosecution. The crude behavior stopped immediately. Unless you actually represent, in your very being, the awesome authority of the Divine Command, no one will heed your teaching. How does Mother give one Her Divine Command? Through profound states of ecstasy.

Every guest is listening to the uneducated sage with respectful attention. An illiterate village man has become the acknowledged enlightener of the best legal and literary minds of modern Calcutta. The Paramahamsa now deepens his probing.

RAMAKRISHNA Dear Bankim, since you have carefully considered the human condition, after reading extensively, please tell us what you perceive to be our ultimate responsibility. What is the knowledge that remains valid and fruitful throughout all conditions of existence, even after the key moment of physical death? Do you accept the heavenly existence of the soul?

BANKIM I do not cherish the slightest attachment to any notion of heavenly existence.

RAMAKRISHNA Excellent! When the physical body drops away, the person who has attained supreme knowledge does not need to enter any higher or more subtle plane of existence, but merges blissfully into the transparent Ground of Existence—not becoming unconscious but becoming Pure Consciousness. However, as long as the individual awareness has not fully awakened, during this very life, into limitless awareness, even the most dedicated, purified person must visit heavenly realms for further transformation and refinement. This individual mind-stream must express itself again through living forms on the planetary plane, either upon this earth or somewhere else in the vast universe. Only the authentic knower of Truth, the *jñani*, is free from the need to be embodied or expressed through some finite mode— whether on physical, subtle, or formless planes of existence.

The mysterious Grace of God returns certain liberated souls into the various realms of finitude and embodiment in order to be true teachers and tender caretakers. But this return is a function of Divine Responsibility, not human desire. Pure Consciousness spontaneously manifests its Primordial Power to teach and transmit Truth, and this miraculous process is what appears as the great guides of humanity, such as Shukadeva and Shankara. This is sheer Divine Action, not human initiative.

Well, Bankim, now please give us your answer. What is our ultimate responsibility?

The Master asks this question to probe and purify the mind-stream of Bankim Chandra, yet he presents it with a playful smile. Perhaps the literary man misunderstands Ramakrishna's spiritual mood, being accustomed to the crude joking of the conventional world. He responds with a misplaced attempt at humor.

BANKIM Sir, if you want my frank answer, I would say that our ultimate responsibility is to eat lavishly, to sleep soundly, and to enjoy reproducing the race.

RAMAKRISHNA Now I see your shallowness. What you are obsessed with, day and night, is involuntarily coming forth from your own mouth. The person who eats garlic with beans involuntarily emits the odor of garlic and beans from his body. The person who gorges on radishes belches the stench of radish.

Once again our Master's directness has surprised and impressed Bankim and the sophisticated people around him. With downturned eyes, the literary giant humbly accepts this severe scolding from the unlettered sage.

RAMAKRISHNA Bankim, you are constantly surrounded, both physically and psychically, by the habitual egocentric tendencies called lust and greed. This is a poisonous atmosphere. Women are regarded not as sacred vessels of the Goddess but as objects for momentary satisfaction. Wealth is regarded not as Divine Mother's abundance, mercifully granted for the welfare of all Her beloved created beings, but as a means to grasp power and to satisfy every obsession imaginable. Your mouth has become a machine that speaks about lust and greed automatically. Your surface mind may soar into impressive intellectual spaces, but your mind's eye is fixated, like the sharp gaze of the high-flying vulture, solely upon dead or dying flesh.

This is not really you who speak in such obsessive patterns, Bankim, but a mind that has unconsciously permitted itself to become calculating, turbulent, and deceitful. This very same mind can become serene, guileless, and innocent by concentrating upon Divine Reality. A mind that has directly perceived Truth, even for an instant, would never jest as you have done, Bankim Babu. You have revealed the impoverished condition of your awareness. What purpose can broad scholarship, brilliance of expression, and commitment to social reform really serve if there is no sound discrimination between what is exalted and what is

merely conventional or habitual? And what kind of *pandit,* or true elder
of society, is he who has not utterly renounced the conventional and
the habitual? This person may be able to quote long passages from
scripture. He may have produced highly technical treatises, composed
in traditional or modern style. But if his mind does not spontaneously
and effortlessly dwell on God and within God, can you call him a
pandit, a man of wisdom?

Certain sophisticated modern people remark about the lovers of God:
"These poor, misguided souls are mad—conversing day and night
about Divine Reality, cultivating no taste for any other subject.
Whereas we have the correct balance. We enjoy philosophy and religion
as well as the pleasures that money, honor, and position provide. We
pray to God, but we also thoroughly pursue the delights of the senses."
These self-willed people are like the magpie, which assumes that it is
the most clever among birds. But have you ever carefully observed the
behavior of the magpie? The moment dawn awakens it, this bird begins
to seek out and consume nothing but refuse. Then it struts about and
chatters self-importantly.

There is shocked silence throughout the elegant residence of Adhar. We
all experience the chastening touch of these fiery words at the center of
our conscience, at the core of our personhood, where one longs for
integrity above all else. As the Master speaks—slowly, stammering
slightly—the radiant smile of Divine Delight never leaves his lips.

RAMAKRISHNA By contrast, those whose thoughts instinctively
move toward the One Reality—in every condition, at every moment—
are like the adept swan of folklore that can drink, from a mixture of
water and milk, only pure milk, leaving the bowl half full of water. The
great swans, the *paramahamsas,* are simply true human beings. Like the
swan flying north in its yearly migration, the true human being moves
powerfully forward in one direction, toward Truth alone, seeing nothing else, enjoying nothing else, seeking nothing else.

Ramakrishna adds, with surprising tenderness: "Please, dear Bankim,
do not take personal offense at my words. I simply must speak Truth."

Bankim Chandra is visibly moved. He replies strongly: "Revered Paramahamsa, I appreciate your uncompromising attitude. I did not come to
you to receive palliatives or flattery. I came here to encounter a person of
Truth."

Bankim Chandra Chatterji is, at this moment, speaking for everyone in the room. Each one of us, wherever we may be along the path, feels humbled and consecrated by this encounter between the ancient *paramahamsa* and the modern *pandit*. Bankim has proven honest and resilient enough to receive probing and purification from a master spiritual physician, from a living manifestation of Truth. For several of Adhar's serious-minded guests, this is the most memorable conversation of a lifetime.

Someone starts to sing. The Great Swan leaps to his feet and enters profound *samadhi*. Bankim pushes through the circle of ecstatic lovers that forms spontaneously around Ramakrishna, and stares in amazement at the blissful sage. He has never observed a human being totally absorbed in Divine Consciousness. Without his noticing, Bankim's expensive woolen shawl drops from his shoulders. He gazes like a thirsty man drinking cool water. Ramakrishna suddenly falls to the floor in prostration, crying: *"Bhagavata, bhakta, bhagavan*—holy scripture, ecstatic lover, and Divine Beloved—are one! Salutations to all the lovers of God and knowers of Truth, wherever they may be!"

12

Ramakrishna Relates
His Intimate Experiences

I N THE DELICATE coolness of early sunlight, companions of Divine
Love are already beginning to arrive in the Master's room, the secret
heart of the Dakshineswar Temple Garden. The Great Swan is seated
comfortably upon a thin grass mat on the circular porch that overlooks
the sacred Ganges, enjoying the morning freshness, the birdsong, the
bright sails on the river. Some of us have spent the entire night together—
chanting, singing, and dancing almost until dawn. We dozed for an hour
or so and awoke again spontaneously, before sunrise, in the mysterious
conjunction between night and day, to find Ramakrishna, who sleeps only
one hour at night, already waving incense before the holy icons on the
walls of his room, intoning softly and melodiously, *"Gita, ganga, gayatri,"*
and dancing blissfully. This Sanskrit phrase invokes the mystic union that
exists between divinely revealed scripture, or *gita*, the sacred manifestation
of Divine Reality as the cosmos, or *ganga*, and the transforming energy
of worship, or *gayatri*. We are consciously plunged, by Ramakrishna's very
presence, into this powerful union of wisdom, cosmos, and worship, this
mysterious identity of heaven, earth, and awakened humanity.

The beloved Rakhal is lying with his head in our Master's lap. The
Paramahamsa shows great tenderness to this profound young man, his
spiritual son whom he regards as the baby Krishna, often feeding Rakhal
with his own hands, placing sweets directly into his mouth as though he
were five years old instead of twenty. An atmosphere like honey—smooth,
sweet, and radiant—surrounds Rakhal, who is destined to manifest as
Swami Brahmananda, a deep reservoir of realization from which a fountain
of advanced practitioners and perfected beings will flow, blessing the

world with their service, their prayers, their very presence. About Rakhal and a few other intimate companions, the Master says: "The *ishvarakotis*— the ever-perfect souls, the timeless rays of light from the Source of Light— are like children of the king. They are given the keys to all the rooms in the seven-story palace. They can climb the steep stairway to the seventh plane of awareness and return at will."

The present owner and manager of the Temple Garden walks by the stone porch on his way to the shrine of Mahakali, Great Mother of the Universe. The Paramahamsa calls out to him in a surprisingly stern tone. Trailokya stops and bows respectfully. The sage very firmly reminds the younger man about a certain performance of sacred theater, omitted from the recent schedule of worship, proclaiming with great seriousness: "The powerful traditions of this Temple, established by your saintly grand-mother, should be observed in all their complexity." Trailokya reassures the Master of his commitment and hurries to attend the morning service. We sense that the God-filled Paramahamsa's presence here at the Temple Garden as a full emanation of Goddess Kali makes the various ritual observances more than arcane or merely pious formalities but absolutely necessary to facilitate the assimilation of the vast spiritual energy being poured forth from day to day. This energy of transformation belongs not just to a handful of ecstatic companions but to the entire future humanity, renewing and realigning all its ancient wisdom traditions, sacraments, and lineages of initiation.

Like a child, the exalted sage of Dakshineswar now turns to us and asks: "Was it correct for me to be so firm with this important man? Should I have even mentioned the subject?" We reassure Ramakrishna about the appropriateness of his remarks, at the same time marveling at the natural humility of this person, recognized by Trailokya's grandmother, founder of the temple, as Divinity incarnate. She always gave him total freedom of expression and spiritual authority concerning the functioning of the entire temple complex, which operates like a vast reservoir and irrigation network of Divine Energy.

Accepting our reassurances with childlike relief, the Paramahamsa enters a different mood. He begins to unfold a dazzling tapestry of transcenden-tal experiences from his sixteen years of rigorous contemplative practices, conducted under strict internal or external guidance in various obscure recesses of the Temple Garden and within its sacred shrines.

We are spellbound. The account continues for four or five hours. The richness of texture, the depth of intensity, the unprecedented scope of these experiences constitute the living scripture that the Wisdom Mother, manifest through Ramakrishna, has revealed for global humanity. As there is always both subtle humor and sheer hilarity in the storytelling of the Paramahamsa, laughter radiates from the open porch into the flower gardens, reaching the ears of those who are bathing in the redeeming waters of the Ganges, and bringing a smile to the lips of the exalted Mother Sarada, who is already preparing her husband's midday meal.

Sarada lives, meditates, and works modestly and selflessly behind palm-leaf screens on the ground floor of the small music pavilion just north of the Master's room. Some of the women companions help with her heavy cooking responsibilities, as she often insists on feeding the many aspirants who circle around this mystic room like bees about a lotus pond. The Divine Consort of Ramakrishna arises so early for her ablutions, prayer, and meditation that one hardly ever catches a glimpse of her. The Paramahamsa helped his young wife develop this discipline of waking very early by playfully pouring water under her door at two or three in the morning. His teachings often take the form of childlike play. But our Master's loving respect and even awe for Sarada are evident. Once she gave a well-known prostitute the inestimable honor of bringing the sage his midday meal. The more conservative companions who happened to be in the room were shocked, and the Paramahamsa himself—who can usually not even sip from a glass of water offered to him or sit on a mat spread for him by a person of unrefined character—simply stared in amazement at his plate of lentils and fried bread. Mother Sarada, who had entered the room humbly and unobtrusively behind the woman of the streets, noticed her husband's inability to touch the food and proclaimed powerfully: "This woman called me Holy Mother and prayed for the blessing, at least once in her life, to feed a manifestation of Goddess Kali. You absolutely must partake of her offering." The Paramahamsa laughed loudly and immediately began to eat with relish and gusto. At another time, Rama-krishna revealed: "If that Being who manifests through Sarada ever becomes angry with me, none of my practices for the benefit of human-kind will bear fruit."

The Paramahamsa is now commenting with a smile about a certain troublemaker, Hazra by name, whom the Mother of the Universe per-mits to harass him from time to time. The insufferably arrogant Hazra takes advantage of the transparent, innocent nature of the sage to

act as a teacher, scolding the Master about his religious and social uncon-
ventionality.

"Hazra comes here now and then to teach me proper behavior." Just
the delicately ironic tone of his voice causes waves of laughter. To laugh
with Ramakrishna is healing. In this instance, tensions we all feel from
being subjected to overly strict or even arbitrary social and religious
conventions are being released.

RAMAKRISHNA Hazra constantly nags me. He insists that my passionate love for the young men who are devoting themselves entirely
to God is particularly inappropriate and that people will think me
strange. That rascal even suggests that I am forgetting God in my
infatuation with these boys. At first I respected his words, as I respect
the words of everyone. I felt greatly disturbed by his admonition—
especially his warning that I might be, even to a minute degree,
forgetting God. Weeping, I entered the Kali Temple and fell prostrate
before the living Goddess expressed there through black basalt,
adorned with red flowers.

The Great Mother of the Universe immediately revealed Herself as a
continuous flash of lightning in the center of my awareness, explaining
that She alone manifests, not only as these pure-hearted young aspirants
but as all human beings without exception and as the entire cosmos.
Not with human words but with a stream of intelligible light, flowing
from Her beautifully dancing Black Form, Goddess Kali made clear
that Her manifestation through consecrated souls is the most intense.
She explained that by falling in love with these souls, I am merging
with Her Wisdom-energy, not forgetting or turning away from Her in
any way. When I realized this, through Mother's wonderful Grace, I
was so moved, so inspired, that I disappeared entirely into the boundless expanse of Her Presence, like a doll made of salt entering the ocean.
I was gone for hours.

Miraculously returned by Her once more into the play of relativity,
becoming aware of my surroundings and my provisional identity, I
became piqued at Hazra. He had frightened me unnecessarily. But this
feeling swiftly dissipated as I realized that Hazra as well is part of Her
Theater. Since that experience, I have enjoyed direct and uninterrupted
knowledge that young men and women who long from childhood for
God-realization and who do not rely upon the conventional world for
any satisfaction are simply Divine Reality, intensely manifest through

the exalted human form. They are God nakedly longing for God, free
from the veils of separation and duality. When I first met Narendra, the
Unsheathed Sword, I clearly perceived that he had no morbid preoccu-
pation with or even passing concern for his physical or social existence.
He was already so sensitive and open to Divine Presence that I had
only to touch his heart center with my fingertips. He penetrated
instantly past the surface of the physical and mental worlds and plunged
into the vision of the highest realm—sheer formless radiance. Returning from what appeared outwardly as a trance state, Naren, unaccustomed to radical God-vision, showed a trace of his commitment to
humankind. He cried, "O Paramahamsa, what did your touch do to
me? I have responsibilities for my sisters and brothers, my mother and
father!" I was moved by his compassion as well as exhilarated by his
spiritual sensitivity. I fell instantly and entirely in love with this soul.
As you know, I cannot survive in this surface world without communing with Naren at least every few days. My longing for him is infinite,
just as my longing for God is infinite. It is just God longing for God.
This is the supreme mystery—the Divine Play as humanity, the *naralila*,
totally unveiled and free from the slightest sense of duality.

Constantly and even desperately I used to question companions, or
anyone who would listen, about why my love for this particular young
man had become so intense. Bholanath, one of the minor administrators of the Temple Garden, gave the most inspiring reply. He explained
from the standpoint of the ancient scriptures, which is always the most
reliable, that someone established on the plane of God-vision—who
can enter and return from highly refined trance states, or *samadhis*, as
easily as moving from waking to dream and back again—cannot enjoy
ordinary shared levels of sensory and mental consciousness without
being in the companionship of pure-hearted lovers of Truth, persons
whose instincts have been sanctified. The very sight of such true lovers
gives the one established in God-consciousness a thrill of delight and
allows for peacefulness of spirit. Otherwise the awakened sage might
feel alien and restless in the environment of worldly convention. This
is why many realized beings wander away into the wilderness or appear
mad. Bholanath's explanation and the elucidation I received directly
from Goddess Kali reinforced each other. Corroboration of revelatory
experience by scriptural wisdom is necessary for a harmonious and
powerful spiritual life, as a strong support for the crushing weight of

greater and greater realizations. No matter how high the bird flies, it can always fly higher. There is no limit to realization, because Truth is an infinite sky. Thanks to Bholanath, I feel a lightness and ease in my whole being concerning Narendra. I can sit in solitude and weep for him with intense love, free from any inhibition. I do not hesitate even to take a carriage to Calcutta and visit Naren in his own small room.

O beloved companions, what uncharted regions of Divine Ecstasy I have passed through! I can only express a particle to you through words. When I begin to recount certain very secret experiences, Mother paralyzes my tongue and I simply cannot form words, although I am fervently longing to share these treasures with you.

After I first received the direct vision of Mahakali, my blissful Mother—Her scintillating Black Form rising out of a golden ocean, with gigantic waves rushing at me from all sides—I remained in a constant visionary state. It was literally impossible for me to tell any difference between night and day, so brilliant was Her Radiance, permeating my entire mind and senses. Undiscerning persons considered me insane. They dubbed me "the mad priest of Dakshineswar." But my madness was the sweet madness of Divine Love, free from the bitterness characteristic of mental and emotional derangement.

After several years of this ecstasy, when I was twenty-three, my beloved earthly mother arranged my marriage to Sarada in order to shock this mind into some sense of worldly responsibility, but I experienced the five-year-old bride as a complete manifestation of the Universal Mother in Her delicate wisdom-aspect as Goddess Saraswati. Thus, for me, the wedding was the highest mystical experience of communion, rather than an imperative to become narrowly pragmatic. Right after this heavenly ceremony, however, the obsessive nature of human existence began to manifest again. The man who loaned the elaborate ornaments for the young bride demanded their immediate return. The child wept. I placated the man until Sarada fell asleep, then carefully and gently removed rings, bracelets, necklaces, and anklets without waking her, praying that the selfish world would never bind or even touch her.

After returning to Dakshineswar from my native village and plunging once more into passionate experiments with Truth, I did occasionally worry about my young wife. How could she survive the painful social pressures of being married to a homeless *paramahamsa* with no worldly sensibility whatsoever? But when Sarada finally came to visit me here at the Temple Garden—sixteen years of age and beautiful with a transcendent Divine Beauty—I no longer worried. Why? Because I perceived that she is a full conscious manifestation of the Goddess. Her personal strength and inner resources are boundless. Such power to assimilate Divine Ecstasy—and to conceal from others her constant ecstatic experience—I have never encountered in any practitioner, before or since. She learned the refinements of spiritual science from me instantly. Whatever I explained, or just hinted at, she understood in its broadest implications and included organically in her daily practice. She once strung a fragrant, seven-strand flower garland for Goddess Kali that produced the actual energy and beauty of the Divine Realm right here on earth. It was a clear sign that Sarada's holy body and mind would be the intersection of heaven and earth for future humanity—a chalice for the immeasurable, inconceivable power and illumination of the revelations Mother Kali is now granting.

O inseparable companions, I existed for sixteen years in the constant storm of Divine Drunkenness. In my painful yearning for God, I was like a bird shrieking for its mate, a kitten mewing for its mother, a cow lowing for its calf. Sometimes I wondered about my own personal future—if only for a few moments—but very soon, past, future, and even the present moment were again submerged in the rapture and unitive knowledge that flooded my being.

Sometimes Goddess Kali would cause me to question the authenticity of my own experiences. Can you imagine such a stern test—to become prepared to renounce the most precious gifts one has ever received? But Truth alone is the path and the goal. I used to pray: "O blissful Mother, if these visions are authentic, please send me an incontrovertible sign. I am an impoverished, illiterate, unconventional temple priest. If the wealthy, sophisticated, highly regarded landowners of this district come to me of their own accord, I will know that my visions are not mere mental projection." And indeed men and women from these important families did visit me frequently, showing much affection and respect, never acting supercilious or superior in any way.

How can I describe the miraculous events that occurred here daily! My spiritual state was incendiary. The mention of any Divine Name or even any object associated with ceremonial worship would cause my hair to stand on end and my body and mind to catch fire with ecstasy.

I was ceaselessly drawn into communion—not just in the Kali Temple, the Radha-Krishna Temple, or the shrines of Shiva, but everywhere in the Dakshineswar Garden.

I worshiped the Goddess as Beauty and Power through the sanctified person of a fourteen-year-old girl who wandered through the temple gates from the nearby village. She was not even slightly disconcerted as I placed flowers on her dusty feet and repeated the mystical prayers and Sanskrit mantras of the ancient esoteric ceremony. After the rather long ritual was completed, during which I clearly perceived this dignified young woman as an embodiment of the Great Wisdom Mother, I placed my forehead at her sacred feet and offered some money which had been ceremonially purified. Not the slightest attachment to conventional forms of female beauty or to the conventional power of money existed in my being.

Such is the offering that every *sadhaka*, every intense seeker of God or Truth, must make in one form or another. Then this very earth will manifest its true nature as the Divine Realm of the Mother. Go forth and enjoy this miraculous creation as companions of Divine Bliss. The Mother projects the entire world, moment by moment, from Her own Ecstasy. Simply remember that all phenomena come from Her, belong to Her, abide in Her, and disappear into Her.

During those first sixteen years of my residence at the Temple Garden of Rani Rasmani, every sacred theatrical performance was experienced as the direct presence of Divine Reality, manifest through the transparent forms of the actors and actresses, no matter how unconcentrated their state of mind or how undisciplined their mode of life. Thus I directly witnessed the entire sacred history of India—the vivid episodes in the holy lives of Sita, Rama, Lakshmana, Hanuman, and countless other earthly and heavenly figures—unfolding its enlightening drama through flesh and blood, space and time. After these performances, I always worshiped with sandalwood paste and flowers the feet of the actors and actresses. Conservatives would stare at me in shock and amazement, crying: "The brahmin priest is worshiping the feet of low-caste persons of loose moral character. This is unacceptable!" Now I perform these spontaneous acts of worship inwardly, beyond the reach of curious gazes. But at that time, I simply could not conceal my ecstasy, even to the slightest degree. What would you do if you actually saw the Divine Incarnation, Lord Rama, and his magnificent consort,

Lady Sita, standing right before your physical eyes, alive and tangible, smiling and offering their blessings? What sheer delight! What madness of delight!

Most often I devoutly worshiped the feet of young women, because of my profound connection with the Goddess. To my vision, these pure and innocent girls were none other than the Divine Mother, Her inexhaustible fecundity of manifestation. What need did I have for temples and images constructed by human hands? I could also perceive prostitutes, though hardly pure and innocent by conventional standards, as sheer Divine Manifestation. One day I encountered a well-known prostitute, dressed in blue, standing beside the holy *bakul* tree in the Temple Garden. She was Lady Sita herself—the purest, most disciplined and courageous among women. Her eyes filled with tears as I approached, and I perceived these as ecstatic tears of longing to meet her beloved Lord Rama, having just been rescued from the imprisonment of the demon Ravana. I fell at her lotus feet and became lost in trance for hours, communing directly with Divine Purity and Divine Love.

Another day, I was taken by carriage to one of the great parks of Calcutta for a refreshing change of atmosphere, hoping to find some respite from the crushing intensity of the constant mystical experiences that occurred within the powerful precincts of the Dakshineswar Garden. But there is no escape from the intensity of Mother's relentless manifestation and revelation. A huge crowd was gathered in the park to observe the ascension of a brightly colored hot-air balloon. The level of ecstasy in this body and mind is immensely heightened when surrounded by large numbers of people, because each human being can be experienced as a direct Divine Manifestation. When the intrinsic holiness of each person is multiplied in a large crowd, the effect upon this subtle nervous system is overwhelming. Trying with great effort to hold on to ordinary relative awareness—just so I could enjoy the festive atmosphere of the park and watch the ascension of the balloonist into the clear blue sky—I suddenly noticed an English boy, dressed in European garb, leaning casually against a tree. The position of his body was similar to the traditional icons of Lord Krishna, whose holy form is represented as bent in three places by the intensity of the Divine Love he incarnates moment by moment. Even with his foreign dress, his light hair and skin, this Western boy became the full embodiment of the youthful Krishna. I became lost in the ocean of Krishna's Love, the undifferentiated *samadhi* of His Love. If my companions had not carefully supported me, I would have fallen headlong to the earth, which had become the sacred soil of Vrindavan, the eternal abode of Krishna.

A similar experience occurred while visiting a country village. The cowherd boys there manifested clearly as the companions of Lord Krishna in the transcendental groves of Vrindavan, lush and green, filled with the music of streams. Through the dust-brown landscape, I ran to these surprised children and placed sweets into their hands and even directly into their mouths. I was filled with the tender intimacy of Krishna's own Divine Love. I humbly requested the young boys to feed me, oblivious of any distinction of caste—for the lovers of God have no caste, no conventional context, no limitation—and oblivious even of the dirt on their hands, which became for my vision the dust on Lord Krishna's lotus feet that actually walked upon this sacred earth. Bowing low before these children, I asked for their blessings, as they were clearly filled with Krishna-consciousness. These were Krishna's constant companions, who bring the cows to graze in the morning light and return them in the cow-dust hour of sunset, when the rays turn red and gold as they stream through the dust rising from the ancient trails.

O beloved friends, without the slightest doubt, you are also the immediate companions of Lord Krishna. If Mother will permit me to reveal this, the One Reality that plays as Lord Rama, Divine Majesty incarnate, and that plays as Lord Krishna, Divine Love passionately incarnate, is right before your eyes, filling this present vessel of body and mind as Ramakrishna. The darling of my heart, my spiritual child who has mystically been carried and given birth from my subtle body, Rakhal, is now resting his head in the lap of Divine Love. When he realizes fully his eternal companionship with Krishna—after much intense meditation and after transmitting the highest spirituality to thousands of persons in the future—he will burst the limits of manifestation and disappear completely into Krishna's Love.

O intimate companions, how consuming my existence was during those early years in the Temple Garden. Even if a millionth part of that spiritual intensity were to enter an unprepared nervous system, it would break into pieces, as when a mad bull enters the open gate of a walled garden, tearing down and uprooting the delicate growth there. Sometimes, for days on end, I had no awareness whatsoever of the relative universe that you habitually perceive around you. This Temple Garden was revealed, to my ecstatic vision, as a vast dynamic play and interplay of various exalted realms. I was so completely defenseless and powerless that Rani Rasmani, the great devotee of Kali, and later her loyal son-in-law Mathur Babu, insisted on keeping me in one of the elegant guest rooms of her mansion here at Dakshineswar. I did not know whether I was residing in a mansion or in a thatched hut, although I lived there for sixteen years before moving to this room nearer to Mother Ganga. One day, in front of the mansion, or *kuthi*, I saw Arjuna's chariot. Lord Krishna was standing in it as the charioteer.

When I was surrounded by the women of that large household, I regarded myself solely as a young handmaiden of the Divine Mother. I even wore a sari, and people perceived with amazement that I walked and moved with precise feminine grace. My spiritual sisters and spiritual mothers felt completely comfortable in my presence, inviting me into their most intimate circles with no self-consciousness. They experienced me as a small boy or girl who has not yet developed awareness of gender. I even used to escort one of the older daughters to her husband's chamber for marital union, walking through the night with an oil lamp, surrounded by her trusted maidservants. I experienced this event as Radha visiting Krishna.

Even now I remain in that blessed state where persons and phenomena are transparent to God, although I have been permitted by Mother Kali to conceal it somewhat. God-vision is always exploding secretly within me. But when this boy Rakhal repeats one of the beautiful Divine Names in a whisper, just barely moving his lips, I cannot control my emotion. The fire of Divine Rapture sweeps through my being, and I melt into the formless ocean of God's Love. This is a Divine Response, not a human reaction.

Although surprisingly diverse, my experiences remain centered around the Feminine—both as the principle of cosmic manifestation and as the transcendent wisdom that unlocks this manifestation, merging it again into the luminous darkness of the Unmanifest. Whereas now I usually see myself as a helpless small child of the Universal Mother, in earlier years I was Her handmaiden—feeding the Goddess, adorning Her with flowers, fanning Her holy image, serving Her and playing with Her in countless ways. Someone once watched me from behind while I was gathering flowers for the worship of Goddess Kali, placing them carefully in a basket carried over one arm. I was dressed in a red sari of Benares silk, the favorite of Divine Mother. This observer was Mathur Babu, both a pragmatic and a spiritually sensitive man who saw many modes of Divine Manifestation pass through this form, reverently accepting them all. He told me later that, while moving through the rose garden, I was absolutely indistinguishable from a woman.

But where there is Shakti, the feminine principle, there is also Shiva, the masculine principle. Once Mathur watched me strolling back and forth on the veranda of his mansion. Through the columns, he could see me moving slowly, deep in ecstasy, pacing first in one direction, then returning. As I walked toward him, this form manifested as Goddess Kali—brilliantly black, with four arms and a ravishing smile. As I turned and walked away from him, this form appeared as Lord Shiva—snow-white in complexion, naked, adorned with bone orna- ments and a living serpent. Mathur began trembling and weeping at this vision, which he tested by looking away several times, but which persisted for more than an hour. These wonderful tears flowed for three days. His body was continuously shaken by tremors of ecstasy. The temple affairs were completely neglected. He was not even able to eat or sleep. At last, he came to me for relief and I prayed to Mother, running my palms down his body, front and back, respectfully request- ing Her *kundalini* energy to subside.

When Mathur returned to a functional state, I scolded him severely. "You pestered, bothered, and importuned me to share some of my mystical experiences. Now Mother has given you a mere drop, and you can finally understand that it is beyond your capacity. Your sacred role is to protect this Kali Temple and the unprecedented Divine Manifes- tation which is unfolding here. Please do not be so foolish in the future."

We laugh delightedly at the tone of voice the Master used to scold Mathur, adopting perfectly a motherly pique, serious yet indulgent. The Paramahamsa is a consummate actor who can play anyone simply by becoming that person. He has, in actual fact, become all roles and dimensions of human and divine experience.

Now the Great Swan leaps to his feet and regales us by imitating, with minute accuracy of detail, the singing and dancing style of a famous woman performer from Calcutta. Such waves of laughter we have never before experienced, as the blissful sage spins from the porch back into his room, almost colliding with Mother Sarada, who is just bringing the midday meal. Bowing before his consecrated partner with palms joined at his heart, Ramakrishna tenderly and playfully proclaims: "How supremely blessed I am to take refuge beneath the shade of this beautiful tree!"

13

Radha and Krishna in Mystic Union

The Festival at Panihati

TODAY PROMISES to be most joyous and dramatic, for the Great Swan of Bliss is invited to attend a festival of *kirtan,* or cosmic dance. The annual gathering at Panihati was inaugurated several hundred years ago by an inspired disciple of Chaitanya, the very emanation and embodiment of Divine Bliss. Even the casual mention of the name Bhagavan Chaitanya stirs intense waves of ecstasy in Ramakrishna's inward being—waves that are communicated to the hearts of those who are in his blessed company, for none of his companions are separate from him. Our Master often remarks: "Just find out who you are and who I am. You will discover the very same Reality. Then you will know—with a certainty more clear and direct than any limited form of knowing—that our companionship is eternal, our beings inseparable."

Mother Sarada, the holy consort and ever-virgin bride of Ramakrishna, wishes to attend today's festival with her husband, whom she regards as her Divine Beloved. Yet Sarada's intense predilection for hiddenness eventually prevails, and she sweetly informs Ramakrishna of her decision to remain within the Temple Garden today, meditating in solitude. To lighten her heart, her playful husband laughs and feigns great relief, exclaiming: "The crowds of pilgrims at Panihati would have pointed at us as we walked together in ecstasy and called us the goose and the gander, the *hamsi* and the *hamsa.*" Sarada, now laughing delicately as well, touches the feet of the Paramahamsa with a deeply traditional gesture of love and reverence. Such energy is released from the flash of visible communion between these brilliant souls, the Radha and Krishna of the present age, that we are struck with awe.

After the Paramahamsa prostrates himself fervently in the direction of Mahakali's Temple, placing his forehead upon the sacred dust as he receives permission from his blissful Mother, the companions of Divine Love depart, riding with the Beloved in a carriage sent from Calcutta by one of the lovers. Small villages are dynamically awakening. The countryside of open meadows is spacious. The sky is a brilliant blue and the morning sun already intense. Ramakrishna is also becoming dynamic, spacious, intense. He shines with a distinctly feminine beauty, in the mode of Chaitanya, who is experienced by advanced practitioners to be Radha and Krishna together in mystic fusion, blissfully playing through a single body—at once male and female, human and Divine, far beyond all notions of duality.

Perhaps this is why Mother Sarada chooses to remain within her secret room at Dakshineswar, hidden behind palm-frond screens on the first floor of the small music pavilion, immersed in contemplative union even as she engages in daily chores. Profoundly inward by temperament, she prefers her husband to manifest both the masculine and the feminine energies of Divine Love before the astonished and adoring eyes of devotees. Later, Sarada will be widely known as Holy Mother. She is destined to reveal the diamond of her true nature before thousands of pilgrims—accepting their adoring worship and granting them not only *darshan,* or a glimpse of living Truth through the human form, but also *diksha,* or *mantra* initiation, transmitting to them the energy that permits liberation into the Truth.

From the still center of a slowly gathering storm of rapture, Ramakrishna jokes and plays as we bounce along the dusty road, moving farther and farther from traces of modern civilization. He appears to be entirely unaware of the powerful Divine Current rising through his being—a volcano of love ready to erupt. The Master is chewing betel and explaining the genesis of this particular festival. Chaitanya gave his companions a clear mandate. Bring the revolution of Love openly, nakedly and freely to one and all, with absolutely no distinction of caste, class, or creed. Again and again, with evident delight, our Master now repeats the fundamental affirmation of Chaitanya: "The lovers of God have no caste. They belong to no conventional social or religious context."

In the sixteenth European century, Bengal was drenched by the monsoon of Chaitanya's great love, which swelled into flood the rivers of his noble companions. The whole planet is destined to be flooded by the same subjectless, objectless love that now streams through Ramakrishna and his lovers—not for the founding of a new religion but to flow through the channels of all ancient wisdom traditions, clearing away blockages of formality and other more subtle obstacles, guiding sincere seekers once more into the purest mystical core of their respective disciplines.

As our elegant carriage begins to approach the temple of Radha-Krishna at Panihati beside the holy banks of the Ganges, we can see thousands of precious human forms dancing in ecstatic waves to the throb of hundreds of drums, punctuated by the unearthly ringing of finger cymbals. A melodious thunder can be heard, even at this distance—the vigorous crying out of the powerful Divine Name, Radha-Krishna. The feminine aspect is mentioned first, for this is the conflagration of Radha's love. The Master is singing very softly, almost under his breath: "O Radha, who wanders in ecstasy through the green groves of Vrindavan, you are ours and we are yours." His face is vividly flushed with emotion. He is evidently merging with Radha, the consort of Lord Krishna.

Our forward progress is now being impeded by crowds of pilgrims. The Great Swan startles us by suddenly leaping from the door of the slowly moving carriage and rushing into the field of dancers, which is like an expanse of amber wheat, waving in the strong wind of fervent devotion. Following him with difficulty through this swirling landscape of ecstatic beings, we find our Master already unified with the chanting party of Navadvip Goswami, the spiritual guide of Mani Sen, who invited us to the festival and kindly brought us in his carriage. Amazed at this spontaneous mode of navigation, we gratefully join Ramakrishna in the circle, dancing with both arms upraised, feeling no sense of restraint, shyness, or even self-awareness. There simply is no conventional world or conventional self anywhere—just a field of flashing smiles, the pervasive fragrance of sandalwood oil, and the rhythmic thunder of the chant. Now and then the revered older guide, the Goswami, tenderly supports Ramakrishna, who is manifesting as a golden-skinned youth of sixteen, as our Master enters *samadhi,* complete absorption in God-consciousness.

Gradually, the surrounding dance circles begin to notice the radiant, free-flowing figure of the Paramahamsa, or perhaps they are just intuitively sensing his exalted presence, because an entirely new level of rapture is being reached by everyone. The lovers are now leaping from the ground as if they have entered another gravitational field. An unimaginable wave of pure love sweeps through the entire festival. It is as if Chaitanya has returned, some three hundred years later, to enjoy the blissful company of his loyal lovers.

Ramakrishna is a superb dancer, free from artificiality or affectation, producing no unnatural gestures, never engaging in mere acrobatics. His movements are unexpected yet rhythmical, none of them appearing random or out of control. In whatever direction he moves, the circles of surrounding dancers spontaneously give way, making room for the divinely inebriated sage, who is like a golden fish swimming freely in a vast, clear lake—sometimes slowly and grandly, other times with blinding swiftness. Tenderness, sweetness, and leonine strength are visible in all his limbs. Lips crimson from chewing betel, his smile is the heavenly smile of Radha, Queen of Love.

Various dancers are now weeping and rushing toward the God-man, showering him with blossoms and flower garlands. Some dancers fall to the ground before him in ecstatic trance. The Paramahamsa stops momentarily, touching them on the chest and returning them to relative awareness. Tears seem to be exploding directly from our eyes into space, rather than rolling down our cheeks. Blissful laughter wells up within us. The powerful yet tender calling, crying, singing, and thunderous chanting, *Radha-Krishna O Radha-Krishna,* sounds to our ears like *Ramakrishna O Ramakrishna.*

We have never seen our Master traversing so many subtle shades of ecstasy. He is like a limitless palette of Divine Colors. His body is now visibly aglow with flame-colored radiance, further awakening sublime devotion within the hundreds of persons who are now circling around his illumined form, which sometimes flows like a gentle stream and other times dances like a cosmic fire.

Suddenly, Ramakrishna stands still in *samadhi,* his wearing-cloth falling from his body, until a companion ties it about his waist again. The chanting modulates to a softer tone, and our Master begins to sing a traditional hymn, improvising exquisite new lines, his heart-melting tenor rising above the murmur of the *mahamantra.*

> Gaze now, astonished lovers,
> upon the companions of Chaitanya,
> who weep tears of love like rivers

as they sing the ineffably sweet Name,
Radha-Krishna, Radha-Krishna.

When the companions of Love
are lost in sacred dance,
the whole world dances with them,
unable to resist their attraction,
swept away by waves of affection.

When these lovers weep,
the entire universe receives
the gift of spiritual tears.
When they are treated harshly,
they respond only with love,
offering to all without exception
the pearl of the Divine Name,
the all-liberating *mahamantra,*
once held secret by the sages.

When the friends of God
drink the wine of love
in their circles of dance,
the universe is intoxicated.
The limited beings we were
have now disappeared.
Only forms of one Love remain,
perennial forms that manifest
blissfully from age to age.

All rules and restrictions
dissolved by ecstasy,
there is no more caste,
no more distinction.
We embrace as equals.
None is untouchable or alien.
No one stands outside
the circle of supreme Love.

The world is completely lost
in the blessed madness of Love.

When lovers chant Krishna's Name,
the universe, held in their hearts,
is chanting Krishna's Name.
Who chants other than Krishna?
What exists other than Krishna?

Negative intentions evaporate
beneath the rising sun of Love.
All sense of animosity disappears.
Who is enemy and who is friend
when only Love shines?

Gaze now, astonished lovers,
on the friends of supreme Love,
who manifest again and again
to purify and dissolve
the world of limitation.
The very earth is trembling
beneath the thunderous dance
of this Divine and human love.

The entire festival is consciously centered on the brilliant figure of the
Paramahamsa, moving in harmony with him as he now dances gradually
toward the Radha-Krishna Temple, which appears to float, like a white
jewel, in the green landscape. The entire evolutionary process of the
Master's timeless dance has consumed some two hours of earthly time.
The Paramahamsa is a dynamic ocean of bliss. Through contemplating his
form, true lovers are now seeing God face to face. Our companion Ram
Datta is in ecstasy, taking handfuls of sand, touching them to the holy
feet of Ramakrishna, and distributing a few grains to each of the hundreds
of devotees who are trying to approach and touch this living flame of
love. Many persons are now prostrating themselves at full length before
the dancing feet of the God-man.

We are among the few pilgrims who can fit into the sanctuary. The
Paramahamsa is now standing completely still before the ancient image
that depicts the mystic fusion of lover and Beloved in cosmic dance.
Ramakrishna is the very Reality toward which this image is pointing. We
are compressed within the dim light of the shrine like grapes being
crushed to make wine. Hundreds of voices around us are crying melodi-

ously to Radha-Krishna, and this poignant cry is being echoed from outside by thousands of voices, operating at full power, roaring like ocean waves breaking on the shore—*Radha-Krishna, Radha-Krishna, Radha-Krishna*. Again in our hearts we hear *Ramakrishna, Ramakrishna, Ramakrishna*. These great waves of holy sound roll across the Ganges, and even those on the far banks of the sacred river are chanting and breathing with us in unison.

14

Meeting Mother Sarada

Where There Is Shiva, There Is Shakti

ABUNDANT RAIN IS falling this morning. Every leaf and flower petal is dripping. The Temple Garden is intensely green and fragrant, its atmosphere inward and mysterious. Mother Sarada is preparing the noon meal on the veranda of the music pavilion, behind screens woven from palm leaves. We help to pour flour from a heavy container and to cut vegetables. Later, we walk beside her, holding a large umbrella, as she brings the food to the northern door of the Master's room, where the resonance of drums, cymbals, and ecstatic voices meets the steady rhythm of large raindrops.

Gongs and conch shells are announcing the formal midday worship at the magnificent temple of Mahakali. But here before us is the Goddess incarnate. Sarada is wearing a simple white sari with broad red borders. A vermillion mark graces her noble forehead. Her hair is thick, long, and very black. She is beautifully adorned with golden necklaces, nose ring, earrings, and bracelets—precious ornaments that were once worn for six months by her God-intoxicated husband while he lived in the spiritual mood of Radha, Queen of Love. Sarada pursues her secluded practice of sanctity in the tiny Nahabat, invisible as a shy bride. Yet she manifests the same intensity of Divine Reality as her sublime husband. "She conceals her colors," the Paramahamsa remarks, "like a village cat who rolls in ashes." There is no distinction in essence between Sarada and Ramakrishna. As Sita, consort of Lord Rama, once explained: "In one form, I am Sita. In another form, I am Rama."

The principal chores are now completed. We can relax. There is no sense going anywhere in this downpour. We are seated on grass mats with Sarada's close woman disciple Yogin and her mother, as well as Balaram's wife and several other women companions of Divine Love. We encircle the diminutive form of Mother Sarada. Someone is braiding her hair, which she always enjoys. Smiling playfully, she remarks: "Remember the Master's words: 'All women are living images of the Goddess.' He even addresses the actresses at the Star Theater as 'my blissful mothers.' " Delighted laughter spreads around the circle.

SARADA One afternoon, the Master came over here to visit. I was gone for a few minutes. When I returned, I saw him reverently offering sacred *bel* leaves before this photograph of his own form. He was repeating in ecstasy: "Here is Divine Reality, perfectly depicted in its True Nature." My eyes were fully opened to his Divinity. I was inspired to ask him for liberation from this earthly plane of existence. He laughed like a boy and replied: "I will incarnate again, and you will not be able to resist the divine attraction to join me. Our roots are inextricably intertwined, like the *kalmi* creeper that covers a pond. Pull one strand and the entire clump moves."

Since that time, I have devotedly worshiped this photograph of the Master, in which he sits cross-legged, smiling, plunged in timeless *samadhi*. Divinity pours in torrents through the beautiful, playful form we call Ramakrishna Paramahamsa. When I rub his limbs with oil before he bathes in the holy Ganga, I can clearly see Divine Light emanating from every single pore of his skin. Once the Master wrote the *mantra* of Kali on my tongue with his finger. For hours afterward I alternated between laughing, weeping, and motionless silence. Ramakrishna simply is Goddess Kali.

What wonderful love and respect he showed for his mother, Chandramani, when she lived with me here. Every morning he would come to salute her, placing his head humbly and tenderly at her feet. He would often say: "I do not regard her only as my personal mother but as the Mother of the Universe." When she passed away at ninety-five, he wept. As a young bride, when I was massaging his feet, I asked my husband his attitude toward me. He answered in a tender voice that filled my heart to the brim with Divine Bliss: "My dear, the Goddess who manifests in the Kali Temple is also fully manifest through your form." When the Master asks my advice, as he often does, I demur, return here to the solitude of the Nahabat, and pray fervently to Goddess Kali: "O Mother, please reveal to me what I should tell him."

The Master has just as many women disciples as men. His affection and compassion for women and men is absolutely equal. He encourages the women lovers of Divine Love to be very strong. Ramakrishna Paramahamsa remarked to one of our spiritual sisters: "Suppose a certain man takes great pains to help you, but you realize he is simply under the spell of your physical beauty. Should you continue to be kind and affectionate toward this man? Would it not be more compassionate to aim a hard kick at his chest and tell him to stay away? You must not be kind to all persons under all conditions. You must discriminate carefully."

The Master's compassion is supernatural. A poor woman arrived at the Temple Garden one Sunday afternoon, bringing four *rasagollas*. They were sweets of excellent quality and obviously represented a huge expenditure for her. The Master's room was crowded with male devotees, as it is today, and she did not feel comfortable entering there to present her offering, so she came here, weeping. At that very moment, we observed the Master burst forth from his room onto the circular porch overlooking the sacred waters of Mother Ganga. He was in a mood of ecstatic restlessness. Suddenly he turned and walked directly through the garden to this veranda. He did not even take the path. His expression was very intense, and it appeared that he was looking for someone. The moment he entered here, his eyes fell upon the poor woman. His spiritual mood changed in a flash and he asked her, with the voice and manner of a small child: "Mother, I am terribly hungry. Can you give me something to eat?" I have seldom witnessed such delight as on that woman's emaciated face. She gave him her *rasagollas*, and he joyfully finished all four, right on the spot, although he had not been able to take more than a few morsels of his midday meal. Chanting KALI KALI KALI, he returned to his room along the path, fully satisfied. We felt entirely refreshed as well. On many occasions, when the Master eats or drinks, those around him become suddenly and miraculously satisfied.

Not just human beings come to take refuge with Ramakrishna Paramahamsa. A mother cat and her three kittens once found shelter at his holy feet, sleeping on his bed with him and showing him much affection. He was greatly concerned that these animals might receive rough treatment at the Temple Garden from workers, priests, or visitors, so he requested one of our spiritual sisters to take mother and kittens to her home in Calcutta. He made the woman promise that these animals would be treated kindly and never given to anyone who might be thoughtless or harsh. The Master would inquire after them from time to time—just as he does concerning his other disciples—always repeating: "Please remember, these cats have taken refuge with me." After about one year, the mother cat suddenly became ill. As the animal was dying, our sister poured holy water from the Ganga into her mouth while repeating the *mantra* of liberation: OM RAMA-KRISHNA, OM RAMAKRISHNA.

What a delicate friendship the Master enjoys with his women devotees! Once he was visiting Mahendra's house. Three young married girls and two older women arrived bearing a large offering of *sar,* a favorite confection of Ramakrishna Paramahamsa, purchased from the finest shop in Calcutta. The moment the Master saw them, he laughed with delight and cried: "How did you discover me here? What sweet have you brought?" They conversed together about spiritual and practical subjects. Suddenly, a rather pompous and conservative male companion of the Master arrived and requested entry to the small reception room. The two mature women moved to one corner, but the Master beckoned the three young brides to hide under the bed where he was sitting. The companion entered, talked for an hour, and left without noticing them. The young women, who had been stifling their laughter, tumbled forth from hiding, seriously bitten by mosquitoes. Tears of hilarity were streaming down the Master's cheeks. He then invited our sisters to share refreshments in the private inner chambers of the house, continuing to offer them rich instruction, ranging from the way to attain God-vision to secrets for developing harmony in the extended family. They did not return to their homes until nine that evening. When a person feels ecstatic love for the Master, she needs nothing else.

The rain is still drumming with steady rhythm. The various frogs and insects of the monsoon season are singing their instinctive forms of praise. The intimacy created by the delightful, gentle tones of Mother Sarada surrounds and embraces us. Who is this humble woman the Paramahamsa recognizes and fervently worships as Mahakali? The longing to understand the mystery of Sarada-Ramakrishna arises in us spontaneously. As she sits on the floor, both feet stretched out straight, rosary of one hundred and eight *rudraksha* beads resting in her lap, a distant look comes over the beautiful eyes of Holy Mother. Gradually, she enters the state of supreme union, eyes wide open yet indrawn. Almost an hour passes in wonderful stillness and radiance. Now the emanation of the Wisdom Goddess begins to speak. She is in subtle ecstasy. Her voice manifests a slightly different timbre.

SARADA It is afternoon and everyone is resting comfortably. The Divine Images have been withdrawn and the temples are sealed. Every phenomenon has become peaceful and transparent. Does God exist only when the eyes are closed in meditation and cease to exist when the eyes are open? All that surrounds us—all this, all this—is Mother's Grace.

Ah, the ceaseless Divine Journey to the earthly plane! There is liberation for creatures but not for God. Wherever there is Shiva, sheer transcendent awareness, there is Shakti, the compassionate energy of manifestation. Shiva and Shakti are always together in mystic union. As the Master teaches: "One cannot consider the Absolute without the relative, or the relative without the Absolute." Shiva and Shakti are once more at play here within the Dakshineswar Temple Garden in the beautiful dancing form of Ramakrishna Paramahamsa. Who can really understand? This is all the Play of God. The love you experience from your parents is God's Love. The compassion you witness in an awakened sage is God's Compassion.

People will never be able to imagine how much Ramakrishna suffers for their sake. The constant fire of his ecstasy consumes the world's impurity and negativity. Even a strong spiritual practitioner can barely cancel out her own negative *karma*. Who possesses the power necessary for world transformation? This is the secret of Ramakrishna Paramahamsa. How soulfully the Master sings: "Behold, the Lord of the humble and the suffering has now come to lift up the humble and the suffering."

All living beings are my spiritual children, and they are destitute beggars. Yet if any call out sincerely—*Mother, Mother, Mother*—Divine Reality immediately responds and descends. Bhagavan Chaitanya was that same descent of Divine Reality. The Lord manifests in human form again and again. The same moon shines in the sky, night after night, simply assuming different shapes, occasionally disappearing but then appearing again. God is the most tender servant of the creatures. They are the living essence of Divine Nature. The Divine pours forth tenderness to the Divine. Simply cry out with a real cry and God must respond. God is the miraculous Tree of Life that fulfills all aspirations. Yearn and you will surely realize God.

This time the Master has taught the entire world the supremely powerful Divine Name—*Ma, Ma, Ma*. He has transmitted Mother's Wisdom-Energy to one and all. She gives birth to beings and universes from Her Womb of primordial Awareness and swallows them again into Her radiant Blackness. Her infinite Awakeness constitutes the liberation and enlightenment of sentient beings. The career of the soul and of existence itself is simply Her Presence, Her Playfulness, Her Grace. Who understood Mother so clearly before the Master came?

Previous sages insisted that life is such intense suffering for the creatures. But who really suffers, God or the creature? The Master reveals that it is God's Suffering. There is no limit to this Divine Passion. Who can imagine how much Ramakrishna suffers? He consciously embodies all beings. There is nothing separate from that One Reality we tenderly address as Ramakrishna Paramahamsa. Occasionally, I ask myself: "Will the creatures of God ever be able to appreciate the infinitely loving sacrifice of God which becomes their experience of creaturehood and, eventually, their liberation and illumination?"

The suffering and longing of creatures is the evolutionary path to mystic union. Divine Reality descends ceaselessly to experience this suffering and to awaken creatures from this suffering. Ramakrishna feels the pain of those who come to him much more intensely than they do. So sensitive and sympathetic is God! God actually knows and understands every degree of suffering from within each particular experience of each conscious being. God does not retreat or withdraw into Divine Transcendence.

Now and then I see very clearly that Ramakrishna has simply become all this—he is the blind, he is the crippled, he is the hungry, he is the oppressed. There are no persons exempt from these forms of suffering, on one level or another. Ramakrishna is the whole creation, longing for reunion with the Beloved. I offer God to whoever comes to me weeping for God. I offer the creatures their own Divine Nature. This is the process of initiation.

My women companions ask me to enjoy more sleep. They say that rising before three in the morning and retiring well after midnight is strenuous. But how can I sleep? I am fully aware of the excruciating suffering of living beings. By silently repeating the Divine Name in the depth of my heart, this universal suffering is gradually transformed into longing and eventually becomes illumination. I see this situation so clearly that it is difficult for me to stop praying in order to sleep, even for an hour. I sometimes think: "Instead of this limited human body, if only I could manifest an infinite Divine Form, perhaps I would be able to do more for suffering creatures."

A large ant was crawling across the floor, and someone intended to kill it. Do you know what I saw? This precious creature was not really an insect at all but Ramakrishna Paramahamsa. I clearly perceived his blessed hands, his holy feet, his luminous face, his tender gaze. I immediately stopped that person from killing the ant. Mother Reality alone has become every form of life. I would like to care for each living creature without exception. As the Master teaches: "Do not be small-minded. Do not pray for gourds and pumpkins from God, when you should be asking for pure love and pure knowledge to dawn within every heart."

15

The Master
Expounds Advaita Vedanta

A LAZY, HOT AFTERNOON in late August. The Paramahamsa is napping in his surprisingly breezy room after the noon meal, cooked deliciously and served gracefully by his beloved Sarada. Our Master describes his mystical relationship with his wife as the intrinsic union between fire and its power to burn, or between milk and its lovely whiteness. These two persons are simply not two, except in conventional thought and perception.

The ceremonial offering of the sixteen traditional articles in the shrines of Radha-Krishna and Mahakali, accompanied by Sanskrit chanting and the ringing of gongs, are now completed. Dakshineswar Garden is silent, save for the continuous praise of the birds and the ceaseless *mantra* murmured by the sacred river. The doors to the places of formal worship are closed, and the Divine Images are enjoying their traditional period of rest. This unveils a mysterious sense of *purna,* fullness or completeness, a sense of pure presence pervading all phenomena in a natural, spontaneous manner. As the ancient sages of the Upanishads teach, completeness manifests from completeness and returns again into completeness.

Ramakrishna opens his eyes, sits up on his low bed, and begins to speak about the exalted insights of Vedanta, the culmination of the primeval Vedic wisdom of India. The Vedas expound the science of cosmic communion with the gods, cosmic harmony, and the heavenly journey of the soul, achieved through powerful rites and awakened *mantras* revealed to *rishis,* the seers of Truth. Vedanta, the dimension of transcendent insight, lies far beyond this sphere of ritual worship, leaving behind the notions of an objective cosmos and an individual soul. This realmless realm—OM TAT

SAT, or sheer transparency—can never be touched by body, speech, or mind. Vedanta shines forth when all shrines are sealed, when all worship is stilled, when Divine Forms and human forms are at perfect rest. As Ramakrishna often remarks: "Only Reality can know Reality."

We place our foreheads on the fragrant floor of the Master's room, prostrating with awe before this *rishi* of the present age, who so clearly manifests the stature of a world teacher by once again bringing spiritual science to its culmination as Vedanta. Yet this leader of humanity dresses like a simple villager. Just yesterday, a new visitor encountered our Master strolling through the rose garden, carefully examining the blossoms, and mistook him for one of the Temple gardeners. The Calcutta gentleman called peremptorily to the Paramahamsa to pick him a rose. Bruising his tender fingers, the selfless sage quickly and quietly complied.

We now observe Ramakrishna as he enters the spiritual mood of teacher. The child of the Divine Mother mysteriously disappears, and we encounter the lion's roar of a fully awakened Buddha. We are deeply grateful for this opportunity to receive the transmission of Vedanta directly from the Source of Wisdom, through the beautiful, bearded lips and sweet speech of Ramakrishna Paramahamsa. He usually presents this radical teaching only to the most intimate of his inner circle. Today, the Wisdom Mother is opening this dimensionless dimension for anyone who happens to be present, visiting from Calcutta on the Sunday holiday.

RAMAKRISHNA The objectless, subjectless insight into the essential nature of consciousness, or *atmajñana,* is radically investigated and unfolded only by a small group of Vedantic scriptures, such as the *Ashtavakra Samhita.* Not many seekers will be drawn to this most uncompromising discipline of direct knowing. Persons qualified for this path of knowledge feel completely comfortable and joyful when renouncing all notions of separate, substantial self-existence. They are the true proponents of *advaita,* nonduality, because they genuinely understand that they do not exist apart from supreme Reality. The knower and the known are simply not two. Reality alone shines: neither two nor even one. Beyond description or calculation.

Your very life-breath must become the conscious, timeless affirmation of Reality by Reality. SOHAM, SOHAM—I am It, It is I. Only the dualistic imagination perceives some separate practitioner who makes this primordial affirmation, SOHAM. To lose completely any notion of separate self, no matter how subtle or instinctive, is the true definition of *sannyasa,* the blessed life of renunciation. Nonduality is renunciation. As long as one imagines oneself to exist independently as initiator or recipient of various actions—either as actor, agent, subject, or object of any kind—then one has not completely renounced. The actual state of nondual knowledge is comparable to falling from a high tree and remaining clearly aware, without tensing a single muscle or feeling the slightest anxiety.

This level of renunciation is usually considered more appropriate for wandering sages or monastic practitioners than for men and women with family and social responsibilities. As long as one holds exclusively the personal view—"Such is my responsibility and I must perform it, because if I do not take the initiative, it will never get done"—one is not prepared to engage in Advaita Vedanta. One may entertain the teaching intellectually but will fail to embody transcendent insight directly.

Nonetheless, regardless of differences in the capacity to understand, this same Truth holds for every conscious being. There never is any duality. The principle of awareness, *atman,* never engages in any activity, although from this pure principle alone, the luminous, transparent, insubstantial universe spontaneously unfolds. When the practitioner is consciously identified, not with any expression of awareness but with the living principle of awareness—breathing SOHAM SOHAM—there remains no sense of intrinsic involvement with polarities such as good and evil, virtue and vice, self and other, existence and nonexistence. However, when one identifies with activity rather than with principle, manifesting an ego that claims to generate various chains of events, then the tensions between polar opposites split that person's consciousness, creating various forms of obvious and subtle suffering. The thick smoke from an open fire blackens the wall behind it but does not affect the very principle of empty space which permits fire to burn in the first place.

My dear friend, Krishnakishore, a radical Vedantist on fire with the most intense renunciation, affirms with total conviction and authenticity: "I am the principle of empty space, within which and by which all phenomena transparently manifest." This great practitioner is not a monk. He attends skillfully to his social and family responsibilities in the same effective way that space permits various phenomena to be displayed. This is an advanced level of realization, an inward *sannyasa,* not a mere intellectual position that any student of the *Ashtavakra Samhita* might claim.

Once one has received the initiatory transmission of Advaita Vedanta from an illumined sage, not simply from a textbook, it becomes fruitful to practice the radical attitude that one is free from individuality, free from particularity, free from any imaginable limits. One can sense when this attitude is approaching true *atmajñana*—omniconscious knowing, without any veils of knower or known, beyond mere playing with words and intellectual posing. How? Just as one distinguishes easily between a ripe mango and a green mango.

You should ceaselessly affirm, with every breath, every heartbeat, every action and intention: "I am freedom from every limitation. I am the principle of timeless awareness." The function of conventional consciousness—in the personal sphere, the social sphere, the religious sphere—is to proclaim various limits, barriers, partitions, distinctions, definitions, and frontiers, and then to submit to these abstractions, gradually becoming entirely enslaved by them. In effect, one is constantly repeating, consciously or unconsciously: "I am not free. I am bound up in all these categories of thought and perception." The conditioned person obsessively and even instinctively repeats: "I am worthless. I am superficial. I am incapable of transcendent insight. I am irrevocably immersed in family, career, and political concerns." This is not a mere verbal repetition but a routine ritual invocation of limited existence by the entire body and mind of the falsely isolated individual consciousness. This state of illusory bondage becomes increasingly vivid and convincing. You should choose, instead, to affirm with your whole being: "I know that supreme Reality alone exists, and this transcendent knowing is itself simply that Reality." How can such nondualistic awareness ever become limited by notions such as bondage, impurity, or imperfection?

The Master is presenting this revolutionary teaching of Advaita with the ferocity of a lioness protecting her cubs. He refuses to permit us to be stolen away by the delusion of duality. Adamantine conviction streams from his blazing heart, brilliant as the noonday sun, igniting our hearts with the ancient Vedantic transmission, the permission to practice this heroic attitude, this renunciation of every context whatsoever.

Yet as the very peak of this revelation, the demeanor of the mysterious Paramahamsa is undergoing an astonishing change. Right before our eyes, he is once more becoming childlike and vulnerable. The manifestation of invincible power is disappearing and complete powerlessness is now unveiled—a naked, simple, humble humanity. We sense this change of spiritual mood in our own bodies as a slight nausea, as if the sage is pulling us back suddenly into our own conventional level of experience in order to examine it clearly in the light of transcendent insight.

RAMAKRISHNA I am severely depressed today. My dear nephew, Hriday, has written that he is dangerously ill. All morning, I have been questioning: "O mind, why are you so miserable about Hriday's situation? Is it *maya* or *daya,* delusion or true compassion?" This is the inquiry every practitioner must engage in, moment by moment. *Maya* is the enslavement to dualistic abstractions. *Daya* is the beautiful functioning of nondual wisdom-energy in the form of tenderness, empathy, and affection. Please tell me, Mahendra, is my dejected mood an expression of dualistic projection and egocentric construction? Or is it unbearable compassion for all beings, the Great Compassion born spontaneously from the womb of the Wisdom Mother?

The most reticent among our Master's companions cannot find a single word to reply. There are unshed tears glistening in Mahendra's eyes. Perceiving the dilemma of his beloved disciple, the Paramahamsa laughs tenderly and speaks in tones of great kindness.

RAMAKRISHNA My dear, you know very well how the power of *maya,* the delusive sense of isolated individual existence, most often expresses itself—as obsessive concern, not only for oneself but for the joys and sorrows of one's own closest friends and relatives. Whereas *daya,* the selfless love and compassion shining from nondual wisdom, expresses itself as even-handed concern for the physical well-being and spiritual evolution of all persons, all precious living creatures, all forms manifested by Pure Consciousness. Now answer the question. Is my depression over Hriday's drastic condition an expression of *maya* or *daya?*

Again Mahendra is speechless. We all know how much Hriday has bothered and even tormented Ramakrishna over the years. Yet this awakened sage, liberated from all conventional limits, is now more intensely concerned than a mother over Hriday's welfare. The Paramahamsa even experiences the pain of the illness in his own body, identifying totally with his nephew's misery.

Mahendra's unspoken attitude is shared inwardly by all of us privileged to be here in the presence of Ramakrishna, who is sheer nondual wisdom and who flows ceaselessly as the most tender compassion for all beings without exception. If our hearts possessed voices, they would cry out in unison at this poignant moment: "O beloved guide, O Ramakrishna Paramahamsa, may the delusive power of *maya* be utterly extinguished in our being and may the transforming power of *daya* flow through us as our very life-breath, just as it flows through your holy person!"

16

The Mystery of Narendra and the Vow of Spiritual Completion

S URROUNDED BY BEAMS of morning sunlight, his body and mind just a play of Divine Radiance, the Great Swan is sitting in his room, the secret center of the Temple Garden. He is delightedly laughing and conversing with friends. The sweep of his conversation is very broad, ranging from intimate details concerning our daily lives—including illnesses, medicines, jobs, and family disputes, details that his highly focused mind retains with astonishing accuracy—to universal teachings about God-realization, which he always describes as "the one and only true goal of human existence."

Ramakrishna's attention flashes back and forth between these different levels swiftly and naturally. In his blessed presence, the ordinary and the extraordinary mingle and fuse, as all separate categories of thought and perception disappear into Divine Mystery. We may be discussing any subject with the blissful sage, in any of the surprising moods he manifests, yet we invariably receive the same transmission of awakened energy. The same blessing flows either through healing affection or as illuminating currents of understanding, through the laughter or tears of ecstasy, or simply as a sense of vast peace and well-being that springs directly from supreme Reality, reasonless and motiveless, without the slightest dependence on any limited sense of satisfaction belonging to the conventional world.

This morning our Master is returning again and again to the subject of Narendra, a brilliant young man of twenty, a sage from birth and even from before his present incarnation into the world of space and time. These two unique beings, Ramakrishna and Narendra, met first on the earthly plane in this very room. Narendra had been studying the journals of Wordsworth, and his British professor, when discussing the poet's states of contemplative rapture, mentioned to the class a certain sage at Dakshineswar who entered similar states of trancelike suspension and absorption. Narendra journeyed to the Temple Garden with only one burning question animating his entire being. With spiritual boldness and total sincerity, he asked Ramakrishna: "Can God be directly and fully experienced, and have you had this experience?"

This revolutionary young seeker of Truth had directed the same question to several important religious leaders and well-known practitioners, always bringing forth responses full of complicated qualifications and other forms of hesitation and equivocation. The Paramahamsa's reply was startling because of its relaxed tone, its simplicity, and its radical, unequivocal nature. Evincing none of the tenseness and self-consciousness that this leading question had stimulated in others, Ramakrishna simply laughed with delight—his eyes swimming with tears of joy as he instantly recognized the spiritual stature of Narendra, inexperienced and somewhat brash as the young man might be. "Of course, my dear," the blissful sage replied with tender affection, "Divine Reality can be experienced much more fully and directly than we are perceiving and understanding each other at this moment." These simple words created a response of complete confidence in the hypercritical mind and passionate heart of Narendra. His highly developed intellectual and moral conscience were completely silent in this historic encounter with his guide, his beloved, his own true nature.

During subsequent visits of Narendra to the Temple Garden, he and Ramakrishna together entered deep states of mediation and union. Our Master carefully explored the sublime dimensions of this *mahatma,* this great soul, discovering precisely how its miraculous incarnation occurred. Narendra will take the name Vivekananda, "Bliss of Clear Knowing," when he becomes the first fully enlightened being to travel from the ancient East into the modern West—arriving, penniless and without formal invitation, to attend the Parliament of Religions at the Chicago World's Fair of 1893 and spending the first night in a railroad boxcar. The blissful sage, enraptured as he speaks, now relives his original revelatory experience of Narendra's advent.

RAMAKRISHNA My awareness rapidly ascends through every illumined level of being, plunging toward the Mother Essence, the dazzling darkness of the absolutely Unmanifest, beyond any possible experience. Suddenly, seven timeless sages appear—a constellation of conscious stars, floating in the boundless awareness beyond all heavenly realms. These seven sages constitute the most subtle transition between relative and Absolute—between the play of Creator and creation, on one side, and the actionless, attributeless Reality on the other. For these primordial, genderless stars of wisdom, however, there are not two sides of Reality but only the inconceivable fusion of Absolute and relative. Their nondual awareness never encounters the Absolute without subtly encountering the relative, never experiences the relative as apart from the Absolute.

A bolt of radiance then emanates from the luminous darkness of the Mother Essence. This mysterious ray manifests as a five-year-old child, golden in color and tender in expression. The child enters into communication with one of these seven brilliant lights, which then begins to manifest in human form, seated gracefully in lotus posture, hands relaxed, palms up, one over the other in the *mudra* of encompassing mediation. This Buddha-figure emerges from its transcendent state of equipoise and expresses love for the child, who is like a flame dancing everywhere around the *muni*, or silent sage, and climbing affectionately onto his lap. This playful process is timeless, beyond all possible worlds, beyond the dynamic of birth and death, even beyond the principle of manifestation. Stammering in a charming manner, the child whispers into the ear of the eternally liberated sage: "I am descending into time. Please help me." The Buddha-figure smiles and a bright ray emanates from its right eye, penetrates through every plane of being like a needle passing effortlessly through many layers of loosely woven cloth, and touches a certain house in the city of Calcutta. That transcendent sage is the focus of boundless awareness which we experience here in the beautiful form of Narendra. The form now before you is the playful child.

This mystical encounter between Ramakrishna and Narendra blossoms like a fragrant lotus within our minds and hearts. We are experiencing both amazement and peace. Without the slightest inhibition, the Paramahamsa is weeping tears of love for Narendra, repeatedly asking us why the young man did not come to join a recent gathering in Calcutta. Our Master suddenly turns to one companion and proclaims: "Ah! Naren is so aloof, so independent! I understand he does not even visit you these days." The body of the divine child shivers once, twice, and he enters ecstasy, speaking aloud with the Divine Mother about Narendra, as if only She can understand and share this burning attraction and longing.

RAMAKRISHNA O blissful Mother, You know how even a glimpse of his form is elevating and inspiring. So much of Your Power is focused through him! His eyes are large and always indrawn, gazing into infinity. He is intellectually brilliant, many-faceted. His gift for music is heavenly. His rich singing voice is impeccable in pitch and spiritually incendiary. In philosophical studies, Naren far exceeds the level of his professors. He is absolutely free from emotional dependency, caring not in the slightest whether any person praises or blames him.

O companions of love, consider carefully. The other day, this glorious young sage—ever-free, ever-realized—was returning to Calcutta from the Temple Garden. He was preparing to walk the six miles. I had to implore him to ride comfortably in the carriage of a certain saintly lover of God. His host humbly requested Naren to sit beside him on the journey. Anyone else would have considered this an honor and a blessing. Not the unsheathed sword of wisdom. Naren took a seat on the opposite side of the carriage from his host, never once glancing at him throughout the entire trip. The wise older man told me about this remarkable behavior, understanding it as a clear indication of Narendra's stature. Nothing in this world—neither royal treasures nor religious honors—will turn my Naren away from his mission of Truth. Truth-force flows from his very pores.

O beloved companions, no one can reach the level of uncompromising spiritual intensity through scholarship alone. Even the most excellent understanding of a sacred text or a radical philosophical treatise does not generate the realization of its living energy in daily life. What is necessary is to pray without ceasing, to reach a state in which the sacred message or the high philosophical teaching is being profoundly assimilated with each breath, each thought, each perception. The essence of contemplative discipline is the constant remembrance of supreme Reality as the only Reality, regardless of the particular religious and cultural tradition through which one moves.

The famous Gauri from Indesh was a profound scholar of the scriptures as well as an intimate lover of God. These two modes can be harmoniously combined. His chosen ideal for worship was the Great Mother of the Universe. His contemplative practice gradually ripened to the stage at which one occasionally melts in ecstasy while repeating the Divine Name that is closest to one's heart. In these precious moments of communion and union between the worshiper and the holy object of worship, Gauri would chant hymns to the Goddess with immense fervor and transforming power. Beside this God-filled Gauri, who had momentarily become a channel for the infinite Power and Wisdom of the Divine Mother, various other *pandits,* men and women genuinely knowledgeable about religion, would appear as powerless and limited as the small green worms that climb laboriously from one blade of grass to another. Listening to him chanting during these moods of absorption, when his voice seemed to shake the entire Kali Temple, I would also be lifted into rare states of mystical experience. Pandit Gauri's main spiritual obstacle, however, was his religious exclusiveness. He narrowly focused his worship on the Goddess alone and could not accept other manifestations of Divine Presence, which are, after all, Her Manifestations. His intellect was constricted, his emotions limited. He took this narrow devotion to extremes. If someone had forced him to pick up a *tulsi* leaf, sacred to Lord Vishnu, Gauri would have used two long sticks to avoid touching it with his fingers.

Both the playful Paramahamsa and his listeners burst into laughter at this comic vision of the dignified *pandit,* vividly conjured by the Master's illumined imagination. As the waves of mirth subside, Ramakrishna breaks into a strangely intoxicating, high-pitched laughter that seems to flow directly from Goddess Kali, expressing Her Amusement at the very idea of placing limits upon Divine Reality. We are all laughing now in ecstasy. Some begin dancing and whirling with the freedom of the Wisdom Goddess, who opens all doors and dissolves all barriers. This storm of Her Bliss continues for more than thirty minutes and then disappears again, as unexpectedly as it came, leaving our upper garments damp with tears of laughter.

RAMAKRISHNA Pandit Gauri and this servant of the Mother now before you shared several months of close contact here at Dakshineswar. Then Gauri suddenly returned to his native village and lived in simplicity and seclusion, without his books or his students. Evidently Goddess Kali, who abides tangibly in this Temple Garden, appeared to him and instructed him. His spiritual life no longer consisted of an occasional heart-melting ecstasy but became constant communion with the Wisdom Mother, enlightening not only his secret heart but opening wide all dimensions of his intellect, emotion, and perception.

One day he reappeared, as unpredictably as he had disappeared. Such unpredictablity is an indication of Goddess-energy. Filled with Divine Delight, eyes luminous with tears, he reeled drunkenly through that door and prostrated full-length before the form now seated here. Gauri had become an overflowing fountain of Mother's illumination—liberal in the extreme, clearly perceiving only one wisdom-energy expressing itself equally through all the ancient scriptures and oral traditions. His inspired interpretation of sacred history opened the minds and hearts of everyone. The ten heads of the demon Ravana, he would teach, are the five organs of action and the five organs of perception when operating under the control of the limited self. The various holy personages in the scriptures he would interpret with uncanny accuracy as symbols for certain qualities of spiritual energy, certain levels of realization. His tender devotion to Rama, the kingly human manifestation of Lord Vishnu, was now just as intense as his fervent commitment to the all-transcending, all-embracing Goddess. She Herself had brought him to spiritual completion.

At precisely this moment, Mother Sarada appears at the door with her husband's midday meal. We all feel the touch of that completion spoken of by the Master as we observe the tender and respectful interaction between these two living figures from sacred history. Sarada-Ramakrishna is a complete expression of Divine Reality. The scripture of their life together has not yet been written with ink on paper but is being composed through mysterious Divine Action in the radiant *mandala* of the Temple Garden, right before our astonished gaze. Each of the companions looks into the shining eyes of the others in this heavenly palace of the Black Goddess, realizing silently that he or she has made precisely the same commitment to completion. Ramakrishna knows about our adamantine vow because he generated it. We now firmly renounce whatever desires or aspirations are partial or incomplete.

Our Master returns to a mood of childlike simplicity. He begins to partake lightly of fried bread with lentils, urged to do so by Mother Sarada, who sits on the floor before her husband, skillfully diverting his mind from its ceaseless upward surge with pleasant talk about the events of the day, spoken in her soft, measured tones. The rest of us rise to take our meal from the Temple kitchen, where every noontime some three hundred persons—wandering renunciates, temple workers, poor families from nearby villages, pilgrims, and visitors—are generously fed. If any guest cannot partake of prepared food but must cook his own meal for religious reasons, rice and lentils are given from the Temple storehouse.

We turn to catch one more precious glimpse of Master and Mother, seated together in subtle union. They are the Divine Image concealed within the heart of the universe and all living beings. Through the gift of companionship with these twin emanations of Divine Wisdom and Divine Love, may our lives be opened and deepened. May we share the experience of Gauri from Indesh, who was transformed by the mere presence of the Paramahamsa, without any debate, without even any words of instruction. May we return, as Gauri did, to this hospitable Temple Garden and to this fragrant chamber, awakened at last into spiritual completion. May we becme God-intoxicated and prostrate with boundless gratitude before these divinely human forms, Sarada and Ramakrishna.

17

Two Great Souls

Ramakrishna's Last Meeting with Keshab Sen

T HE CARRIAGE BEARING the Great Swan stops in front of the elegant Lily Cottage on Upper Circular Road. Here the renowned religious leader and social reformer Keshab Sen is experiencing the final days of his earthly existence. Once, the God-intoxicated sage arrived at this stately mansion, repeating: "Mother told me to eat an ice cream at Keshab's house." Keshab was politely protesting that no ice cream shops existed in that neighborhood, when a vendor unexpectedly rolled his ice-packed cart into the driveway of the estate. Ramakrishna finished his ice cream like a happy child, then grasped both hands of the dignified Keshab, and they danced in rapture, calling out the most intimate Divine Name: *Ma, Ma, Ma*—Mother, Mother, Mother.

Relatives and disciples of Keshab now gather eagerly around the cab door as Ramakrishna steps out, plunged into an ecstatic mood, his body supported by his companions. Servants with solemn faces lead us respectfully to the second floor veranda south of the formal reception room. Here Ramakrishna offers his profound respect to Keshab's mother, remarking to her: "Blessed is the womb that bore such a son. Many important people have been delighted and elevated by Keshab's teaching." This venerable woman, Sarada Sundari Devi, visits the sage regularly at Dakshineswar.

Sitting down cross-legged on a divan, our Master now enters meditation. A long period of silence ensues. Thoughts disappear from our minds like birds flying into the sky of the Paramahamsa's timeless awareness. Finally, he opens his eyes.

Ramakrishna now becomes extremely restless to meet with his beloved Keshab, complaining to some of the followers who are present: "Come, now! Why should I not go directly to him in the inner chambers? Why this formality? Why strain him to walk out here?" A certain Prasanna, an intimate student of Keshab's and a pure-hearted practitioner, replies courteously and humbly: "Reverend sir, he insists on getting dressed to meet you. He will be here in just a few moments."

"Nonsense!"—the Master is crying aloud, intensely agitated, yearning to commune with his inseparable friend—"It is all of you who are creating, with every thought and perception, this false sense of separation, these formal rules of communication."

Attempting to soothe the fiery sage, Prasanna gently and sweetly begins to describe Keshab's present mood. "Beloved Paramahamsa, the noble Keshab Sen is now a completely different person. His impressive scholarship and his dignified bearing as cultural and religious leader have been removed. He talks blissfully with Mother Kali just as you do. Experiencing Her Response inwardly, he calls out to Her with love. He laughs and weeps with ecstasy." The moment Ramakrishna hears these words, he enters deep *samadhi,* total absorption in the Mother, beyond any form of expression whatsoever, human or divine.

His body trembles subtly for a few minutes, particularly the thumbs, as if a powerful electrical current is consciously focusing and adjusting itself through the entire nervous system. Then the human form becomes perfectly still, except for a wonderful smile playing continuously across bearded lips. The eyes are partially open, unwavering, focused upon some ultimate central point. The figure appears to increase slightly in size, as if expanding into the boundless space of Divine Presence. Usually, we would see the hair on his forearms and calves standing on end, as though these limbs were bathed with static electricity, but it is winter, so the sage is wearing a green flannel coat, a green shawl thrown around his shoulders, and a green cap drawn down over his ears.

Ramakrishna's God-filled form is seated upright on the sumptuous divan, not leaning against its colorful bolsters and pillows. His beautiful meditative equipoise seems barely to touch the ordinary world of space and time. The family and disciples of Keshab gaze in amazement, and we the companions gaze as well, for one can never become accustomed to the miraculous sight of human reality merged consciously and completely with Divine Reality.

Fewer and fewer life signs are manifesting in the Master's body. No movement of breath is discernible. Experienced yogic adepts as well as medical doctors who examine the Paramahamsa in deep *samadhi* fail to detect even a heartbeat.

For more than an hour, we simply sit in the presence of this Divine Mystery. As the sun sets and the brief twilight passes, great peace descends palpably upon the entire household of Keshab Chandra Sen. When oil lamps are lit in the reception room, the Great Swan begins to show signs of returning into the realm of common awareness. Subtle trembling now comes in waves, as the rhythms of breath and heartbeat are reestablished. Supporting him under the arms, his legs moving almost mechanically like a puppet, we are able to bring the Paramahamsa into the warm light of the large room. He murmurs, like Radha longing for Krishna: "Take me to Keshab! Take me to Keshab!" Blinking and gazing around at the elaborate furnishings, the sage speaks softly to his blissful Mother, the Great Mother of the Universe. Everyone listens in perfect silence.

> RAMAKRISHNA KALI MA KALI MA KALI MA. Such earthly magnificence was necessary for Keshab's mission, his prophetic call to open the eyes of modern culture to Divine Reality, to impress even the wealthy and the Western-educated with the ideal of God-realization, to open minds and hearts that were closed to transcendence. But nothing on earth will be necessary for him now. Only You, O blissful Mother. Only You.

Catching a glimpse of his beloved spiritual son, Rakhal, who has been sitting beside him the whole afternoon, Ramakrishna is surprised and cries out tenderly: "My dear, so you are here, too, at the sunset of Keshab's earthly life. What joy to be together!" Gazing into the broad face of Rakhal, which shines with Divine Light like a full moon, our Master once more looses his tenuous hold on the human form and the human environment, slipping into the mysterious borderland between our collectively constructed world and the primordial realm of the Goddess. He looks around suddenly in joyous surprise, just as when he glimpsed Rakhal, and laughs aloud.

> RAMAKRISHNA O Goddess Kali, I see that You as well are manifesting here during the auspicious final days of Keshab. Ah, how beautifully You are dressed in Your brilliant red sari of Benares silk. How magnificent You look, Mother, with the mystic silver keys to every dimension tied in the corner of Your cloth. This must be a special occasion indeed. But please sit quietly beside me. Do not dance and ignite my being

with Your Fire of Ecstasy. I want to retain consciousness of conventional space and time. This will be my last meeting with Keshab in his earthly form.

Regardless of his plea for spiritual sobriety, the Paramahamsa enters a state of intense inebriation, displaying the symptoms of one intoxicated with strong wine—his center of gravity disappearing, his speech becoming indistinct, his eyes floating upward. Sometimes, during these moments, he speaks a language entirely unintelligible to the companions; at other times the highest teachings flow spontaneously from his lips. Such is the case this evening. The large group of people, filling the spacious reception room in Lily Cottage, lean attentively toward the Paramahamsa to decipher his slightly blurred yet eloquent words.

RAMAKRISHNA Body and soul! Sheath and sword! Vehicle and driver! This conditioned evolution, this physical nervous system, will inevitably disintegrate. A certain point in the natural process of disintegration is called death. Whatever is born within time must die within time. Whatever relative conditions come together must separate again, must transform again. This is the body. This is the world. But for the soul, which is a unique facet of the infinite diamond of Divine Reality, there is no death, no disintegration, not even transformation.

Consider the delicious betel nut. When the kernel is fully ripened, it no longer sticks to the shell, but when the nut is still even slightly green, it is difficult if not impossible to separate the kernel cleanly from the shell. After ripening into God-realization, into full spiritual maturity, awareness no longer identifies with its visible or subtle vehicles. The principle of awareness and the various experiential vehicles of awareness are no longer imagined to be stuck together. They belong to entirely different orders of reality.

At this moment of elevated concentration, Keshab Sen enters the room through the eastern door. Those of us who have been awed by Keshab's powerful discourses, delivered in the important lecture halls and liberal temples of Calcutta, are now shocked to see his emaciated form, barely able to stand, leaning against the wall for support. We remember the joyous vision of this excellent man, dressed in a white robe, standing in the Brahmo Temple, tears of spiritual emotion causing his eyes to shine as he addressed his dignified and intelligent followers on the new direction their ancient civilization must take. Much of his congregation would also be shedding tears. Most precious, however, is the memory of Keshab Sen—at the adamantine insistence of Ramakrishna Paramahamsa—delivering a lecture from the steps of the Kali Temple in Dakshineswar to the various devotees of both Keshab and the Master who happened to be present that afternoon. What joy the Great Swan experienced upon witnessing the vigorous oratorical style of Keshab, perceiving beneath its surface the living power of the Universal Mother.

With great difficulty and evident pain, refusing any assistance, the venerable leader of the Brahmo Samaj begins to sit on the floor before the Master. Ramakrishna leaps immediately from the large divan and joins his beloved friend on the Persian carpet. They sit together cross-legged, almost knee to knee, gazing at each other with unalloyed love. Now Keshab, palms joined at his heart, bows low before Ramakrishna, bending fully at the waist and remaining with his forehead at the lotus-feet of the Master for several moments. The silent profundity in the room is inexpressible.

As Keshab rises from this deep bow, the Paramahamsa is once more lost in ecstasy, a heavenly smile illuminating his countenance, conversing animatedly with his blissful Mother, the awesome Goddess Kali, about the destiny of the magnificent soul of Keshab Sen, this person of universal vision and empathy. Speaking as loudly as his weakened condition permits, Keshab calls out to the Master: "I am here, revered sir. I am here with you, longing to converse and commune with you."

Keshab takes the left hand of the Paramahamsa—the mystical hand, consecrated to the esoteric worship of the Goddess—and tenderly strokes it, hoping that the sage will return to the level of awareness at the twelve-petal heart chakra, where human conversation becomes possible for him once more. But the Wisdom Mother keeps Her precocious child in *bhava samadhi,* the state of partial absorption in which he remains so drunk with Divine Love that She alone can speak through him. This Divine Speech occurs at the sixteen-petal nerve center at the throat level in the subtle body of the human being—a body quite distinct from the visible, biological body.

The words that now stream from the smiling, bearded lips are at once music, nectar, fragrance, and radiance. As the sage so often explains: "There is only a transparent boundary of light distinguishing the embodied being called Ramakrishna from the open space called Mahakali." With great spiritual thirst, Keshab is drinking in this refreshment and illumination flowing directly from the heart of the Wisdom Goddess through the pure mind of the Paramahamsa.

RAMAKRISHNA As long as human consciousness continues to identify itself with *upadhis*—with various superimposed personal and cultural images—it remains conditioned to perceive multiple centers of individual awareness, such as Keshab, Prasanna, Rakhal. But when consciousness awakens to its own essential nature, as timeless and conditionless, then limitless awareness alone exists, perceiving only itself through all forms of life, through all configurations of manifestation. The entire universe, including its coherent laws and its amazingly diverse conscious beings on various planes of being, is simply an expression of primordial awareness— subjectless and objectless, ever-awakened, by nature peaceful and blissful.

Supreme Reality is not merely undifferentiated. It manifests subtly as various levels of power and clarity through different conscious beings, although always remaining the one secret essence of every phenomenon. Pandit Vidyasagar did not understand this wonderful mystery—the differentiation that unfolds spontaneously within the One Reality. He held an oversimplified view, asking, "How can it be true that God, Who is universal Justice, has endowed particular persons with greater spiritual capacity than others?" I laughed with abandon at his naiveté, replying: "If your view of God is correct, dear sir, then why can one person sometimes manifest the power of fifty persons? Why, for that matter, have we taken so much trouble to come visit you and listen to your words?"

Any soul through whom Divine Reality displays its Power and Wisdom with much greater intensity and clarity—such as the beloved Keshab Sen, who has stirred the spiritual consciousness of so many—is like the inmost chamber of God's palace. The Divine Beloved longs to play joyously and rest peacefully within the heart of the consecrated lover. This is why certain persons manifest unique spiritual powers. What is the sure sign of such an intimate confidant of God? Soul-awakening power, wisdom, and love are focused through this man or woman.

The primal Power, or *shakti*—which contains the entire spectrum of Divine Energy and which is the principle and very possibility of cosmic manifestation—is identical in essence with the inconceivable, attributeless Reality, the absolutely Unmanifest. They are simply not two. Water is water, whether it remains still or breaks into waves.

The Unmanifest is an infinite diamond and the display of manifestation is the variegated radiance of that diamond. There is no gem without its brilliance, nor can the gem's brilliance exist without the gem. There is no Absolute without the relative, and no relativity can exist apart from the Absolute. There is always butter in buttermilk, whether it is churned or not.

The Unmanifest is an infinite serpent, and the cosmic play of Mother Shakti is the graceful and powerful movement of that serpent. *Shakti* is the one Divine Reality, which consciously becomes the entire universe—lawful structures and miraculous manifestations, including all the precious beings abiding on earthly, subtle, and heavenly planes. The Unmanifest spontaneously shines forth as *shakti*, and *shakti* is simply the luminous darkness of the Unmanifest. Mother Energy and Mother Essence are not two!

After God-realization, which is the conscious union of the manifest with the Unmanifest, the same Reality is experienced as all dimensions of being and also as the dimensionless Ground or Source of Being—the open space of unconditioned awareness. Every conscious being we gaze upon is then perceived to be God. Inanimate structures as well are God. Mother showed me even the marble floor of Her Temple to be Pure Consciousness. But the most complete Divine Manifestation, surprising as it may seem, is this very human reality, this subtle nervous system—a potential expanse of illumination greater than the physical cosmos and greater than the eternal heavenly realms.

Among human beings, God is expressed most clearly through selfless lovers who love only for the sake of Divine Love. These are the pure in heart. These are the sattvic lovers within whom the most exquisite harmony and balance prevail. They experience no trace of obsession with any egocentric desire. They have awakened as the brilliant, boundless play of Divine Love, lost eternally in the mystery of its own Divine Romance.

The fully enlightened human being, who encompasses and transcends both earthly and heavenly realms, has awakened into unity. This is the mystic fusion of *purusha*, Pure Consciousness, and *prakriti*, the boundless display of creativity. This high-energy fusion is sheer bliss. It is the innate union of aspectless and aspected, resembling in joyous intensity the procreative union between masculine and feminine. Can there be a father without a mother or a mother without a father? Yet this mystic mother-father union is infinite, rather than the finite phenomenon we know from the common experience of sexual union.

To be aware that it is nighttime presumes that one has experienced daylight. Conversely, to know when day arrives, one must have been through the night. To know the bliss of union, one must have experienced the suffering of separation. Do you understand all this, Keshab?

The noble eyes of Keshab Sen are glistening. He laughs with surprised joy at Ramakrishna's personal question, delivered as the Paramahamsa suddenly comes out of *samadhi* and notices the physical form of his ailing friend. Keshab's demeanor is now no longer marked by debilitation and pain, nor by the sorrowful prospect of parting from his family and coworkers. His mission has been the spiritual and moral reeducation of his culture, including the secular education of women, for which purpose he founded Victoria College. Keshab has now clearly transcended this earthly vocation.

The Master asks again, very pointedly: "Do you understand all this?" Still holding Ramakrishna's hand, this prominent leader, well known throughout India and a personal acquaintance of Queen Victoria, responds with the traditional humility of a disciple before his guide: "Yes, revered sir, I understand and deeply appreciate your teaching."

The sage's response is like a flash of lightning: "This is not my teaching. Mother alone knows. There is no one under the sun who is my disciple. Quite the contrary, I am the ardent disciple of everyone."

Just as suddenly as he emerged into personal contact with Keshab, the Paramahamsa returns into *samadhi*. This time his mood is the ecstatic, childlike worship of the Goddess. He cries aloud in an electrifying voice.

RAMAKRISHNA O blissful Kali! Who is teaching other than You? As Shakti, You vividly project and suddenly dissolve the insubstantial images called the world. Tenderly You preserve and protect the lives of all Your precious creatures, who are sparks of Your own Divine Life, finally reembracing them into You. O Mother, You grant whatever blessing souls may desire on their particular level of evolution—whether they long for wealth, pleasure, righteousness, or total liberation. This small child before You cannot exist for an instant apart from the graceful presence of his Universal Mother. You know absolutely everything and I know absolutely nothing. This child only delights in Your blessed Sustenance and Your blissful Play. O Mother Kali, You completely transcend the speculations and manipulations of the mundane mind.

Once again the Great Swan is propelled from *samadhi* by the Divine Power and fixes Kali's burning gaze of love upon Keshab. "Beloved friend, do you now, at long last, truly understand my spiritual mood?"

Lost in the Paramahamsa's own ecstasy, Keshab is transfigured. An unearthly energy is radiating from his emanciated form. "Yes, revered sage, it is true. Everything you say is absolutely true."

At this dramatic point in the final earthly meeting of two great souls, with many tear-filled eyes focused upon them, Ramakrishna unaccountably enters the mode of crystal-clear sobriety. He now speaks in a normal tone of voice, displaying the relaxed wisdom and subtle humor of complete spiritual maturity. The fire of ecstatic awakening, roaring wildly through the hearts of everyone in the room, is now skillfully brought under control, transformed from one moment to the next into a gentle, warm radiance. Beaming delightedly, the Paramahamsa converses with the great leader as if nothing unusual has happened to his friend. Not once does our Master make mention or even take notice of the physically weakened condition of Keshab. He speaks instead, and rather sternly, about the spiritual weakness, or immaturity, of modern liberal religious views, particularly the attitudes of Keshab's own community.

RAMAKRISHNA Keshab, please explain why the members of your Brahmo Samaj dwell so much on conventional notions about God. Does profound awakening really come about by repeating over and over that God created sun, moon, stars, mountains, and oceans? Can real intimacy with the Creator ever be attained merely through enthusiasm over the creation? This is like the person who continuously praises the beautiful design of a garden, while making no sustained effort to meet and converse directly with the designer. Which holds greater interest, the garden or the one who originally envisioned the garden? Is Divine Reality so distant that one can only engage in vain speculation about it from afar? No. The goal of human life is to meet God face to face, to realize Mother here and now.

After drinking deep from the wine of Love at the tavern of the Divine Beloved, one takes no interest in estimating how many wine barrels may be stored in the vast cellar of the establishment. One is in love not with the tavern but with the beautiful Keeper of the tavern. One is not romantically inclined to the wine but passionately attracted to the glorious Pourer of the wine. You need only a few sips of God's strong wine to become genuinely drunk with love. It is this true inebriation, this mystic communion and union, that your followers must seek, Keshab, not social reform, science, philosophy, theology.

An extremely wealthy man who had developed a conventional, external devotion to the Creator once requested me to pray that he might offer all this worldly possessions at the Feet of God. Unable to remain politely respectful of his important social station, I replied sternly: "These are desirable riches only to your limited understanding. What can acquisitiveness and egocentricity offer to God, Who is sheer selflessness? To God, your worldly wealth is less significant than straw, less valuable than motes of dust."

Someone once robbed the Radha-Krishna Temple at Dakshineswar. Mathur Babu became righteously indignant and stormed into the sacred place, complaining to the Divine Mother that She had failed to protect the golden bangles and other costly instruments of ceremonial worship. I became aghast. Even though Mathur, the manager and owner of the Temple Garden, was in a rage and no one dared approach him, the mysterious Power which resides here, in this glass case, flashed forth like lightning: "Beware, Mathur. Your words are absurd, inappropriate, even dangerous. To Divine Reality, these golden ornaments, jeweled crowns, silver trays, vessels, and implements are mere clay. The Mother of the Universe, in Her Aspect as Goddess Lakshmi, is good fortune itself, wealth itself. Should God weep and repent just because a desperate man has stolen some temple property and left you with a slight financial inconvenience? How bizarre your spiritual priorities have become!"

My dear Keshab, can anyone bring the totally free and unpredictable Mother Shakti under tight, rational control—whether by wealth, scholarship, elaborate ceremonies, or social reform? Divine Reality responds only to selfless love, because God is Love. What could infinite Love desire other than love itself? Would boundless Love yearn for golden ornaments, stylized rituals, abstract institutions? Divine Love longs only for true lovers—for heart-melting devotion, for astonishing intensity of feeling, for diamond-sharp discrimination between deceitful love and pure love, for courageous renunciation, moment by moment, of every self-serving impulse that may cleverly masquerade as love.

The fact remains, Keshab Sen, that seekers can only understand Divine Reality in terms of their own level of inner experience, no matter how sincerely they try to adhere to advanced teachings that they may read or hear. Therefore, the tamasic worshiper of Divine Mother, the devotee who is still violent and unrefined, is convinced that Goddess Kali takes pleasure in animal sacrifice. The rajasic worshiper, who is still obsessed with personal gratification, cooks delicious, expensive dishes to offer, with great ritual elaboration, before a regally adorned image of the Mother. The sattvic worshiper, who is becoming a true lover, no longer engages in any external show. The delight of mystic union is inward and invisible. This blessed person may offer simply a few drops of Ganga water and a few green leaves from the sacred *bel* tree. Flowers and oil lamps can be dispensed with. After perceiving that every blossoming plant is a spontaneous offering to the Mother, I could no longer pluck flowers for formal worship.

No one may even notice that the sattvic worshiper is performing worship. Occasionally, a small plate of puffed rice may be placed informally before the sacred image of Divinity. On the most auspicious days for praising the Goddess, this lover may prepare some sweet rice pudding by boiling milk down to a thick cream, just as his own being has been condensed into essence over the fire of Divine Love.

The supreme lovers, however, transcend the three categories of tamasic, rajasic, and sattvic worship. They are so childlike that they can only cry *Ma, Ma, Ma* while dancing, weeping, and laughing. Lost in ecstasy, they are incapable of making formal offerings, chanting scriptural passages, repeating *mantras*. They can no longer even perceive the Mother as separate from themselves, being completely dissolved in Her. Many times, when I enter the Kali Temple, I cannot prostrate before the Divine Image. Which one is Her and which one is me? When I take a red flower from the silver tray and attempt to place it at Her Lotus Feet, my hand moves instead to the crown of my own head.

My beloved Keshab, do you know what is happening to your physical system and why? You are being taken by Mother Kali into the supreme childlike state beyond worship. Your offerings to the Lord and service of the world are over. The intense longing that has flowed through your body during the years of our friendship is now taking precedence. People may perceive it as illness, but it is really the process of spiritual completion. You are encountering the sacred river Karmanasha, Destroyer of the Sense of Duty. It is blissful to plunge into this swift current. All sense of being able to initiate actions, from spiritual teaching and social reform to even the simplest personal responsibility, now comes to an end.

At the initial blossoming of ecstatic emotion, one does not understand its radical implications. Such purified and sanctified emotions gradually efface the function of self-assertion and self-perpetuation. Only years later can one clearly notice their effects. I often sit and observe large steamships passsing the Temple Garden, far out upon the holy waters of Mother Ganga. They seem to float by insubstantially, without sound, weight, or impact. But some time afterward, what a surprising roar and commotion is created by the waves they have generated, crashing against the stone embankment of the Temple Garden! These waves eventually erode the mortar, and large stones fall into the sacred river. The impact of spiritual intensity is now upon you, Keshab. The mortar of convention has been eroded. You are falling into the river of Divine Peace. You are entering the liberating current of the Karmanasha.

When the mad elephant of holy rapture enters the hut of this physical body, composed merely of mud and thatched palm leaves, the frail structure is brought down. Yet the process of effacement begins gradually, like a house catching on fire. At first, a few flammable items in the inner chamber may be ignited from a single candle on the shrine. Finally comes the roar and brilliant light as even the very foundation is destroyed by huge flames. Precisely so, dearest Keshab, the fire of knowledge first consumes such obvious impurities as anger and selfish desires, which are harmful to others. Gradually, these liberating flames spread throughout the entire structure of egocentricity. Finally, even the physical body is radically purified by Mother's fierce Wisdom-energy. Sometimes the body does not survive the process. Such is the present case.

But the integral stream of consiousness is never destroyed by Her merciful process of deep purification. The conscious stream must continue to be purified by flowing on and on. You may think your evolutionary experience is over, Keshab Chandra Sen, but it is not so. Mother will not release you from physical incarnation in this hospital of relative existence as long as the slightest trace of spiritual illness remains. You will never receive permission to leave the hospital until this disease of egocentric thought and egocentric activity is completely cured, leaving no chance for a relapse. The doctor is very exacting and skillful. This is why you were committed to his loving care in the first place. Would you wish anything other than the finest, most advanced treatment?

Keshab is laughing like a man in vigorous good health. Everyone joins him, and the joyous tumult that always surrounds the Great Swan bursts forth like a downpour of healing rain. Even Ramakrishna is shaking with mirth over this image of the hospital and the doctor, the path and the guide. The clairvoyant sage is clearly indicating that Keshab, sincere aspirant and great soul that he is, must take another incarnation in the complex realm of earthly embodiment before attaining spiritual completion. Yet our Master has unveiled and described the process so vividly, naturally, and humorously that no one feels depressed or overwhelmed by the prospect of greater effort and further evolution. The Paramahamsa, inexhaustible fountain of the Mother's Wisdom, continues to elucidate the spiritual function of physical illness, this time from his own personal experience. Refreshed by laughter, the attention in the room is again sharply focused.

RAMAKRISHNA My nephew Hriday, who attended on me during the early days of my adventure at Dakshineswar, used to cry out in amazement: "Uncle, never before have I seen or even heard any account of such ecstasy for God and such acute illness and suffering." This body was wracked with severe diarrhea that neither traditional nor modern treatments could cure. It felt as if millions of termites were disintegrating my nervous system. Yet a constant stream of advanced contemplatives and mysterious adepts continued to flow through the Temple Garden. I was conversing, singing, and meditating with them night and day. A certain medical doctor from Natagore was called to examine my case. He finally discovered me, somewhere on the sacred grounds, surrounded by wandering sages, avidly discussing Truth or God in the light of one initiatory lineage or another. He exclaimed: "The man is absolutely crazy. He is so emaciated that there is barely any substance left other than bone, yet still he is engaged in ceaseless philosophical inquiry." This body somehow managed to survive the storm in order to bear even more rigorous spiritual burdens. You see, Keshab, appearance or disappearance depend entirely upon Mother's own sweet Will.

With soothing tenderness, the Paramahamsa now sings some lines from a mystic hymn very close to his heart.

O Mother of this vast universe,
all action is accomplished only
through Your unpredictable Will.

> You take counsel with no one.
> No one other than You knows why
> You manifest every phenomenon,
> every living being, every event.
> Your Manifestation, O Mother,
> awakens, purifies, sanctifies,
> and deifies the human soul.
> You accomplish Your own Goals
> through this inscrutable Play.
> Men foolishly claim responsibility.

The atmosphere of Lily Cottage and the space within our hearts is freshened and made fragrant by the Master's song, his voice sweeter than any we have ever heard. After ornamenting the last line with surprising melodic development, the Paramahamsa bursts into the high-pitched laughter of the Goddess, manifesting Her feminine Energy completely. No one joins this time. We simply gaze in silence at Divine Mother manifest, experiencing astonishment and adoration.

RAMAKRISHNA The expert gardener removes soil from the rare roses, exposing their roots to the morning dew and thereby causing the plants to flower more intensely. This is why you are being shaken to your very roots, Keshab, so you will blossom even more beautifully in your next incarnation.

Keshab Sen and Ramakrishna Paramahamsa collapse into each other's arms with laughter. No trace of heaviness, sorrow, or solemnity now remains.

RAMAKRISHNA Whenever I am informed that you are even slightly ill, dear Keshab, I become restless, like the lover who longs only for the happiness of the beloved. This profound attraction I feel is because you are a lover of God as well as a lover of humankind, which is the fullest expression of the Divine. Hearing about your recent serious illness, I shed tears in the secret hours before dawn, praying to Goddess Kali with my whole being: "Mother, Mother, Mother! If You remove Keshab, who will there be among modern religious leaders that can understand my spiritual mood, and to whom I can freely express Truth?" Weeping uncontrollably, I traveled by country boat to the awakened image of Mahakali in Kalighat, offering fruits and sweets at

Her dark blue Lotus Feet and praying for your spiritual evolution and illumination, in whatever form it might manifest.

The companions of Divine Love are extremely moved to glimpse the depth and intensity of our Master's affection and yearning for his intimate friends, realizing that he cares and prays in this same way for everyone who has taken refuge with him, interceding ceaselessly with the Great Mother for our swift progress along the path to God-consciousness.

RAMAKRISHNA When I first encountered you in this lifetime, Keshab Sen, you were seated in silence, surrounded by loyal adherents. It was at a lovely garden house on the banks of the sacred river. I recognized you immediately, and Mother caused me to cry aloud: "Ah, here is someone who has lost his tail!" Your disciples were about to take offense at this rude, disheveled priest and have him removed from your presence. But you dissuaded them and asked them to listen. I elucidated: "When the tadpole drops its tail, it can begin to live both on land and beneath water. This man before me can breathe the clear air of Divine Reality as well as move beneath the obscuring waters of the habitual world."

When I first gazed at you, you were meditating. I clearly perceived that your mind was submerging in supreme Reality, like a fishing bob that is pulled underwater by a huge fish. Keshab, you have invited the modern world to listen to Mother's Wisdom, and She has blessed you. Seeing you this evening, after conversing and communing with you, I can honestly say that there is no anxiety at all in my heart concerning your spiritual well-being, although for the last few days I have experienced a kind of nervousness that I might not be able to meet with you again during this life.

The venerable mother of Keshab Chandra Sen now appears in the same doorway through which her son entered the reception hall—her head bowed humbly, covered by a fine yet simple sari, her palms joined, fingers slightly interlaced. One of Keshab's relatives calls out to the Master: "Revered sir, here is mother. She is saluting you." Ramakrishna smiles ecstatically and makes a delightful gesture, indicating his attitude—who is there to salute whom, when all is simply the Mother? The matriarch whispers a few words, and Umanath calls out again from beside the doorway: "Sir, mother requests you to cure her son's illness." The Paramahamsa now turns directly to face the white-haired woman with tears streaming down her cheeks. Lovingly yet strongly, he addresses her.

RAMAKRISHNA Respected mother, other than the Divine Mother of the Universe, there is absolutely no one who gives illness and removes illness. Please meditate with your whole being upon the Great Goddess, who graciously bestows bliss to the heart under every circumstance. She alone can remove sorrow by transforming it into the intense yearning to merge with Her.

Turning back to his beloved Keshab, Ramakrishna earnestly and intimately advises him, as if the two were alone together somewhere.

RAMAKRISHNA My dear friend, you must pay no attention to the sorrow and discontent being expressed by your family members and loyal followers. Speak only about the allness of God. Think only about the allness of God. Do not permit your mind, even for a moment, to sink into the conventional categories of birth and death, pleasure and sorrow.

This extremely serious mood is transformed again as the Paramahamsa begins to laugh in a carefree, youthful voice. We find ourselves laughing for no reason whatsoever other than the Master's own laughter. Taking Keshab's emaciated forearm tenderly into both his hands, Ramakrishna playfully weighs it and proclaims with a brilliant smile: "Your arm and hand are very light, Keshab. It means you are purified. Hypocrisy and deceitfulness make a person's hands and arms heavy." Everyone is laughing again, a healing and illuminating laughter that we experience as the most delicious nectar—the nectar of timeless awareness.

Once more from beside the eastern door, Umanath calls out respectfully: "Revered sage, mother is asking you to bless Keshab."

The Paramahamsa becomes serious once more, almost agitated, responding with great firmness: "What is all this about? There is only one Reality. God alone can bless. I am nothing. I am no one." The Great Swan soars into ecstasy. He sings with poignant beauty the same lines from the mystic hymn to Goddess Kali, repeating them several times in heart-melting tones.

> O Mother of this vast universe,
> all action is accomplished only
> through Your unpredictable Will.

> You take counsel with no one.
> No one other than You knows why
> You manifest every phenomenon,
> every living being, every event.
> Your Manifestation, O Mother,
> awakens, purifies, sanctifies,
> and deifies the human soul.
> You accomplish Your own Goals
> through this inscrutable Play.
> Men foolishly claim responsibility.

The numerous persons present here in the elegant reception hall, including the mother of Keshab, are lifted entirely out of the dense atmosphere of personal will by the soaring energy of these few lines of music and verse. Once again the playful Paramahamsa transforms this moment of exalted silence into laughter. Rocking with mirth, he teaches by parable.

RAMAKRISHNA God laughs uproariously, with infinite Divine Humor, when human beings claim cosmic ownership or cosmic responsibility. This intoxicating laughter of Divine Reality is generated when two brothers decide to divide their ancestral land, stringing a line across this one sacred earth and foolishly proclaiming: "This side is mine, and the other side belongs to you." The entire universe not only belongs to God alone, but is simply a manifestation of God. How can human beings imagine that their abstract boundaries and definitions carry any ultimate significance? God laughs again when the medical doctor or the folk healer proudly assures the family of a child who is desperately ill: "Have no fear whatsoever. My techniques will certainly be powerful enough to cure your child." No one can possibly save the life of a person if the inscrutable Divine Will is calling that soul forth from the veils of physical existence.

Ramakrishna gazes at Keshab meaningfully. We sense the palpable presence of this transcendent Divine Call to come forth from space and time. At this precise moment, the leader of the Brahmo Samaj returns to the level of ordinary consciousness and begins coughing painfully. The wracking sounds continue for a long time, coming in wave after wave. Exhausted, Keshab is forced to retire and leaves the room with difficulty as he had come, leaning against the wall for support.

Yet the atmosphere does not become heavy or depressed. Delicious refreshments are served to the Paramahamsa, who is now seated again on the divan, and the other guests partake of them as *prasad*, food which has been offered to Divine Reality and which has thus become filled with healing and enlightening energy. Keshab's son, a young man with clear features, is introduced to Ramakrishna and sits near him. A family member requests the sage to bless this youth. Responding with an entirely different tone than in the previous instance, our Master speaks ecstatically.

RAMAKRISHNA I have not received permission from my blissful Mother to bless anyone. I do not even have permission to exist apart from Her. I have never begged Goddess Kali to grant me any personal power whatsoever—whether healing or any other form of intercession. I only weep and supplicate ceaselessly that I can express in every moment the purest love for Her. She is none other than Pure Love, you know.

As the Paramahamsa enters a uniquely tender mood—speaking in gentle tones, smiling sweetly—he caresses the back of Keshab's son. The family members beam with joy, recognizing that the requested blessing is emanating spontaneously from the Great Mother through the mysterious, unpremeditated actions of Her child. The sage now moves his hands in subtle patterns up and down the spinal column of this fortunate son of the household, as he speaks frankly about the young man's father.

RAMAKRISHNA Is Keshab Sen just a common, limited person? Not only does he inspire confidence and respect from powerful worldly men and women, but ecstatic lovers of God are also drawn to him and profoundly enjoy his company. I once visited the great practitioner Dayananda, who happened to be waiting for the imminent arrival of Keshab Sen. This holy man actually arose several times from his meditation seat to see whether Keshab had arrived. It was clearly a form of spiritual yearning. This was strange, because Dayananda was a Vedic traditionalist and Keshab does not accept the necessity of complicated rites and sacrifices, nor does he even accept the existence of the forms of Divinity mentioned in the Vedas. But the venerable Dayananda still loved Keshab immensely and would respond to the liberal religious view of the younger man: "The supreme Lord has created such vastness and complexity. Why could He not create various deities and reveal various sacred rituals as well?"

This generosity and broadness of spirit displayed by Dayananda was precisely the same quality he admired in Keshab Chandra Sen. Our beloved Keshab, you see, is free from the proud and doctrinaire attitude of narrow-minded religious leaders. Countless times, when persons came to Keshab with intense aspiration, he would send them to the Dakshineswar Temple Garden. He never tried to confine, contain, or dominate the seekers of Truth. If his disciples had doubts that were particularly difficult to resolve—the resolution of every doubt that may arise along the path being the responsibility of the genuine guide—he would send them directly to Dakshineswar. Conversely, I always advise those who visit the Temple Garden immersed in intellectual problems about religion: "Go to Keshab if you need further discussion. Mother has specially designed him for that."

Keshab and I share intimately on every level because we are part of the same current within the mysterious ocean of the Mother Reality. Goddess Kali sent us to Calcutta together. I have always cherished admiration for Keshab's broadness and bold universality. I have always prayed to my blissful Mother to increase the spiritual power She is entrusting to Keshab. I have requested Her to conceal me and reveal him. He is a *mahatma*, a great soul, manifesting right here in the midst of Calcutta society.

Quite unexpectedly, the Paramahamsa arises to leave. His body appears to be lifted from the divan by some force other than will or musculature. Suddenly, he is just standing, like a shaft of intense light, in the center of the room. The disciples of Keshab, deeply moved by the Master's generous confirmation of their teacher's spiritual stature, now gather around Ramakrishna lovingly, feeling themselves also to be part of this living current of Divine Mother's unprecedented manifestation at Dakshineswar. They accompany us down the stairs from the veranda to the dark street where the carriage is waiting, horses snorting expectantly, their hooves clattering against the cobblestones. The Paramahamsa notices that the oil lamp on the ground floor has burned out. Turning to the family and close disciples of Keshab, he speaks strongly.

RAMAKRISHNA This house should always be well lighted. A single lamp is not sufficient. As the proverb teaches: "A residence without light is an invitation to poverty." In this case, the residence is the modern world and the lamps are the pure-hearted lovers, consecrated to Truth alone and vigorously committed to the education and inspiration of humankind. Be sure this precious residence remains fully illuminated!

As our carriage pulls away into the luminous darkness of the full-moon night, we recall a time when Keshab and some disciples visited the Paramahamsa at Dakshineswar. After much searching, they found the sage in the remote jungle area of the Temple grounds, seated beneath the Panchavati, the grove of five sacred trees that were planted by our Master's own hands some thirty years before. Ramakrishna often requested us to place our foreheads on the sacred earth of the Panchavati, joining us in this powerful traditional gesture of reverence and explaining simply: "I have experienced so many divine visions here." In dappled sunlight beneath the spreading branches of the banyan tree, the two friends conversed for a while. Suddenly, Keshab became inspired and proclaimed: "Beloved Paramahamsa, with your permission, I would like to announce your message of religious harmony to the entire world, East and West. It will infuse tremendous good into the life of modern society, on every level. It will inaugurate an era of global peace." Ramakrishna immediately entered ecstasy at these eloquent and sincere words, and responded from a transcendental dimension of awareness.

RAMAKRISHNA Dearest Keshab, it is not necessary to communicate through lectures and periodicals the universal message that Mother is manifesting here at Dakshineswar. The Divine Power and Wisdom that are flowing through this body will spontaneously and effortlessly spread among pure minds and hearts. The crushing weight of hundreds of Himalayan mountain ranges would not be able to suppress this force of Truth.

Some days after their final meeting, when he is informed of Keshab's death, Ramakrishna weeps. Sobbing like a child, he stammers: "Keshab's passing is like losing half my life. He was a wide-spreading banyan tree, giving shade and comfort to thousands. Where else will one be able to find such a generous shade tree? I am like the palm or betel nut, which casts barely any shadow at all." Then the Paramahamsa bursts into laughter and enters ecstacy.

18

The Paramahamsa Transmits Spiritual Intensity

O Brother Madhusudana, Please Come!

E ARLY ON FRIDAY the fourteenth, we journey from the crowded metropolis of the modern world to visit the primeval Temple Garden. It is the auspicious day of the full moon. We find the God-intoxicated sage, clad in only a thin cloth in the chill morning light of December, sweeping the path north of his room. "Mother Kali walks here barefoot," Ramakrishna explains in a childlike manner. "I am clearing the way for Her delicate Lotus Feet."

He greets us as if he were expecting us. Shining with the inner heat of *yoga,* or mystic union, Ramakrishna is the perpetual full moon of Divine Knowledge and Divine Love. Deeply moved, we prostrate before him in the traditional manner, placing palms, knees, and forehead on the sandy path where Divinity walks. The sage surprises us completely by prostrating as well, the crown of his head almost touching ours. As we stand up again together, we are already laughing. Our somewhat romantic, misty mood of devotion is dissipated by the unexpected humor and naturalness of his friendship. Ramakrishna possesses the rare ability to put everyone at ease, allowing us to feel that he is best friend, confidant, brother, and equal in every respect.

Hand in hand, feeling like childhood companions, we enter his fragrant room. He feeds us fruit, sweets, and water, placing delicious morsels directly into our mouths and whispering endearments into our ears. As we sit together intimately on the floor, he inquires in detail about our health, our family, our contemplative practice. Ramakrishna's mind is so pure, so disciplined, so powerful, that to be the focus of this attention is almost overwhelming. But whenever we feel tears of gratitude rising to our eyes, he skillfully diverts us with some hilarious remark or gesture.

Other seekers of Truth are gradually arriving at this place of pilgrimage, like bees of hummingbirds drawn to an open flower by its subtle, all-pervading perfume. Because of the presence of these sincere aspirants, the divine child is propelled by his Wisdom Mother into an entirely different mood. He moves onto the small bed, settling into radiant equipoise. Advanced teachings begin to pour through him as from a fountain. We have been transformed once more into humble, devoted disciples, seated with awe at the feet of a God-realized sage, the rarest of beings in any universe. Humor and naturalness continue to grace the Master's words.

RAMAKRISHNA The mature spiritual person, one who is truly awakened, need not remain involved in social responsibilities or religious observances. The sense that one must, or even can, initiate any action begins to disappear as one realizes that only God acts. This realization is the final fruition of all aspirations and disciplines. When the fruit appears, the flower petals fall from the tree. Passages from holy scripture will flutter away from the mind like petals in a strong wind. The *mantra,* the condensed inward invocation of Divine Presence, may remain active for a while, but eventually even these sacred words will blow away, leaving only the primordial resonance—OM OM OM—which is not just a word passed down by tradition but a humming tone at the center of awareness, audible at the core of every sound in the universe. OM is the open portal to supreme Reality.

How long will it be necessary to practice various levels of religious discipline? As long as you do not shed tears and feel tingling sensations coursing throughout your body while repeating one of the precious Divine Names, you are still subject to the structures of moral and religious training. How does a small child learn to wake from a sound sleep in order to use the bathroom? Until this ability develops, the child must continue to wear diapers.

This outrageous analogy, used often by our Master, brings forth gales of laughter. Sometimes the playful Paramahamsa suggests that gurus are like soft toys for children to chew on while they are cutting teeth. He cherishes no sanctimonious attachment to any religious form. He is a *jivanmukta*, a soul liberated from human convention and limitation while still living on earth. Often Ramakrishna will say: "Follow conventions of purity and piety only as much as absolutely necessary. Persons who are obsessed with religion cannot attain profound wisdom."

VISITOR Revered sir, how should one regard money and the efforts to obtain it?

RAMAKRISHNA To worship God in order to generate material success or to be victorious in some litigation is not the sign of a true practitioner, who simply remains open to whatever gifts of abundance flow spontaneously and mysteriously from Divine Reality. This attitude of grateful receptivity does not preclude working hard at some honest occupation. Yet even when engaged in personal effort, the lover of Truth experiences the miraculous flow of Divine Sustenance, and therefore can never be obsessive about earning or saving money. Such a person becomes constitutionally incapable of being obsequious, servile, slavish, or deceptive in order to receive material or emotional compensation of any kind. The ecstatic lover cares only for Truth, not for money, adulation, or power.

Nevertheless, surprising abundance often comes to such a person. The true lover humbly regards even minimal subsistance as a gracious gift from the vast storehouse of Divine Abundance. These true lovers no longer even instinctively reach out to grasp, becoming instead sheer receptivity. They are capable of receiving Divine Grace through a single glance, breath, or heartbeat—even through tribulation. The lover of God is like the daughter or son of an infinitely powerful king. This royal princess or prince is always relaxed and confident under every circumstance. The *Bhagavad Gita*——which functions as the Torah, Gospel, and Quran of Hinduism—describes this person succinctly as "one who remains spontaneously content with whatever comes." The person who loves Truth alone, free from any self-centered motivation whatsoever, can gratefully receive the gifts of basic sustenance or immense wealth from any direction whatsoever. By not desiring it, this person purifies it and uses it generously for the common good.

VISITOR Revered sage, how should the spiritual seeker exist in the practical, mundane world?

RAMAKRISHNA Exist in the ordinary structures of family, religion, and society as the mudfish lives in the soft mud at the bottom of a lake. The fish does not consider this mud distasteful, but is also never confined there, being capable at any time of swimming into the spacious, crystal-clear water, without even a particle of mud adhering to its body. To cultivate love for Truth, one must occasionally come forth from the conventional environment into spaciousness and clarity. To retire now and then into blessed seclusion, even in one's own house or heart, is necessary—for several hours, for several days, for a month, for a year. Swim peacefully through clear waters of solitude, illuminated by the sunlight of Truth. Then you can return compassionately to the denser, more obscure realms of social responsibility, without becoming disoriented by them. The mudfish never gets lost in the mud, which is simply part of its natural environment. The body of the fish is never stained by mud. Certainly you can live at home, surrounded by your extended family, attending your place of business daily. Simply maintain the sense of perfect freedom, clarity, and expansiveness—moment to moment, under every condition. Who cares if the world is strewn with thorns? Simply put on sandals and walk over them. The sandals are the knowledge that God alone exists.

VISITOR Honorable sir, I was under the impression that the householder's life is an obstacle to spiritual progress and that full realization is impossible in the context of worldly enjoyments and responsibilities.

RAMAKRISHNA One can awaken fully into Divine Presence only if one feels a fundamental freedom from all limited, egocentric motivation, whether connected with family affairs or religious pursuits. The person who cultivates commitment to liberation from self-involvement experiences his own personal selfishness and various collective forms of selfishness as a forest fire dangerously out of control, threatening the lives of all conscious beings. The person of dispassion clearly perceives that the obsessive attachment to spouse and children which seeks to own and control their lives is like a deep well with no way of escape. One would be very foolish indeed to fall into such a well. Such uncompromising insight into the nature of pervasive selfishness might inspire one to enter a monastery or become a wandering renunciate. But one will discover the danger of egocentric motivation in these other ways of life as well. The person whose heart belongs to the radical path of total freedom, total renunciation of self, simply refuses to exist within any conventional categories, even for a moment. No family, no monastery, no wandering life, no self. Nothing but God. Nothing but Reality. Such persons, whether they live a monastic or a family life, have no complicity with the ego world, no sense of diplomacy toward the ego world. Hence conventional opinion often regards them as insane. I used to be known as the mad priest of Dakshineswar. Temple guards and even other priests have kicked me as I lay in ecstasy within the various sacred shrines, unable to respond. I never reported these incidents to the authorities. Why report the conventional world to the conventional world? The thief, dressed as a policeman, pretends to investigate his own crime.

The delusive power that makes the selfish, habitual environment so dangerous is simply the instinctive urge to perpetuate the limited self and its limited existence. This becomes the atavistic drive to possess, to dominate, to control, to consume. Sexuality, when it is not spiritually consecrated and elevated, is an obvious instrument of this delusive power. So is the obsession with wealth and hierarchical position. But this delusive power, this *maya*, begins to dissipate by itself the more it is recognized, confronted, refuted, unmasked. Some people enjoy wearing disguises—even a full tiger skin with head, tail, and claws—in order to frighten their friends, perhaps during twilight in a rural village setting. The friends at first may scream out in dismay, but the moment they penetrate the disguise, they laugh and shout: "This is no tiger. It's only you." The prankster smiles and goes away to fool someone else. Just recognize the power of *maya* for what it is—mere empty pretense—and it withdraws spontaneously, although the prankster-ego does return again and again, under an astonishing array of disguises.

Beloved friends of Truth, no one can cultivate radical freedom simply by wishing to do so or even by desperately trying to do so. One must deal skillfully with various subtle tendencies—those inherited physically, those imposed socially, and those deposited in the mind-stream by previous incarnational experience. This complex tapestry of mental and physical tendencies is difficult to unravel. Listen to a story. Once a forest yogi, advanced in concentration but lacking in wisdom, invited a powerful king to retreat with him into the wilderness in order to be liberated from the heavy cares of the kingdom. The sovereign, who was actually a hidden sage, replied: "Dear sir, I am afraid you would be disappointed. I could easily divest myself of palace, courtiers, and refined comforts to live in your forest retreat. However, the subtle tendencies within me to create and rule a kingdom would still remain active, attracting various persons and events to fulfill themselves. Your peaceful, solitary retreat would gradually become a busy *ashram* and eventually the burgeoning center of a new empire."

The Paramahamsa requests his friend Mahimacharan to chant from the *Mahanirvana Tantra*. He listens raptly with palms joined at the heart, a single tear shining like a bright pearl at the outer corner of each eye.

> I bow only to You,
> timeless Cause of Time.
> I bow only to You,
> Pure Consciousness
> that displays all worlds.
> I bow only to You,
> Reality without attributes,
> my sole refuge,
> only adorable One,
> One who purifies,
> One who protects.
>
> I bow only to You,
> the absolutely Unmanifest,
> inconceivable, indescribable.
> I bow only to You,
> light of meditation,
> nondual awareness.
> To You alone
> do I bow.

To our great surprise, the whole day has passed. There has been an illuminating series of questions and responses, punctuated by mystic hymns and rich, extended silences. Most casual visitors are returning to Calcutta. Night falls. One by one, our Master is sending forth his inner circle of companions into the Temple Garden to reflect, pray, and meditate in solitude. To some he is recommending the mysterious recesses of Mahakali's shrine, to others the wilderness atmosphere of the Panchavati, the grove of five sacred trees where he has performed so many austere yogic disciplines for the sake of awakening all humanity. The skillful sage knows precisely which contemplative prescription to give each seeker of Truth.

He follows up carefully on the effects of his spiritual medicine, requesting us to describe our dreams, visions, and other unusual symptoms and experiences. Sometimes he even adjusts our physical posture as we are sitting in meditation, or places his hands on certain psychic centers within the body, activating their particular elevating and liberating energy. Sweetly, he reminds us: "Does an angler catch an immense carp every day? Does such a fish strike immediately when the baited hook is cast into the water? Do not abandon your concentrated daily efforts!"

The Great Swan never transmits exactly the same guidance to different persons—unlike those sects which force individuals, regardless of their unique needs, to aspire to a single ideal, to confine themselves to a single mode of practice, to breathe a single atmosphere. The Paramahamsa often proclaims with laughter, referring at once to the bamboo flute, to the subtle body, which contains seven lotus-centers, or levels of awareness, and even to the biological form: "I have an instrument with seven holes. Why should I play a monotone?"

Ramakrishna now directs one of the companions of Divine Love to the hallowed banks of the Ganges, giving him specific instructions suited not only to his spiritual temperament but to the particular needs of his soul at its present stage of awakening. If one knows the combination, the lock opens instantly. Just a few hours of concentration, when following precise guidelines suggested by the Paramahamsa, can open the door to an entirely new dimension of experience which might otherwise remain inaccessible, even after one has completed rigorous traditional practices.

The aspirants spread out eagerly into the mystical landscape of our Master's *mandala,* the twenty acres of the Dakshineswar Temple Garden. Ramakrishna blesses and sends each one forth with a unique map composed of his gaze, his touch, his word, and his subtle presence within our hearts. These are living maps to the location of certain Divine Treasures to be discovered again during modern times for the benefit of humanity as a whole and for the renewal of sacred traditions.

The Great Swan is now completing his instructions to the beloved companion being sent to meditate near the stone embankment of the holy river.

RAMAKRISHNA You must generate the purest childlike faith and confidence in the words of your guide and the wonderful revelations that await you—not sometime in the distant future, but tonight. You must develop, here and now, the intense yearning of a newborn infant for its mother. That level of primal intensity is like the red line on the eastern horizon. Perceiving that vivid color, one knows intuitively with every cell that the golden sun is about to rise. When one feels this spontaneous concentration and consecration, within a few moments or a few days, one will directly experience God. The fact that God-vision follows intense yearning is even more certain than the rising of the sun over the earthly horizon. One who weeps for God will see God.

Listen to a story. A boy named Jatila was frightened to walk to the nearest village through the jungle that surrounded the remote dwelling of his family. His mother, wishing that her child's fear be allayed, advised Jatila to call upon his secret, invisible brother to make the journey with him and to protect him in every way. She taught Jatila a powerful name of Lord Krishna: Madhusudana. The boy was very content with the companionship of this invisible brother, whose presence the child now felt as he was going to sleep at night and when he awoke in the morning. One day, on his way to the village school, Jatila heard a deep growl in the undergrowth and instinctively cried out: "O beloved brother, Madhusudana, you must come to help me!"

Jatila looked around expectantly, but his secret, invisible brother did not appear. The boy began to weep with abandon, sobbing: "Brother, brother, how can you leave me when I really need you? Brother Madhusudana, come! Please, come!" Lord Krishna, the very heart of Divine Reality, could not resist the profound attraction of this pure faith and intense yearning. The Lord emanated instantly and appeared before the tear-filled eyes of the child as a radiant human figure, glowing like a dark-blue jewel. Speaking tender words, the awesome Lord of the Universe quieted the sobbing child, led him to the edge of the village clearing, and then faded into transparency like a rainbow. Krishna's last words to Jatila were these: "Call me whenever you need me and I will come. Visibly or invisibly, I will certainly come. Never be afraid of any condition, person, or event for the rest of your life on earth, and then return joyfully and peacefully to me. I am your friend."

We all disperse into the Temple grounds with this confidence in Divine Friendship, pursuing our various forms of contemplation with the contentment of Jatila, feeling the constant presence of his invisible brother. Late at night, some are seated cross-legged on the second floor of the southern music pavilion, open to the sky, elevated above the Dakshineswar Garden. We are gazing at the sacred river and the brilliant, moonlit domes of the Kali Temple. All manifest Being seems merged in the radiance of the full moon. We are literally in another world. This parallel universe is permeated with Ramakrishna's presence. It is a *mandala,* a mystical palace beyond space and time, spontaneously emerging from the Paramahamsa's seamless awareness, from Universal Consciousness. We can hear the sacred Mother-current murmuring melodiously in the stillness.

Suddenly, a beautiful cry arises. With calm movements, lost in the open-eyed meditation on pervasive peace which the Master has prescribed for us, we turn our gaze and see the companion sent forth to the bank of the Ganges. He is standing beside the silvery waters calling out, with intense earnestness and immense love: "O brother Madhusudana, brother Madhusudana. Please, come! You must come!"

19

The Ideal of Feminine Love

RAMAKRISHNA IS reclining comfortably and informally on the floor of his room, basking in the intimate companionship of the lovers, as if he were simply one of us rather than Divine Love itself. Whenever any companions visit him, the Paramahamsa becomes euphoric, sometimes caressing our faces or holding our hands and dancing in delight, crying MA MA MA. He can appreciate us much more than we appreciate him.

He is our master in every way—in humor and even in humble service. One of the young disciples, a peasant boy whose function is to attend to the sage's very simple needs, recently received a handsome pair of sandals from a wealthy Calcutta devotee. A wild jackal stole one of them from the north porch of the Master's room, and Latu was distressed—not from attachment to the sandals but out of respect for the gift, coming directly from the Lord through the hands of a devoted lover. Ramakrishna, although apparently immersed in *samadhi*, noticed these details, slipped out of the room, and searched the jungle. One hour later, to our utter amazement, the smiling sage returned with the missing sandal.

This morning Ramakrishna is generously praising the devotion to God demonstrated by the well-known aspirant Devendranath Tagore. Our Master has been invited to the large Tagore household on several festive occasions and has personally probed and tested the spiritual commitment of Devendranath. During these visits, the radiant holiness of the Great Swan has permeated the many children in this distinguished family, one of whom, Rabindranath Tagore, is destined to become a poet of world stature, through his delicate songs transmitting to the entire globe the fragrant atmosphere of Indian civilization.

The Master's thoughts now take a new direction.

RAMAKRISHNA There is significant difference between a genuinely good person such as Devendranath, a dignified man of the world who is also engaged in the path of contemplative development, and the ecstatic lovers gathered in this room—especially the younger persons here who have never made the unconscious pact with the conventional world which dampens the fire of love for God. These radical young men and women—or older persons who have kept their revolutionary sensibility undiluted—not only contemplate Divine Reality day and night, but their every breath and even their ordinary physical actions are totally God-oriented and therefore fragrant with Divine Presence. Persons who have already contracted a complex series of compromises with conventional thinking, perception, and behavior remain veiled. Their minds are obscured by the conscious and unconscious drive to uphold convention, although they may also experience sincere devotion to God or genuine commitment to Truth.

Take Mathur Babu as the example of an excellent man, sincerely devoted to the service of the Mother, both through the traditional Divine Image and in this living form now before you. Mathur once approached as I was conducting worship in the Kali Temple, handed me a lotus blossom, and requested that I offer it at the sublime red-soled feet of my Mother. Since I was entirely merged in the flow of the worship—in which one offers all physical sensations, all emotions, all thoughts, and all worlds—I also offered this flower presented by the owner of the Temple Garden, knowing him to be a sincere devotee of the Goddess. Unfortunately, Mathur was embroiled in a serious lawsuit and was convinced that my offering would bring him a favorable legal judgment. I began to detect the stench of the selfish world, completely incompatible with the spirit of selfless worship. I experienced pain in my body while attempting to offer this lotus, just as when my hands became cramped and paralyzed by the touch of gold or silver coins. If I so much as tie a knot in the corner of my wearing-cloth to carry medicine, my breath stops and my limbs refuse to function.

A similar event occurred with the founder of the Dakshineswar Garden. Rani Rasmani once slipped into the back of Mahakali's Temple as I was lost in ecstatic communion, far beyond all the rubrics of textbook worship. I was seated on the shrine next to the sacred image, which I perceived not as composed of black stone but as sheer aliveness, as all-pervading consciousness. After offering the same red flower at

Her Feet and then upon my own head, I was fanning Mother with a yak-tail fan. During this extended worship, Rani Rasmani allowed her mind to dwell intensely on the threat of a certain lawsuit. This energy of self-interest disturbed the flow of communion with the living Goddess. Mother moved through this body like lightning. Without the slightest premeditation, I strode to where the noble lady was seated in the semidarkness and slapped her lightly across the face. She understood my action instantly as a warning from the Goddess, and kept at bay her temple guards, who were ready to pounce on me and thrash me with their bamboo poles.

To realize God, to merge completely with the Great Mother, is like threading a needle. Not even one invisible fiber can deviate from perfect single-pointedness. No energy current in the physical or subtle body can be flowing in another direction. Not a single conventional concern can make any basic claim upon the mind or senses. But single-mindedness and devotion are not enough. What unwavering devotedness was shown by the mother of Rati! She used to visit the Temple Garden almost daily, even though the journey was difficult. She remained attentive to the teachings that occur in this room. Though poor, she always arrived bearing offerings. Her loyalty appeared to be selfless in every way. But the dangerous countercurrent in her being was concealed in this very single-mindedness. She was an almost fanatical worshiper of Lord Krishna. Even though she experienced her beloved Krishna through this form of Ramakrishna, when she noticed that I partake lightly of the nonvegetarian offerings from the Feet of Kali, she stopped coming. My reverence for the beautiful black Warrior Goddess was blasphemy to her. Her religion, intense as it was, proved to be a mere conventional, egocentric commitment—not to the living Truth that she was actually experiencing in this place, but to abstract categories, to cultural inhibitions, to personal preferences and opinions. She was a religious person, not an ecstatic lover. Her devotion was one-sided, her fervor selective. She will have to wait until the moment of death for her illumination. She is not part of my inner circle.

Unable to remain very long on this mundane plane of conversation, the description of the force of self-interest, Ramakrishna glances out at the midmorning sun floating in the blue sky. Immediately he enters *samadhi*, mystic union with the glorious sun of knowledge and bliss, source of all the light rays that we call the universe. Our Master's luminous countenance, eyes wide open and unblinking, remains directed slightly upward. There is no evidence of any conscious function in this relaxed form. The smile of Goddess Kali lights his face. His lips are tender and expressive. There is no strain, tension, or grimace of yogic effort to concentrate upon a meditative object or to suppress any mental or physical functioning. He is simply filled to overflowing with Mother's Energy, the hair of his beard standing on end like the petals of a *kadamba* flower. Head, hands, torso, and limbs are still as the statue of a meditating Buddha.

After a timeless interlude, rich in silence, the Great Swan comes forth again from the state of supreme identity, just as suddenly as he entered. Turning toward one of the persons in the room who practices a rather dry technique of philosophical reasoning, he speaks pointedly. We are amazed at this instant transition to the plane of human conversation, for the process of regaining relative awareness after deep *samadhi* often takes hours. The more we become acquainted with Ramakrishna, the more we discover him to be ever new, ever original.

RAMAKRISHNA You should know, Hazra, that the sublime and ineffable state of *samadhi*, total absorption in Divine Presence, is reached most directly and naturally through selfless love. Vedantic reasoning, although coherent and convincing, does not really elevate the entire consciousness. Recently, at a circle of *kirtan*, while chanting the glorious Names of God with uninterrupted remembrance, a vision flashed before my eyes—whether inner or outer eyes, I do not know. Like a black storm cloud that builds on the horizon, the dark blue Krishna was moving among the *gopis*, his beloved female consorts, who were lost in rapture, moving like supple green trees lashed by the wind of ecstasy. My form was following directly behind Krishna's—closer and closer to perfect union with the Lord. The intensity of love expressed in this epiphany was unbearable. I was catapulted into the formless midnight sunrise of *samadhi*, where there is no Krishna, no *gopi*, no manifestation of any conceivable kind. Just sheer awareness, transparently aware.

At other gatherings of the lovers, if the hymns of union are sung intensely enough, I can no longer bear the exquisite beauty, the living poetry of Radha's supreme love, and I am literally thrown into *samadhi*, sometimes so profoundly that vital signs disappear and the devotees fear that I may have cast away the physical body. Of course, I can discard this visible form forever in *samadhi*, but I return because Mother desires me to taste Divine Love in the blissful company of the lovers.

Still inebriated by this conversation, the Paramahamsa stands outside his room, completely naked, and takes a full ablution with Ganges water from a small gourd-vessel, needing to be steadied on his feet by the pure hands of his most intimate companions. Ramakrishna often instructs us: "To live spiritually while surrounded by the mundane world, always keep your mind divinely intoxicated—a mild inebriation of awe, wonder, sweet gratitude, and mystic union that stays with you every moment." Now he returns and sits on his bed, still naked, unselfconscious as a five-year-old. No one feels the slightest shyness or embarrassment in his presence.

The blissful sage continues to speak with prodigious enthusiasm about the ecstatic love that great women mystics feel for the storm cloud of Divine Love called Krishna. He is identifying himself totally with the unbearable attraction experienced by these marvelous *gopis* on every level of their being. As Ramakrishna often teaches: "The *gopis* would place their invisible subtle bodies beneath Krishna's Lotus Feet lest his soles become bruised by the harshness of the world." These are not simple milkmaids, as the sacred history suggests, but great *yoginis* and *dakinis*—female beings who are highly evolved in the path of selfless, nondual awareness. These are the female warrior companions of Goddess Kali, transforming themselves and playing as the gentle lovers of Lord Krishna.

Early in the adventure of his *sadhana*, after wearing women's clothing for six months in a state of profound identification, Ramakrishna actually became the supreme *gopi*, Radha, Queen of Ecstasy, in order to realize oneness with Lord Krishna through the deliriously sweet Way of Honey, as this mode of contemplative practice is traditionally described. Our Master took the direct path of nondual love into the impenetrable depths of mystic fusion and supreme identity, where subject and object are instantly consumed. As a result, he can distribute the nectar of Radha's love to whomever he wishes, whenever he is inspired to do so. Later, when Ramakrishna attained mystic identity with Lady Sita, another queenly manifestation of Divine Reality, she proclaimed to him as they were disappearing together like a rainbow into the blue sky of formlessness: "I bequeath you my smile." The heart-melting feminine smile of the Paramahamsa can instantly create a God-intoxicated state, as his companions, both men and women, know so well.

Ramakrishna teaches about *jñana* and *bhakti*, unitive knowledge and unalloyed love: "*Jñana*, being masculine, is obliged to stand and wait in the outer court of Mother's mysterious palace, while *bhakti*, being feminine, is invited to come directly into Her Presence, without the slightest veil or formality." His sweet voice now rises to a fervent feminine pitch as our Master extols the ideal of ecstatic love.

RAMAKRISHNA Beloved friends! Holy companions! Please accept as supreme and adopt with your entire being the passionate and selfless attraction of the *gopis* for the dark blue jewel of Divine Love, their incomparable Divine Beloved, Krishna of Vrindavan. Sing their ecstatic songs. Breathe their perfumed breath. You must! You must!

Right before our eyes, Ramakrishna bursts into flames of love that consume the conventions of space, time, and separation. He sings with the voice and gestures of a female consort, as we all float together in the luminous ocean of undifferentiated love.

> Tell me, friends of Love,
> how far is that dark grove
> where the Blue One waits,
> languishing for love?
> Where is that secret heart?
> The Lord of the Universe dwells there
> in the enchanting form of my beloved,
> the dark blue, long-haired Krishna.
> His fragrance engulfs my soul.
> I am overcome with longing.
> I cannot take one more step.
> KRISHNA KRISHNA KRISHNA!
>
> I cannot return to structures
> of habit and convention.
> Even if I never reach You,
> I will abide in the wilderness,
> crying out Your sweet Name.

RAMAKRISHNA O friends of God, look carefully at any traditional icon of Lord Krishna. His countenance is delicately feminine—without any trace of coarse sensuality, without any sharp edge of masculine energy. He enchants the hearts of men and women equally. Is Lord Krishna really dark blue? Gaze directly into his eyes. You will experience only brightness.

20
Avatara Meets Wandering Sadhu

Bouncing along in the enclosed cab of a carriage, we barely notice the colorful world streaming by because the Paramahamsa's conversation is so intriguing and so nourishing. We are on our way to visit Ram Babu—a visionary lover of Ramakrishna, a prominent Calcutta gentleman whose convictions about our Master's spiritual stature are exalted and intense. He openly and courageously announces Ramakrishna as *avatara,* a full descent of Divine Reality into its own projected cosmos. This is a rare affirmation in the Western-influenced, agnostic climate of cultured Bengal, but Ram does not care about the sophisticated opinions of his peers. He is devoted only to Truth.

The classical *avataras* of Hindu tradition manifest simultaneously as male and female beings in human relationship as well as in mystic union. The name of the feminine counterpart appears first, because of the primacy of Mother Reality, the distinctive incense of Tantric tradition. The Mother is the womb of nondual wisdom. The indivisible being, Sarada-Ramakrishna, is regarded by Ram Babu, along with most of our inner circle, as a contemporary manifestation of Radha-Krishna and Sita-Ram.

Since we are traveling to visit someone whose faith in the *avatara* is so strong, the Great Swan is spontaneously entering the mood of Divine Incarnation, which is one among many parallel spiritual attitudes that the Universal Mother expresses through his transparent form. Accompanying us today is Mani Mallik, a modern unitarian Hindu, who does not accept the possibility of the Divine Descent as a human being. The sage is patiently instructing his somewhat sceptical friend.

RAMAKRISHNA As you sit to meditate upon Divine Reality—call it whatever sacred name you will, from whatever wisdom tradition—you should begin by radically opening your mind and heart to the one Presence, which is innately free from any form of characterization, any form of limitation. This means to divest yourself of emotionality as well as conceptuality. No images or concepts whatsoever should be superimposed upon God, who is utterly beyond speech and mind.

Such modeless meditation is difficult to sustain for more than a few moments. It is difficult to stare into the naked sun at noonday. But the moon is easy and delightful to gaze upon. The moon is none other than the sun's overwhelming radiance taking beautiful form. Thus it is healing and natural to gaze for hours, or even constantly, upon the full moon of the *avatara,* a divinely human being who is nothing other than God's Light, expressing itself through the form of perfect humanity.

For the *avatara,* there are no fundamental considerations of body and soul, nor is there any spiritual path, which is the interplay of these dimensions of awareness called body and soul. For the *avatara,* there is no *karma,* no limiting or binding impressions from the history of personal and collective embodiment. The genuinely human body and mind of the *avatara* is an opaque covering. Beneath this veil, there is no individual soul, no eternal facet of the Divine, but instead there resides the complete Divine Reality, with infinite facets.

Practitioners, adepts, saints, sages—these are individual souls, evolving toward the absolute universality with which the *avatara* begins, from the moment of physical birth and even during the prenatal state. As the Master is now explaining to his attentive companions, the body, mind, and will of the *avatara,* although completely human and thus vulnerable, are the delicately constructed glass case in which the Divine Treasure is on display. The humanity of the *avatara,* Ramakrishna often repeats, is like the crystal of an oil lamp, through which only radiance is visible in the darkness of night.

Individual souls evolve naturally toward the full awareness of their intrinsic perfection, their infinite nature. After merging consciously with the Only Reality, souls may choose to shine forth again as conscious rays of that Reality, during their present or future incarnations. The *avatara,* by contrast, simply is the Only Reality from the beginning—not a ray from that Reality that emanates or returns. The *avatara*—manifesting graciously from age to age, from civilization to civilization throughout history—is the boundless magnet for souls, the uncreated energy of Divine Grace, the very possibility of the mystical path, even the very possibility of cosmic manifestation.

More than slightly intoxicated by these teachings, which come not from textbooks but from direct experience, we arrive at Ram's recently acquired garden house. Alighting drunkenly, we are ushered toward an open-air sanctuary where the lovers are waiting. The Great Swan is delighted by this peaceful grove of holy basil, or *tulsi,* sacred to Lord Vishnu, Divine Source of the avataric descent of Rama and Krishna. Again and again, Ramakrishna exclaims: "Here it will be easy to meditate upon Divinity." We remember his lucid remarks about the *avatara,* through whom humanity can meditate upon Divinity with the greatest intimacy and ease, eventually merging with the Lord in superconscious union.

Trembling with devotion, Ram Babu offers ceremonially before Ramakrishna a large platter of fruits and sweets. The divine child tastes some at random, then tenderly distributes the rest as God-filled *prasad* to the companions of Divine Love, gathered here beside a moon-shaped reflecting pond, enjoying the delightful company of Divinity in human form.

Nearby, a wandering renunciate, or *sadhu,* is seated beneath a spreading tree. Ram generously opens his new garden to all contemplative practitioners. Surrounded by lovers, who are like dim stars around the full moon, Ramakrishna now strolls over to greet this dignified holy man.

"Revered sir," our Master begins in the humble traditional mode, "to what monastic lineage do you belong and what formal title should I use to address your holiness?"

"No titles, no background. Some people call me a *paramahamsa.* Most people do not call me anything. Nameless, formless."

"What a thrilling attitude. I am Shiva! I am Shiva!" Ramakrishna shouts this supreme affirmation—SHIVOHAM SHIVOHAM—at full volume, the hair of his arms and beard standing on end as if a great wave of static electricity has washed over his body.

The God-man and the *sadhu* now sit in deep silence, facing each other. We gather around them. Ramakrishna finally addresses the ascetic wanderer, speaking to him in Hindi rather than Bengali. "Beloved brother, Mahakali is insisting that I reveal another spiritual attitude to you." The white-bearded *sadhu,* somewhat surprised, looks attentively at our Master, senses his unique presence, and prepares to receive guidance directly from the Mother of the Universe. None of us feels that the encounter is accidental or insignificant. Advanced practitioners are often mysteriously guided to Ramakrishna for certain refinements in their meditative practice that no sacred text can offer and that no narrowly focused traditional guru can transmit.

RAMAKRISHNA My dear formless and nameless friend, the omnipresent process of creation and dissolution, the sheer dynamism of Divine Power, is your blissful Mother. The nameless, formless Reality, the transcendent awareness in which you are now permanently awake, is precisely the same Reality that you perceive blossoming around you. *Brahman* is not different from *shakti*. The perfectly peaceful Absolute is not different from the playful relative universe. They are simply not two realities. Nor are they two dimensions of the same reality. They are not even two perspectives. Not two! Absolutely not two!

Ramakrishna enters deep absorption as he reveals this teaching of radical nonduality. The physical body of the God-man undergoes an amazing transformation. The *sadhu* is scrutinizing this spontaneous *samadhi* with knowledgeable appreciation. The Master's muscles seem to have become flowing water. He continues to speak eloquently, while remaining in ecstasy.

RAMAKRISHNA *Brahman* is a shoreless ocean. *Shakti* is the omnipresent, interdependent action of its waves. The spaceless, timeless expanse of nondual awareness is a mysterious instrument with infinite possibilities. Mother is its spontaneous music. As long as Her inscrutable Will keeps consciousness manifest through the human form, one is tempted to think that there are two realities—the formless God and these confusing mirror images called the universe. But no, my friend. There is no such twoness whatsoever. There is no superknowledge separate from or opposed to ordinary ignorance. There is no day as a reality apart from night. There is only wholeness or completeness—beyond night or day, beyond ignorance or knowledge, yet containing both, manifesting both. How to describe this dynamic plenitude? Not with words from any scripture or philosophy. What is simply is!

As our Master delivers this enigmatic yet powerful phrase—*What is simply is!*—he opens both hands in a gently explosive gesture. His graceful, tapered fingers are like the petals of an exotic flower. A radiant silence arises the moment Ramakrishna performs this spontaneous *mudra,* this statement of Truth through a gesture of the body alone. What was adumbrated by the words of the God-man is now being transmitted full force to our inward being. No scripture will ever be adequate to the ineffable teaching that flows through the *avatara*. The *sadhu* is noticeably affected.

After an indefinable interlude that extends into twilight, these two timeless companions arise without haste and link arms. Together they stroll back to the carriage, whispering secrets and laughing like childhood companions. Respectfully, the *sadhu* helps Ramakrishna climb into the carriage. Our Master's eyes are swimming with Divine Bliss. "Not two. Only Mother!" These are his last words to the advanced practitioner, who has now been transformed by the Wisdom Goddess into a completed sage. The naked limbs of the ascetic shine with a new light. There is a new tenderness in his expression.

As we draw away slowly from the small circle of lovers, the hooves of the horses clattering on the stone drive, our Master is already talking to Ram, who is accompanying us, about this new companion.

RAMAKRISHNA The *sadhu* is very lovely. He possesses a refined spirit. Please arrange to bring him whenever you visit Dakshineswar from here. The Mother Reality that abides mysteriously within this form immediately recognized the *sadhu* to be a realized soul, one who has genuinely awakened into formless awareness. This is admirable. But supreme Reality is expressed perfectly through forms as well. Mother expresses forms formlessly and manifests formlessness as form. There are many other subtleties about Divine Manifestation that cannot even be hinted at through language. The Absolute miraculously incarnates before our very eyes as the relative universe. This inconceivable Completeness can even become focused as a particular human being, without tearing the fabric of humanity. The *avatara* engages in natural human activity while teaching, demonstrating, and experiencing only Truth. From that Completeness alone springs forth the omnipotent, omniscient manifestations called Shiva, Kali, Krishna. The sacred mantras OM SHIVA, OM KALI, OM KRISHNA are simply forms of a single OM, the primordial nature of awareness. The *avatara* is precisely this original OM, and therefore effortlessly embodies the Divine Forms and the formless Divine Attributes revealed through all sacred traditions.

Tears are running down Ram's cheeks. His profound understanding of Ramakrishna as a full Divine Descent is being confirmed by the very

Source, expressing itself intimately through the charming, sweet, slightly stammering speech of Ramakrishna Paramahamsa. But the selfless sage never exalts his own position. Smiling delightfully, he addresses his most adamant disciple.

> RAMAKRISHNA Beloved Ram, suppose the matriarch of a vast estate sends a young child from her own family to invite everyone to a sumptuous feast. Naturally, those who live on this estate will look upon the child with the same special affection and respect that they feel for the benevolent owner, their benefactress and protectress. In this sense, the boy and his powerful mother are regarded as one. Her wish is made clearly known through him. The royal, generous, universal invitation of the Wisdom Goddess comes through the mouth of a child. I am that mere child.

His devotion undaunted, Ram Babu replies: "But to see you, sir, is precisely the same as seeing God."

Ramakrishna responds: "Do not ever make such a rash statement again! The wave is contained by the ocean. The ocean is not contained by the wave." Repeating the words *nirakara brahman,* the philosophical term for formless Reality, the sage now slips into *samadhi,* like a pearl diver disappearing into the blue depths.

21

The Mood of the Divine Child

Ramakrishna Breaks His Arm

AS MAHENDRA ENTERS the room, humility radiates from his very pores. He prostrates full length before the Paramahamsa. Mahendra's noble face with large eyes, graced by the long beard of an ancient Indian *rishi*, a seer of Truth, is full of concern. His impressive figure melts entirely into devotion as his forehead lightly touches Ramakrishna's feet. He is bringing a fresh white cloth to change the sling on our Master's arm.

Some days previously, the Paramahamsa, retiring as usual to the remote pine grove to answer the call of nature, unexpectedly entered ecstasy. He fell on his left arm, yet felt the intense pain of the break only when his mind returned to relative awareness. Usually, someone attends the sage wherever he may wander in the large Temple Garden in order to prevent just such an occurrence. But Ramakrishna dismissed his attendant at the edge of the grove. It is the only area of personal privacy that remains in his daily existence.

Since this injury, the Great Swan has remained constantly in a childlike state, passionately inquiring of everyone who enters his room why he broke his arm and how to assuage the pain. The serious-minded young Rakhal is unable to be patient with this openly childlike behavior, considering it unseemly for a God-realized sage, who is traditionally viewed as beyond both physical pain and mental distress. Others among the companions of Divine Love look upon this event as Mother Kali's way of teaching us that Her miraculous child, Her emanation, is fully human, completely vulnerable, and utterly dependent upon Her inscrutable Will. Ramakrishna is free from the self-satisfaction of the adept who considers himself above and beyond the universe and its suffering beings. He calls this subtle sense of superiority "the ego of knowledge." The blissful sage of Dakshineswar has even transcended sagehood.

After inquiring briefly about Mahendra's health and his difficult family situation, Ramakrishna, unable to control his emotion, bursts into tears: "If I am merely an instrument, operated by the omnipotent Mother of the Universe, why should part of this instrument have been broken?" The most reticent disciple does not venture any reply but concentrates on renewing the sling around the injured arm, bound by a splint. The childlike Paramahamsa winces and cries out with pain, even at the most delicate touch of Mahendra.

When this process is finally completed, Ramakrishna complains like a five-year-old of being terribly hungry and asks Mahendra whether he has brought any delicacies from Calcutta. Rakhal is trying to be patient with the situation. His brooding expression is intense and very beautiful. Ramakrishna glances at his spiritual son and immediately enters *samadhi,* lost in the ocean of Divine Intensity and Divine Beauty. Gradually returning to the perception of space, time, and individuation, the divine child begins to repeat: "I want to eat sweet *jilipi* and drink cool water." Beginning to sob like a small boy, he converses with Goddess Kali: "Mother, Mother, Mother! O Brahmamayi, O Dream Power of the Absolute! Why have You done this to me? My left arm is seriously injured, You know."

Turning to the seekers of Truth seated on the floor, some of whom are astounded to witness the great sage in such a childlike mood, the Paramahamsa pleads: "O friends, please tell me that I will be all right again, that the pain will disappear, that I will be able to offer flowers with the left hand, sacred to the Wisdom Goddess!" We all murmur consolations and assurances as one would to a suffering child. Ramakrishna, tears streaming down his cheeks, requests his dear companion Adhar to stroke his feet.

The companions are accustomed to the physical nakedness of the Paramahamsa when he dances without restraint and the wearing cloth falls from his radiant, amber-colored body. But this emotional nakedness is very unsettling. We experience anew our own childlike vulnerability, our complete dependence on the Mother's Will. Listening to the Paramahamsa crying for Her, a surprising new intimacy with the Divine Mother begins to unfold within our being.

Suddenly, the Great Swan chants aloud the mystic seed syllable that invokes formless, attributeless Reality. Three times it rings out, with deep resonance—OM, OM, OM. The atmosphere of the room is instantly elevated to the most rarified plane of awareness. Every mote of dust is fully charged with Divine Presence. We begin to dissolve into luminous space. Ramakrishna is also surprised by this sudden thunderbolt of transcendent knowledge.

RAMAKRISHNA O blissful Kali! Why are You causing me to mediate on the primordial OM? Mother, please do not plunge me into Your formless Ocean of Consciousness. Do not absorb me into the state of *brahmajñana*, Your subjectless, objectless awareness. Mother, I want to make merry with the lovers. I want to play. Keep me simply as Your child. From this blessed state, I can adore You, plead with You, complain to You. A small child is easily frightened and desperately needs its mother. I long only for my Divine Mother. Her alone do I need. With all due respect to the transcendent knowledge of the Vedantic sages, I do not desire it. Mother, please give that kind of dispassionate knowledge and invulnerability to the proud adepts who seek it. Grant me only pure love for You. I long desperately for Your Presence, for Your Smile, for Your Touch. O You Who are composed of sheer bliss! O Anandamayi Ma! O blissful Mother!

Repeating again and again this most beautiful epithet of the Goddess, Anandamayi Ma, tears streaming from his reddened eyes, the Paramahamsa, unable to life his voice in song because of physical pain, recites the cry of complaint to Kali, composed a century before by the inspired Goddess-worshiper Ramprasad.

> O glorious Mother Kali,
> listen to the complaint
> that rages in my heart.
> Even though I am wide awake,
> knowing that You alone exist,
> even with the guidance and protection
> of Your Omniscience and Omnipotence,
> the deceitful robbers called
> ordinary conceptions and emotions
> have entered the house of my mind
> to steal my precious treasure—
> pure love and pure devotion.

Somewhat calmed by Ramprasad's song—at least no longer sobbing uncontrollably—Ramakrishna continues to speak directly with the Black Goddess: "What did I do wrong, Mother? I do not even perform any action at all. You alone are the sole initiator of activity for the entire universe. I am the instrument, You the sole wielder of the instrument."

Turning suddenly toward Rakhal, the Master opens wide his half-closed eyes and speaks in a mood of penetrating sobriety.

RAMAKRISHNA I know that you are plagued by limited views of what is proper behavior. Please do not defraud yourself with trivial considerations, my dear. Let us all weep with abandon at the way these deceitful robbers—these common, habitual assumptions—have broken into our house. They steal away with the inestimable treasure of ecstatic love, without even being able to understand or enjoy what they have stolen.

The Paramahamsa now begins to play like a convalescent child who has momentarily forgotten his delicate condition. Soon he has the room filled with laughter by his naughty antics, mimicking and teasing everyone, both verbally and with hilarious gestures. As the sage frolics about, Mahendra has to repeat constantly: "Sir, please be careful. Remember your injured arm."

Just as unexpectedly, Ramakrishna enters the mood of wisdom. We no longer perceive a child before us, but a God-realized master of the highest stature and refinement. He addresses us with profound earnestness.

RAMAKRISHNA O friends of Truth, none of your meditative disciplines will be of any ultimate value unless you realize directly—here and now, before continuing even one step further along the path—that *akhanda satchidananda* alone exists, that you simply are indivisible Being, Consciousness, and Bliss, that Mother performs all action, including your own acts of devotion and meditation. Your aspiration to realize Truth is simply God longing for God. Constantly discriminate, with the sharpest, most uncompromising accuracy, between your ordinary assumptions—about the world, about yourselves, about God—and the actual Truth, which is total unity, all-encompassing oneness, perfect simplicity. Discriminating this way, with illumined intellect and open heart, do not hesitate to renounce your assumptions and obsessions, moment by moment.

Absolutely nothing can substitute for this constant process of discrimination and renunciation—not pilgrimage, not prayers, not meditation, not even ecstasy or Divine Grace. Without discrimination and renunciation, the energy of your prayer or your ecstasy will be momentary, like a sizzling drop of water on a red-hot iron pan, all sound and no substance. The aspirant who is still enslaved by conventional thinking—whether personal, social, or religious—may experience the flow of Divine Grace for a few seconds, perhaps when contemplating the beauty of a flower or sensing the awesomeness of a sacred shrine. But moments later, habitual thought and perception return to the falsely assumed existence of impurity, negativity, division, separation. True contemplative practice cannot be carried on just a few moments or a few hours at a time. An insatiable restlessness, a dynamic longing to merge completely with Divine Reality, must surge from the center of your being—while waking or sleeping, working or playing.

There should be no procrastination, no waiting for some supposedly proper or auspicious time—either later in this life, in Paradise, or in some future incarnation. If a beloved son or daughter continues to insist on receiving his or her share of the ancestral land, loving parents will eventually respond, transferring the deed even though the youth may still be a legal minor. God will certainly respond to your prayers for illumination if you experience intense restlessness to return consciously to your own original source, through intimate communion and radical union.

Divine Presence brings us forth from itself and as itself. We can claim, here and now, our just inheritance, our birthright of unity. God is our spiritual father and mother fused as one Reality. If our knowledge of unity is strong enough, we can insist, even demand. I used to cry desperately: "Reveal Yourself to me, O Mother, O supreme Reality, or I will take my own life."

In a less extreme spiritual mood, one can pray tenderly to the Great Goddess: "O blissful Mother, You alone are able to awaken Your child into Truth. You who protect every creature as a spark of Your own Life must recognize this child, too, as composed solely of Your Radiance. I have not received transcendent knowledge from Your bliss-bestowing Hands. I have not developed mental discipline through long hours of worship and meditation. I do not experience the unquenchable fire of pure devotion. I am nothing. You alone exist. Please merge me consciously into Your Reality."

A luminous silence reigns. Tears fill our eyes as we gradually understand that the Master is initiating us into his own rare mode of intimate, prayerful, childlike longing. All proud sense of self-effort, self-discipline, or even self-realization disappears from our hearts. Only Mother's Grace remains. Here is the secret to complete renunication.

Shaking his right fist and kicking both feet against the bed exactly like a small child having a tantrum, Ramakrishna is now calling out again to Divine Reality: "Mother, I cannot live without You. Not even for an instant!"

22

Upward-Flowing Energy of Kundalini

THE PARAMAHAMSA'S broken arm is still bound with splint and sling, but he no longer pays the slightest attention to his physical condition, constantly dissolving into the immeasurable ocean of *samadhi* and miraculously coming forth again to teach humanity. Yesterday, the God-intoxicated sage was conversing with Goddess Kali: "Those who come here driven by religious fantasies and selfish desires will see this broken arm and go away again. They will no longer pester me for limited results. Mother, You have played a very clever trick here." Singing *Ma, Ma, Ma,* he then merged into Her, neither speaking nor moving for many hours.

The atmosphere this afternoon is pleasantly relaxed. It is Sunday, when many persons from the busy metropolis of Calcutta come for respite to the peaceful Temple Garden, seeking our Master's delightful company. Several private carriages have drawn up north of the sage's room. Ramakrishna is humming softly—OM KALI, OM KALI. Someone offers him a beautiful new sandalwood fan. Exclaiming, "Good, good, OM KALI MA," he fans all the holy icons in his room and finally the radiant icon of his own form.

Two connoisseurs of art are now regaling the Paramahamsa about an exhibition at the Asiatic Museum: "Many maharajas and other important collectors have loaned rare works—couches and other articles of furniture, beautifully designed, inlaid with silver and gold. The craftsmanship and artistry are well worth seeing."

Ramakrishna laughs with abandon. Finally catching his breath, he speaks in a playful tone: "Yes! Absolutely! It is important to view such an exhibition. You will gradually realize that the gold and silver furnishings of maharajas are like discarded leaf-plates to be licked clean by wild dogs. That will be an important refinement of your spiritual life." Everyone now laughs with similar abandon. Laughter is the central channel for the Master's transmission of radical wisdom. We can feel the clarity and radiance of his spiritual freedom bubbling up within us as laughter. Even the two connoisseurs, though somewhat disconcerted, are genuinely laughing. The small room has now become, as Ramakrishna often describes it, a vast marketplace of joy.

RAMAKRISHNA When I first began to visit Calcutta with my nephew Hriday, he was always wide-eyed. "Uncle, uncle," he cried one day. "Look there! The English Viceroy's residence! Is it not like a royal palace, with its great white columns?" I glanced at the impressive structure, and Mother Kali clearly revealed it to me as a mere pile of clay bricks.

More laughter springs up and floods this blessed room with the clear water of wisdom, healing our subtle obsessions about wealth and power, sweeping away both anger and envy, directed toward maharajas from the Orient or the Occident.

RAMAKRISHNA Divine Reality alone exists. Its splendors, including golden couches and brilliant constellations, are mere temporal flashes of what is essentially timeless. It is like the magician and his magic feats. Observers become mute with astonishment when they enter the hypnotic trance projected by a powerful magician and begin to perceive his wonders and miracles. But whatever occurs under individual or collective hypnosis—although it is being tangibly and vividly experienced—remains fundamentally unreal. In the case of magic feats experienced under hypnosis, the mind of the magician alone is real. In the case of the universe, only the nondual awareness that we call Divine Reality is actually present. The countless phenomenal events are products of hypnotic suggestion. Mother alone is real, and all else is the splendor of Her Magic, or *mahamaya*.

One of the liberal modern thinkers in the room speaks enthusiastically, as if he has not even heard the Master's remarks: "Revered sir, at the museum exhibition there are various fascinating scientific demonstrations. There is a huge electric light, almost as brilliant as the sun. It caused me to reflect upon the greatness of God, who creates both electricity and human intelligence." The Paramahamsa smiles, responding gently and patiently.

RAMAKRISHNA Dear Manilal, the cosmic creation is certainly a marvelous magic feat, but what does it really consist of? Is this universe composed of electric forces or human intelligence? Not at all. Divine Presence alone manifests as the entire cosmos—as all its subtle material forces and all its spiritually conscious forms of life. There is simply nothing other than God before our eyes, before our scientific instruments, before our rational minds.

Crying out the words "all this" the radiant Paramahamsa describes a large, graceful arc with his right hand, beginning and ending at his heart center. We feel this gesture as if it is moving with great power inside our own heart, opening us completely to receive the nectar of his wisdom-speech, which is not description but initiation.

RAMAKRISHNA All this! All this is *akhanda satchidananda,* the transparent Ground of Being, absolutely blissful consciousness, subjectless and objectless. Creator and creation are both *satchidananda.* Even *maya,* the hypnotic force of delusion, is simply *satchidananda.* Not only the visitors and the various exhibitions, but the entire museum is indivisible Being-Consciousness-Bliss.

I visited your famous Asiatic Museum once. The curator showed me some fossilized bones. Just think, an animal lying surrounded by stone for thousands of years becomes stone. How much more powerful and fruitful it is to remain surrounded by God-realized persons! After just a few years, one becomes God.

Laughing heartily and lifted into a distinctly higher state, Manilal responds: "Beloved sage, if you come to visit this exhibition, you will generate enough illustrations and instructions for ten or fifteen years." The Paramahamsa smiles broadly.

RAMAKRISHNA The exhibition I would love to attend would contain paintings of wandering yogis and yoginis, men and women fully engaged in the actual process of yoga, or mystic union. This is not just physical or mental exercise, but the Great Yoga, which leaves nothing outside or inside—only God. At my ideal exhibition, there would be a large painting of a naked yogi with long, matted hair, seated in full lotus—right foot on left thigh, left foot on right thigh—eyes closed in unwavering meditation. Beside his graceful form glow the dying embers of a large log; behind him, the red eastern horizon. Another painting would depict a tantric adept wearing a deep red shawl and bone ornaments, plunged in the darkness of a new-moon night. As he smokes hemp from a water pipe, his face is illuminated by the charcoal fire that blazes up as he takes a powerful draw. His half-closed eyes, inebriated with love for Goddess Kali, are indrawn in expression like a mother bird hatching her eggs. This exhibition would truly kindle spiritual awareness and profound aspiration, just as gazing at a wax fruit can make one thirsty for a delicious ripe mango.

The main obstacle to yoga, or conscious union with *satchidananda,* are conventional thoughts on the instinctive level, such as "I am male" or "I am female." From these assumptions arise abstract notions, such as "I need a sexual and emotional partner to fulfill me." The confining structures of wealth, power, and hierarchy then begin to multiply uncontrollably. True yoga becomes possible only when the mind and heart are purified—blissfully emptied of all these habitual assumptions and fantasies.

The seat of all-purifying transcendent insight is the subtle lotus center between the eyebrows. At least, this is where the energy of insight is experienced as long as we retain the provisional notion of a body in space and time. By the pressure of routine thought and perception, the current of primordial awareness in inadvertently and even forcibly relocated from the forehead center, where it manifests naturally as liberating wisdom, into the subtle lotus centers correlated in the physical nervous system with the organs of evacuation and reproduction. The result is an obsession with possessing, manipulating, and enjoying power, in all its various egocentric forms. Through authentic contemplative disciplines, under the careful observation and guidance of a selfless adept, this living current of awareness, or *kundalini,* is once more oriented upward through the navel center, heart center, throat center, and forehead center, eventually reaching the thousand-petaled lotus, the golden crown of the subtle body, where full enlightenment occurs. All limited power structures and ego structures then blissfully dissolve, including the universe falsely perceived as a place of negation and separation.

The most effective discipline, however, is friendship and constant companionship with God-conscious men and women. Living among weavers, one gradually learns to distinguish a forty-one- from a forty-two-strand thread, simply by touch. One should avoid the popular notion of yogic discipline as some secret, powerful technique of visualization and concentration that the individual can use at his own discretion. This ambitious kind of yoga increases the energy of egocentricity rather than genuinely releasing us from ambition, whether personal, social, or religious.

Through the elevating companionship and wise affection of holy persons—those in whom the upward-flowing current of *kundalini* is awake and established—one gradually loses all concern over public opinion and the superficial standards of popular judgment. One renounces all culturally induced hopes and fears. One becomes a free yogi, wherever one may be located—in a remote village or in the center of Calcutta. The constant discrimination and renunciation of egocentric thought and behavior then become easy and natural. Through this delightful holy companionship, concentration and willpower spring up spontaneously rather than being manipulated and tainted by strange, ambitious physical and mental disciplines.

One then perceives directly through the eyes of the *rishis,* the ancient seers of Truth. One actually experiences the intrinsic unreality of limited self, limited family, limited society, limited religion. One instinctively renounces what one genuinely knows to be unreal. This genuine knowledge alone constitutes true control of the senses, thoughts, and emotions, not some artificial process of suppression and repression. At any sign of serious danger, the turtle withdraws within its shell. This is a natural, spontaneous process which nothing can reverse. At the slightest sense of unreality, the realized yogi withdraws consciously into Divine Reality.

The person who has not courageously confronted the basic unreality of conventional structures—including both individual and collective egocentricity, including as well the very notion of a substantial universe—can never sincerely love the Real or long intensely for the Real, much less become Reality. Such a person may pretend to love God, or may even wish to love God, but true sincerity, truly guileless conviction, remains impossible. Why? Because of divisive thinking—basically, the sense that there is God plus some order of existence other than God. This illusory category—"something or someone other than God"—is what now receives the majority of your attention, Manilal Mallik. Give up this dualistic thinking, this subtle hypocrisy!

The Paramahamsa's thunderbolt of wisdom strikes the sophisticated Manilal at the very center of his being. All the companions in the presence of the Great Swan feel equally chastened. We awaken with a sudden jolt into greater clarity. We decisively reintensify our commitment to knowing Reality and becoming Reality. Companionship with the upward-flowing energy of Mother Kundalini is transforming indeed!

23
Secret Rhythm
of the Wisdom Mother

ENTERING THE HOLY atmosphere of the Master's chamber at about eight this morning, we find him already passionately engaged in conversation. On the walls behind and beside him hang sacred icons. There is Goddess Kali, Divine Manifestation of Pure Consciousness; Radha-Krishna, Divine Descent of Love; Sita-Ram, Divine Emanation of Beauty, Majesty, Power, Justice; and Jesus Christ, Divine Incarnation of the Logos, the eternal Creative Wisdom of God. These and several other great spiritual transmissions flow into the dynamic expanse that we call Ramakrishna Paramahamsa—each maintaining its integrity and distinctness there, like the discrete currents in one vast, planetary ocean.

RAMAKRISHNA Beloved friends, please remember that the most complete manifestation of God, on any plane of being, occurs through the medium of humankind. This is the drama of Divine Descent, the *avatara* who is simply God at play within God. You may wonder: "How is it possible for limitless awareness and limitless bliss to express itself fully through a limited nervous system? This human vehicle is driven by hunger, thirst, need for sleep, reproductive urges. It is tremendously vulnerable to disease. It is hypersensitive to sorrow and weeps as well with longing. How can God become a human being?"

The answer lies right before your eyes as the entire range of manifestation. All these limited forms and relative processes are simply *satchidananda*—Being Absolute, Knowledge Absolute, Bliss Absolute. Through how many conscious beings is this supreme Reality weeping and suffering, being born and dying! If it is possible for Divine Presence to manifest, moment by moment, as this vast universe—

including heavenly as well as earthly planes of being—certainly it is possible for God to focus completely through a radically purified human body, mind, and heart.

Lord Rama, full embodiment and conscious expression of Divine Reality, nevertheless wept for his beloved consort, the holy Lady Sita. He did not withdraw into some invulnerable Divine Transcendence. God enters entirely into the humanity of the *avatara,* and God is expressed perfectly through every atom of that humanity. There is no limit to the miraculous power of the Divine to incarnate consciously as a particular living being or to manifest as the natural processes of the creation.

Listen to the figurative language of the Puranas, so rich in spiritual meaning. Lord Vishnu incarnates as a ferocious sow, a powerful mother-protectress, in order to defeat a particularly virulent strain of demonic energy. After the Divine Victory is accomplished, the Lord does not wish to return to transcendental existence, but thoroughly delights in the earthly play of space and time, even through this relatively unrefined body and mind. Divine Reality actually gives birth in its form as the sow and enjoys the process of suckling its young. The heavenly beings, bound by their heavenly conventions, become greatly disturbed by this incomprehensible Divine Play. They request assistance from the Warrior of Wisdom, Lord Shiva, the expression of Divine Transcendence. Shiva emanates into space and time and manifests an impressive Divine Form before the incarnated Lord Vishnu, imploring Him to return to His heavenly mode of being. The sow simply continues to suckle her young ones. Then Shiva, with His diamond thunderbolt of Wisdom, swiftly and painlessly ends the limited existence of this life form, and Lord Vishnu comes forth, like a bright sword from its dark sheath, laughing in ecstasy. The Lord of the Universe immediately manifests again in his abode of Pure Consciousness, beyond earthly, subtle, and heavenly planes—the abode which he has never essentially vacated. Many secrets about Divine Descent are hidden in this sacred history.

In deep silence, the ecstatic lovers meditate together on the mystery of complete Divine Expression, this mystery which we see embodied directly before us as Ramakrishna Paramahamsa. Gracefully clearing away the accumulated weight of religious inhibitions, regulations, and distortions, the *avatara* mysteriously descends to make spiritual progress swift, sure, and easy for many, not just for a few. The *avatara* is not an individual soul and therefore does not seek to attain liberation, but descends again and again to open the way of liberation from self, to become a sublime object of worship and adoration for countless conscious beings who are awakening and evolving. As Ramakrishna often cries out in ecstasy: "O Mother, if for the good of humankind I must be born and suffer a million more times, I will joyously bear it."

VISITOR Revered sir, what is the exact nature of the life of the soul after physical death?

RAMAKRISHNA As long as a person remains ignorant of ultimate unity—as long as one experiences oneself as a separate, individual center of consciousness, no matter how spiritually advanced—there will be the perception of a process of being born, dying, and being reborn. This manifestation will occur either on the earthly plane of the cosmos or on various subtle and even formless planes. But why remain fascinated by this phenomenal process? The moment that supreme knowledge blazes above the mind's horizon, the obscuring mist of birth, death, and rebirth dissipates. Then Consciousness alone is conscious. There is no separate stream of consciousness to return into this world or to wander through the delights of heavenly realms. There is no separate conscious being who comes into this world in the first place. Nor is there a world that exists independently. To supreme knowledge, or *brahmajñana,* the physical universe and the nonphysical realms are revealed as Pure Consciousness. The entire cosmic drama continues to manifest, coherently and lawfully, but is simply *akhanda satchidananda,* indivisible Reality-Consciousness-Bliss.

You may sincerely wonder: "Why this play of relative experience and supreme knowledge?" There is no conventional rationale for this cosmic process of manifestation and awakening from manifestation. Consider a common artisan who is making clay pots for yogurt. He forms them by hand and spreads them out to bake in the sun. Since he works quickly, without much concern for uniformity, some of the pots are thinner and become baked sooner than others. Now suppose a sacred cow, wandering unrestrained through the village, walks over these freshly made pots. The vessels already baked hard are broken into shards by the cow's hooves. Laughing aloud, the liberated sage who lives disguised as a simple potter, throws these shards away. The crushed pots that are still soft, he melds into a large lump of clay to fashion into new pots.

So long as you are not fully baked by the blazing sun of knowledge, when the hooves of death crush your form, you must return to the hands of the Cosmic Potter. The space within the hard-baked pots has become one with universal space. This is liberation. Only useless shards remain.

Consider another image. When rice is boiled, the grains become soft and delicious, but they cannot be sowed again to produce a new crop. This boiling process is the awakening of supreme knowledge. The person of liberating wisdom, completely cooked, becomes nourishment for humankind but cannot be replanted again in the earth of separation, division, individuality.

Rich silence intervenes between the bursts of illumination that shine forth from the Paramahamsa. We are permeated by the secret rhythm of the Wisdom Mother. The lovers listen with rapt attention. Conventional time disappears.

RAMAKRISHNA Lover and Beloved, the soul and its precious Lord, are not two separate entities. They are part of a continuous flow. The individual life of the soul is not essentially distinct from infinite Divine Life. Nevertheless, as the devotional scriptures reveal, there is a dramatic relationship between the human and the Divine. Human lover and Divine Beloved are not merely interchangeable. The quest for realization unfolds as *I* and *Thou*, until the lover attains maturity. Then there is only *Thou, Thou, Thou.*

This body is like a crystal bowl containing the water of awareness, which is the mind in its conditionless, innate purity. Supreme knowledge is the sunlight, illuminating this clear medium of awareness. Across a still pond, one perceives the golden path of the setting sun. This is how Divine Forms manifest in the context of living sacred traditions, which are collective mind—large bowls of water. The flash of transcendent insight reveals that *brahman,* or boundless sunlight, alone is real. All its reflections upon the surface of awareness are dreamlike or insubstantial.

The ego structure—which is the persistent notion, constantly regenerated and renegotiated, that one is an independent center of consciousness—is like a stalk of grass floating in the clear water of awareness, appearing to divide it into two dimensions, subject and object. When this apparent division is removed, the small bowl of individual awareness is revealed as none other than the shoreless ocean of *satchidananda*. Remove this floating barrier, this superimposed abstraction called ego, and there remains only bliss-consciousness, only reality-consciousness. But as long as the slightest superstition of twoness persists—the faintest optical illusion of this and that, here and there, life and death, soul and Lord—the awakening to supreme knowledge cannot occur. The sage who is established as panoramic awakeness functions spontaneously and appropriately in every possible situation without any sense of separate ego. The individual mind of the sage is like a line drawn on water, like a moon in the daytime sky.

Beloved Naren once told me that he would prefer to stand cautiously at the very edge of the ocean of Divine Bliss—to sip the nectar of ecstatic union but not to fall into the fathomless depths and lose consciousness. I scolded him for indulging in such superficial understanding: "You foolish boy, how can one lose consciousness by merging with Pure Consciousness?" The sage immersed in the ocean of *samadhi* is capable of remanifesting a transparent, provisional ego in order to teach the path of mystical knowledge, to inspire lovers along the way of Divine Love, or to engage skillfully in any other form of compassionate service. The sage encounters no barriers whatsoever. One who has merged with supreme knowledge never takes a single step out of rhythm.

There are certain signs that indicate an authentically awakened person and that clearly distinguish such a person from anyone who falsely claims to have reached the single goal of all evolution and aspiration. A genuine *jñani,* a knower of Truth, cannot possibly harm any living being in any way.

However unconventional the *jñani*'s actions may be, they always benefit the greatest possible number of conscious beings, skillfully accelerating their progress toward full awakening. Often the mature *jñani* manifests the guilelessness, transparency, and openness most closely approximated by a small child. As the wise proverb teaches: "An iron sword that touches the alchemical stone turns into pure gold." Gold is soft. It cannot penetrate armor or even hold a sharp edge. The *jñani* may wield this golden sword of wisdom with the fierce attitude of a warrior, but such action should be correctly understood as an intensification of tender compassion, not as wrath or aggression.

From some distance, a burnt string looks precisely like a real string. But it can be blown away by a single breath. It cannot tie knots. The same is true of the provisional ego projected by the *jñani*. The closest analogy to this playful ego of the mature sage is the attitude of the small child who has no rational attachments. This child may carefully shape a palace from sand. If anyone, even his mother, so much as touches this creation, the child cries. Yet a few minutes later, laughing, he knocks it down himself. One moment, a child will manifest great attachment to its wearing-cloth, absolutely refusing to part with it under any circumstances. The next moment, this same child will walk away naked, leaving the precious cloth behind on the ground. Such is the mood of the knower of Truth, who may maintain an elaborate household and teach many disciples but who is capable at any moment of leaving conventional life to live on the crowded streets of the holy city of Benares.

The secret of the *jñani*'s dispassionate mood, his freedom from all contexts, is the direct knowledge that dreaming experience and waking experience are essentially similar. A certain knower of Truth, who happened to be a poor woodcutter, was immersed in a beautiful dream. He was the royal father of seven wise and gifted children, an enlightened king, protecting and guiding a prosperous and peaceful kingdom. His companion suddenly awakened him. They were in the cold, dark forest, resting on a bed of damp moss, with large loads of wood to carry home. "You have just destroyed a dream world of great fruitfulness and delight," cried the woodcutter. "But that was a mere dream, and this is reality," his companion replied. "No, my dear friend," the hidden sage exclaimed. "Please understand on a deeper level. My kingship and fatherhood in the dream are neither more nor less real than my present station as an impoverished and childless laborer."

Transcendent knowledge, or *jñana*, opens directly into the timeless and boundless expanse of awareness called *atman*. The awakening as sheer awareness sometimes occurs through the contemplative process of *neti, neti*—"it is neither this nor that." By ceaselessly applying the method of *neti, neti*, the *jñani* disidentifies with every possible configuration of awareness and returns to the essence of awareness. But there is a level of maturity beyond even the sublime dispassion and transcendent vision of *jñana*. The most mature among the knowers are called *vijñanis*. They dance, laugh, weep, and sing in relaxed communion with

Divine Reality, experienced as an inconceivable fusion of transcendence and immanence, formlessness and form. The *vijñani* becomes *purna*—simplicity, peacefulness, plenitude.

There are three levels of spiritual maturity. Some have read or heard from reliable sources about milk as a nourishing liquid, white in color. They are the humble students of religion and the faithful practitioners who are aspiring to the vision of God. Others have actually seen milk. They have directly contemplated its astonishing whiteness. Some have even tasted milk. These are the incontrovertible witnesses to God's existence, the *jñanis,* the knowers of Truth, authentically free from every doubt. Finally, a few highly evolved persons can reach out and drink milk any time they wish, and can nourish others with it as well. These are the *vijñanis,* the fully awakened sages. They play with God, speak directly with God, lose themselves in God, and reappear as God—manifesting fresh spiritual moods every few moments, never mechanically repeating any teaching or any mode of behavior.

One must pass through *jñana* to ripen into *vijñana.* The royal way is ceaseless application of *neti, neti*—the sensibility that refuses to identify with any finite pattern, any limited experience whatsoever. This process goes on steadily, like the heat of a cooking fire. "I am not the physical elements, nor electric or magnetic forces, nor subtle materiality or energy of any kind. I am not the information provided by the senses or the rational mind, neither am I the intuitive mind or the ego structure that appears as a separate individual center of consciousness. Nor am I any form of cosmic law, either physical or metaphysical. I am not collective consciousness. I am neither Creator nor creation."

As one continues to climb in this way toward the open roof of wisdom, one spontaneously eliminates each of the steps, aware that it is not yet the roof. One does not have to force oneself to leave behind any particular step if one has genuine momentum—the unflagging aspiration to climb to the top of the stairs, to attain the final panoramic vision. When one actually reaches the roof, however, one discovers with great surprise that it is not essentially different from any of the steps. Both steps and roof are composed of the same insubstantial bricks of Pure Consciousness. One then dances with the bliss of unitive knowledge on the open roof, even descending the stairs again while continuing to dance. One joyfully realizes that *brahman*—the inconceivable, indescribable Reality—manifests as every step or level of experience, from first to last. A single sense perception is *brahman,* no less than a beatific vision of the Divine Face. The opening of a single flower is *brahman,* no less than the unfolding of the constellations.

Boundless Consciousness, without separate subjects or objects, miraculously manifests as materiality. You may wonder how *atman*—sheer awareness or transparency—can appear as what one senses to be impenetrable earth and stone. To clear this and every doubt, simply remember that Divine Presence is capable of any manifestation whatsoever. God will never be limited by what people perceive as the bounds of possibility, no matter how expanded their relative knowledge may become.

After blossoming as *vijñana,* the sage can move comfortably in any dimension of the world—city, village, forest retreat. It is simply God living within God. This divinity of all beings, structures and dimensions can be clearly perceived by the organ of supreme vision that develops naturally as soon as the mind becomes pure enough. This gnostic eye can penetrate all imperfections, all partial manifestations, all surfaces. When I worship a young woman as the Goddess, at first I am aware of her limited awareness—cultural prejudices, personal preoccupations. Suddenly the gnostic eye penetrates through these veils and sees her clearly as the blissful Mother of the Universe.

Those who are blessed to be present in this mysterious room are tasting the delicate milk of *vijñana,* flowing abundantly through the pure mind and the radiant body of the God-man who often repeats, enigmatically: "The *avatara* is the udder through which the milk of knowledge flows." through the power of the Master's words, we can feel the awakening of this timeless eye as an inward humming and tingling, as a slight swimming or swooning. Gratefully we look around at our brothers and sisters, gathered in this secret palace of the Wisdom Goddess, surrounded by fragrant twilight and serenaded by the songs of the boatmen and the services in the various temples. A single phrase of the Paramahamsa rings in our hearts: "God living within God."

Somehow an entire day has passed in the long silences between mystic hymns and illuminating conversations. We are exhausted, but our spiritual sense is sharper than it was this morning when we arrived at the Temple Garden. After some twelve hours of ecstatic discourse, overflowing with the brilliant energy of the Mother's Wisdom, Ramakrishna's bearing remains exactly the same. He now rises to visit the Kali Temple for the formal evening worship. It is almost nine. The sage steps into slippers, his soles too sensitive even to walk over the smooth stones of the temple courtyard. As he strolls in the vanishing light toward Mahakali's Abode, he reels like a drunkard and is supported discreetly by his young, bare-footed companions. As we watch from the southeastern veranda of Ramakrishna's room, the emanation of the Goddess disappears through the mysterious, dark portal of Her nine-domed Temple. God living within God.

24

Special Worship of Kali

The Master Meets a Young Actor

GODDESS KALI IS receiving special worship tonight in the sanctuary of Her Temple. The complicated ancient ceremony begins to unfold in the blackness after dusk and continues until the red light before dawn. Classical ragas are played ceaselessly from the southern music tower during this sacred night of the dark moon, several instruments intertwining rhythmic patterns and melodic lines. Every corner of the temple structure and its graceful colonnade gleams with oil lamps, their illumination distinctly golden. The Temple of the Great Mother is reached by ascending seven steps—the mastery of seven planes of awareness, the blossoming of seven lotus centers.

We are privileged to be with the child of Goddess Kali in the *garbha,* the very womb of Her Temple. Here is the awakened stone image of Bhavatarini—the Tara, or Savioress of manifest Being. Her sanctuary is only fifteen feet square. Upon a thousand-petaled lotus crafted from silver rests a white marble image of Lord Shiva—supine, lost in ecstasy. Four silver pillars hold the crimson silk canopy. There is an overwhelming fragrance here, above and beyond the sweet emissions of flowers, fruits, and burning incense. It is the perfume of the Black Queen, who is fully awakened by the worship offered through Her own Emanation, the childlike Paramahamsa beside us, seated on a small red carpet before the Divine Image, surrounded by large trays of delicious offerings. He is dressed in a new, red-bordered cloth and is gently waving a white yak-tail fan to refresh the Wisdom Mother on this warm Indian night. Formed from black basalt, wearing a red sari of Benares silk and a golden crown, the beautiful *murti* of Mahakali is merely thirty-three inches tall, but appears more vast and magnificent than the hundred-foot-high, nine-domed temple where She graciously resides.

The elaborate formal worship complete, Her Feet are now covered with scarlet hibiscus blossoms and by fresh green *bel* leaves touched with sandalwood paste. She is striding dynamically toward the south across the immaculate breast of Lord Shiva, Her right foot on His chest, Her left on His thigh. Surrounding Her are the esoteric symbols for various currents of spiritual energy—lion to the west, sacred trident to the east, jackal to the southeast, black bull to the south, and to the northeast, a great swan. To the northwest is the royal bed where Mother Kali rests in the afternoon. There is a silver glass of cool water for Her to drink and a gleaming copper vessel of Ganges water for Her to bathe.

The Mother wears a mystic pearl necklace of seven strands, a chain of stars, and a golden garland of human heads—ego structures mercifully severed by Her sharp Sword of Wisdom. The beauty of Her aquiline nose is enhanced by a golden nose ring with a pearl pendant. Her earrings are golden fish. She has three eyes, the one in Her forehead being Her Eye of Wisdom. She has four arms. Strongly confronting all negativity, one of Her left hands holds a sword, and the other left hand bears a freshly severed human head by the hair. Unveiling primordial harmony, one right hand is uplifted, palm forward, giving the blessing of fearlessness, and the other right hand is open, palm upward, in the gesture of boundless generosity. The Mother's arms are adorned with various ornaments made of gold, set with jewels. One of her anklets is a *panjeb* used by the women of upcountry Bengal and was procured by Mathur Babu at the earnest request of Ramakrishna.

The inspired sculptor of this image practiced intensive contemplation of Mahakali for six months before setting to work. While immersed in his holy task, this consecrated artisan would take only one light vegetarian meal each day. The completed *murti*, or embodiment, was installed and awakened in a grand ceremony conducted by a certain ardent young priest, just nineteen years old, who was later to be known as Ramakrishna Paramahamsa.

The Great Swan is now speaking in a mood of profundity. His resonant voice fills the entire temple space, the entire sacred cosmos.

RAMAKRISHNA My Mother is the principle of consciousness. She is *akhanda satchidananda*—indivisible Reality, Awareness, and Bliss. The night sky between the stars is perfectly black. The waters of the ocean depths are the same. The infinite is always mysteriously dark. This inebriating darkness is my beloved Kali. Mother is now running up and down the stairs of Her Temple in sheer delight, Her tangled black hair flowing free. Her anklets are making musical sounds. Can you hear? Can you see?

Reality with attributes, *saguna brahman,* has been unanimously declared by the Vedas, Puranas, and Tantras to be Mahakali, the primordial energy of awareness. Her Energy is like the rays of the sun. The original sun is attributeless Reality, *nirguna brahman,* boundless awareness alone. Proceed to the Original through its Radiance. Awaken to nondual Reality through Mother Kali. She holds the key.

The passionate lover does not care for formless Divine Presence. The small child wants only its mother. But the vision of the *ishtadeva,* the aspect of Divinity most intimate to the heart, is equivalent to supreme knowledge, for the *ishtadeva* is actually the practitioner's own infinite nature, limitless awareness.

Mother, is it You or I? Do I peform any action, think any thought? No! No! It is You alone. You listen through my ears to all these words of teaching. I am not listening. Only You.

Ramakrishna suddenly notices the blissful countenance of Lord Shiva, lying face upward beneath the Goddess. Like an excited child, he exclaims: "Look! Look! Here is the living Shiva." As a result of his initiatory words, we can clearly perceive this marble image as conscious, alive, breath suspended in *samadhi.*

With a woman's touch—becoming more and more divinely intoxicated—the Paramahamsa now straightens the Mother's sari and rearranges Her ornaments more attractively. He is murmuring tenderly: "O Mother, how can I offer my life and mind to You, when it is You alone Who have become my life and mind?" We begin to shiver and tremble slightly with ecstasy, tasting a mere drop from the lake of nectar called Goddess Kali.

The eyes of the divine child now fill with tears as he sings hymn after hymn to his Divine Mother in the flickering lamplight, gazing steadily upward toward Her brilliant black Image, garlanded with red flowers. It is the most inspiring sight we have ever beheld. Finally, Ramakrishna arises and throws himself into full-length prostration. We join him. Dawn is already blossoming.

The grand worship is concluded by a performance of sacred theater in the colonnaded patio before the Mother's Temple, where She can observe through large double doors, swung open wide. The Paramahamsa and his companions watch the drama with profound attention, participating inwardly, plunged in the mood of Goddess-worship, which reveals every being and every event as Her Reality alone. As our Master often remarks: "I see the reflection to be precisely the same as the original, the rays the same as the sun."

Naturally intimate with all souls, the blissful sage makes friends with the professional actors, and they return with us to his room for light refreshments. Ramakrishna is floating free, a feather on a breeze. The complete, authentic worship of the Goddess has been accomplished, and the Paramahamsa is transmitting Her sublime satisfaction. He begins conversing tenderly with one of the actors, a young man of open gaze and clear complexion. The room is already flooded with early morning light.

RAMAKRISHNA Your performance was harmonious and accurate. The person who possesses the sensibility and discipline to excel in acting, singing, instrumental music, or classical dance can engage in meditation with that same commitment and quickly become adept— but only if his motivation is sincere. As one practices the disciplines of one's art intensively and regularly, so should one practice *japa*, the inward repetition of the Divine Name closest to one's heart. This gradually concentrates the mind within God. One should occasionally offer flowers, candlelight, and incense with graceful movements, creating an atmosphere where Divine Beauty can vividly manifest. This practice gradually transforms one's entire daily life into worship. Finally, one should plunge into the silent depths of nondual awareness. Such alone is true meditation. The breath becomes so subtle that the diaphragm barely moves. This experience gradually merges one with God.

Ramakrishna opens his eyes wide and intimately asks, "Are you married, my young friend? Do you have children?"

"Revered sir, my daughter died, but now another child has been born."

A profound sigh escapes the Master's lips. He always suffers even more sorrow than the person who is bereaved, and by this mysterious action lightens the emotional burden of death. Then the sage offers uncompromising teachings that remove a much more terrible burden—the spiritual distortion of life.

RAMAKRISHNA Birth and death. Death and birth. How swiftly the drama unfolds. And you are still so young. As the folk song laments: "My husband died just after our marriage, leaving me so many nights to sleep alone." My dear young man, you are beginning to experience the empty nature of temporality. What you have been taught and conditioned to call happiness and contentment are only momentary flashes. The entire conventional world is like the hog plum—mere pit and bitter skin. Partaking of this strange fruit, one's ability to digest spiritual teaching is seriously impaired. Nevertheless, many persons acquire this taste. I tell them: "All right. Go and eat hog plum. But come back here when you get indigestion."

You are engaged in the glamorous profession of theater, consuming applause and adulation. But these are insubstantial and possess no nutritional value. Your full, handsome face will gradually wilt and your cheeks become hollow. Your belly will protrude from self-indulgence.

You may wonder why I stayed to watch your performance, why I appreciated it so much and invited you here. I was attracted by the precision of the rhythm, the instrumental music, the singing, and the gestures. These were signs of spiritual potential. I became interested in meeting you, but then Goddess Kali appeared before the eyes of my heart and indicated that She alone is acting through all bodies and through all minds.

The young actor is receptive to the wisdom of the Great Swan, whom he begins to question eagerly about burning issues in his own life.

ACTOR Revered sage, what is the proper distinction between the primitive sexual urge and legitimate sexual desire?

RAMAKRISHNA The primal drives to reproduce and to survive are the roots of the tree. All the self-centered desires that a person may experience—whether legitimized by convention or not—are the branches of this strongly rooted tree. One cannot simply uproot it entirely and continue to function on the earthly plane. But one can thoroughly redirect the energy of desire away from selfish ends toward the loving service of humanity and the loving worship of Divinity. These two forms of selfless love are essentially the same and should be fused. With the most intense passion imaginable, long for the insurpassable delight of mystic union with God, in which every pore of the body becomes like a sexual organ.

It is very honorable for husband and wife to assume the sacred roles of Bhairava and Bhairavi in the Tantric practice of sexual union. The motivation is no longer reproduction or gratification but the longing to attain *samadhi*, to merge with God. No bliss on earth or in Paradise can compare with the infinite bliss of *samadhi* attained through the union of *shiva*, Pure Consciousness, and *shakti*, the Divine Energy that manifests the universe, moment by moment.

Instead of remaining obsessed with the mundane world, become obsessed with the ultimate experience, mystic union—not just for yourself but for all living beings. Rather than being proud of your natural gifts, be proud of your high spiritual calling. Thus obsession, pride, and other negative emotions will be radically transformed.

The initial, astonishing vision of God gradually blossoms into intimate communion and culminates in union. This process is not possible unless we offer our entire being, both body and mind, to Divine Reality alone. Offer Mahakali the energy of desire, including all drives and urges. Offer your marriage, your child, your theatrical performances, your breath, your life—only to Her. Do not use them for yourself. Do not subtly offer them to yourself. Merge them entirely with Mother Reality. As long as you regard any event or activity in your life, including your physical body, as other than God, your mind will remain divided and the conscious union of *shiva* and *shakti* within the nerve channels of the subtle body will be impossible.

The more one seeks personal gratification, even in the smallest details, the less Divine Bliss one can experience. The constant quest for egocentric pleasure not only defrauds you of your birthright, which is infinitely blissful awareness, but mere pleasure-seeking inevitably produces suffering, both for yourself and for others.

A certain adept, living alone in the wilderness, received his spiritual instruction from twenty-four gurus, one of whom was a giant heron. From this noble bird he learned the simple yet powerful method that frees one from the anxiety and suffering that always attend the quest for gratificiation. The heron, while flying to her nest with a large fish, was chased by voracious crows. These loud, aggressive creatures were diving at her from every direction, driving her earthward. There appeared to be no escape for the graceful bird until suddenly the heron simply dropped her burden. The crows followed the fish, and the heron soared to freedom. Drop the very notion of selfish enjoyment. Right now! The loud, conflicting voices within and around you will cease, and you will soar into the silent, open sky.

Any degree of wealth can become a magnet for the negative energy of obsession. Brothers and sisters live happily and peacefully together as part of one extended family until the ancestral land is being divided. Dogs lick each other and sleep side by side until a single scrap is thrown among them. Young actor, stay in harmony with your brothers and sisters, your parents and friends. This harmony will greatly enhance your spiritual life. If the actors in a play are not in perfect concert, as you well know, a truly theatrical effect is not produced. Please visit this room whenever you can. These companions are your mystical family. Look around you. This is a gathering of bright jewels.

ACTOR Revered sage, our troupe takes three months for vacation during the rainy season. It will be our honor and joy to pay an extended visit to Dakshineswar. We have heard the name Ramakrishna Paramahamsa from many sincere seekers and advanced practitioners. They say you are like a person who can dance freely while balancing a brimful pitcher on your head.

RAMAKRISHNA Yes, dear younger brother. Keep your mind on the pitcher, on God-consciousness, while performing the complex dance of responsibilities, including your family life and your career in theater. In my native village of Kamarpukur, where I grew up far from the sophistication and distractions of Calcutta, I used to spend hours watching the woman who prepares flattened rice. With her right foot she pushes a heavy beam, suspended by ropes, and keeps it swinging. With one hand she turns the rice paddy in the earthen mortar, where the large pestle plunges downward with tremendous force, propelled by the weight of the swinging beam. With the other hand she cradles her baby, sometimes nursing it as well. She keeps an eye on the fire, which needs to be stoked regularly, and roasts the flattened rice in a pan, browning it without burning it. In addition, she converses with her customers, not only about the money they owe but about certain details of their lives. Her other small children are running about noisily, and occasionally she scolds them. The inward part of her attention, however, is always fixed on the constant rhythm of the plunging pestle. If she does not remove her hand at the correct time, it will be crushed.

Young actor, in precisely this manner fix your inward attention on the task of God-realization, which is the central rhythm behind all roles and relations of surface existence. This takes intensive practice, unwavering alertness. Give seventy-five percent of your mind to God, and operate with twenty-five percent in the world. You will be able to participate effectively in every responsibility.

ACTOR Revered sir, is there valid rational or empirical proof that the soul is independent of the body?

RAMAKRISHNA There is a great deal more than proof, my dear. Proof of any kind is always somewhat indirect, partial, or questionable, whereas all-encompassing Divine Presence can be experienced directly, fully, and incontrovertibly. By engaging in authentic disciplines, your nervous system, both physical and subtle, is prepared to receive and assimilate the tremendous impact of God-vision. Then the living Divine Reality takes the initiative and enters completely into the human consciousness that has been sufficiently prepared. This Divine Initiative is called the Grace of God. It is absolutely necessary. Limited human disciplines, no matter how powerful, can never compel Mother to manifest.

The ancient *rishis,* the seers of universal Truth, directly and fully realized *atman,* or their own true nature, to be boundless awareness. This ultimate realization at the root of all civilizations is not possible through faith, through reasoning, or through scientific investigation. Conventional religion is limited by cultural conditioning. Philosophy is limited to what can be apprehended by the rational mind. Science is limited to the information provided by the senses or by instruments that extend the senses but remain on the material plane. Supreme Reality simply cannot be approached by the ordinary intelligence, which is focused through cultural norms, reason, and sense experience. To awaken and develop accurate and reliable spiritual sensibilities, one needs to seek out awakened sages and to abide humbly and patiently in their holy company. The untrained person can barely discern the major pulse in the wrist. An apprentice in the ancient healing arts, who lives in the company of adept traditional practitioners, gradually learns to distinguish seven progressively more subtle pulses along the forearm, using them to diagnose invisible conditions in the complex realm of the human body.

The sensitive young man's entire demeanor is transformed as he recognizes the depth and subtlety of Ramakrishna's wisdom and begins to feel the attraction of our Master's selfless love. The sweet taste of this Divine Love reveals even the purest parental love to be limited by conventional and personal considerations.

ACTOR O noble Paramahamsa, I understand now the incorrectness of my very mode of questioning. I have been more aggressive than receptive.

RAMAKRISHNA Yes, you are ready to practice *tapasya,* the inner discipline that generates heat and intensity throughout the subtle nervous system, the practice that awakens the upward-flowing energy of realization. This can be done very simply through loving repetition of the Divine Name in the heart center. No complicated external or internal ritual or method will be necessary for you. The Names of the Goddess or of Baby Krishna produce very swift results.

Religious people speculate constantly about the final goal—salvation, beatific vision, mystic union—but they seldom actually attain it during this earthly life. Why? Because they remain satisfied with studying and chanting the scriptures, with praying at certain specified times, with performing various ancient rituals. Can anyone attain God-consciousness simply by studying and contemplating the Vedas and the Vedanta? Even the most exalted scriptures give only a hint about the nature of the One Reality. There always remains a clear distinction between the study and worship of God and actual God-realization.

One cannot become intoxicated by planting and harvesting hemp, nor by repeating the name for this active substance, nor even by rubbing it over one's entire body. One must actually swallow some. Similarly, my young friend, you must become intoxicated by Divine Presence. Discover Mother's Energy within your very own being! It is never possible to explain or describe true spiritual inebriation to a person who has not experienced ecstasy and who may not yet be mature enough. Can one explain the delights of sexual union to a five-year-old child?

The actor has now entered an intense mood of inquiry. His eyes are shining, his whole body is alert. His ordinary mind and senses, his personal and cultural habits, have been bypassed by the spiritual skill of the sage. In this heightened state, the radiant and gifted young man finally poses the real question, intimately addressing the Great Swan with his whole being. "Beloved Paramahamsa, how can one actually realize *atman*? How can one become boundless awareness?"

At this high point of communication between seeker and guide, various devotees suddenly enter the room, bringing food that was offered in the Kali Temple during the all-night workshop. The peak of concentration now becomes a marketplace of joyous commotion. The young man is looking with some consternation toward his newly discovered spiritual friend, while the Paramahamsa is actively discussing meal arrangements for Rakhal, whom he adores as the child Krishna, experiencing himself as Yashoda, Krishna's mother. But this particular mood swiftly passes. Ramakrishna tenderly takes the actor by the hand and leads him onto the western porch that overlooks the expanse of the Ganges, already filled with colorful sails as the boatmen begin to ply their trade on the holy waters.

The two new companions stand together in silence, shoulder to shoulder, gazing over the river of Divine Knowledge and Divine Peace. Several of us join them.

RAMAKRISHNA You asked me about realizing *atman*. Limitless awareness is precisely what you are at this very moment. You must now consciously yearn to be what you really are. Every cell of your body, every strand of your consciousness should experience this longing— not because of any lack or absence, but with the clear sense that timeless awareness already belongs to you. It simply is you. Become like the person who suffers an infection which causes him to perceive every dimension of his visual field tinged with the color yellow. Visible structures remain in play, but they are all faintly golden. *Atman* can be intuited as a pervasive golden radiance—inconceivably rich, supremely subtle.

My dear young actor, consider your own professional experience. When you take a theatrical role seriously, your thoughts and even your instinctive movements gradually become pervaded by that character, that atmosphere. So play the role of your true nature, which is indivisible awareness and bliss. Allow the intense atmosphere of this role to permeate your entire body, speech, and mind. Soon you will realize that *atman* is not a role but the essence of all roles.

The actor has become illuminated. With the confidence of direct God-vision, he gazes into the sacred landscape with sacred eyes. Joyously, Ramakrishna and his highly receptive young friend, hand in hand, rejoin the uproar and laughter of the playful companions of Divine Love, those who are spiritually liberated during this life on earth. The two sit together inseparably on the floor of Divine Reality, in the room of Divine Reality. They are living, breathing Reality.

Suddenly, the child of Goddess Kali enters an unusual ecstasy. His eyes are dancing. He is not withdrawn into *samadhi*. His voice is loud and clear.

RAMAKRISHNA Divine Reality is not invisible. Look around you. Here! Here is the visible *brahman,* the transparent ground of Being. Mahakali reveals Her Temple to be composed entirely of bliss-consciousness. The black stone image, the worshipers, the gold and silver implements of worship, the large chandelier, the black and white marble floor of the shrine, the sacred earth beneath—all is sheer consciousness. To realize this is the ultimate aim of every contemplative discipline. All is Consciousness! Cherishing this goal alone, ecstatic lovers fall madly in love with their Supreme Beloved. *Jai Kali Ma*! Victory to Mother Kali!

The Paramahamsa now offers everyone his *salaams,* the greeting of Divine Peace in the Islamic manner. Joyfully, he sings:

> A fakir has arrived,
> absorbed in divine moods.
> Holy is this one
> to both Hindu and Muslim.

Smiling broadly, our Master turns to Mahendra, his amanuensis, and asks: "Am I really liberal-minded? Please tell me!"

25

Great Swan
Meets Orthodox Pandit
Ramakrishna and Shashadhar

RAMAKRISHNA IS seated in the home of his beloved companion Ishan. He remains as serene among the city noises of Calcutta as when surrounded by the quiet of the Temple Garden. Wherever he travels, the Great Swan is englobed by peace—*shanti, shanti, shanti*.

A white sheet has been spread on the floor and white pillows placed near our Master, who is wearing a white cloth and a white woolen shawl informally covering his honey-colored body. He resembles a joyous infant, even with his full black beard, streaked with silver. Since this is a High Holy Day in Hindu tradition, Divine Ecstasy is streaming through the Paramahamsa's very pores. The sacred calendar radiates directly through his subtle body, revealing itself as Divine Initiative, not human convention. The Paramahamsa is waiting eagerly to visit Pandit Shashadhar, who is one of the notable teachers now attempting to reaffirm religious orthodoxy in the face of the liberal cultural developments in this modern Asian metropolis, this confluence of East and West, this greenhouse for future planetary civilization.

When the appointed hour arrives—four o'clock tea in the British pattern—a few companions climb into a hired carriage with the God-drunken sage. He is seated cross-legged, already in *samadhi*, physical eyes partially open, inner vision merged in the shoreless ocean of Light. As it is the rainy season, a constant drizzle has made the road muddy. Beneath a dark gray sky, the other companions follow on foot, some carrying black British umbrellas, others simply throwing their upper cloths over their heads, Indian fashion. The slowly moving vehicle bears this rare Divine

Treasure through narrow, twisting lanes. Today is the Car Festival, during which the Lord of the Universe is paraded through the streets, focused through an ancient image. The lovers of Ramakrishna feel that their Car Festival is being celebrated this way, blessed with a living, contemporary image, composed of pure consciousness.

Upon arriving, the sage is led respectfully to a well-appointed drawing room in the house where the Pandit is an honored guest. Shashadhar rises and bows to Ramakrishna with reverence. The Pandit's lectures, delivered with sincerity and charismatic eloquence, have attracted significant numbers of young Hindus to return from their fascination with Western Christian influences to the perennial religious tradition of their ancestors. The bearing of the teacher is tranquil and noble.

At the very sight of the Pandit, who is wearing a long string of *rudraksha* beads sacred to Lord Shiva and the Goddess, the Paramahamsa enters *samadhi*, standing still, a subtle tremor of ecstasy coursing throughout his entire body, tears glistening at the corners of his eyes. Speaking from this heightened state, our Master, his powerful gaze fixed upon the younger man, stammers over and over: "Quite excellent. Quite excellent." We guide the God-man to a beautiful Persian carpet, where the Pandit joins him.

Attaining sudden sobriety, Ramakrishna addresses the popular religious teacher: "Please tell me how you give your lectures and why you deliver lectures at all."

Somewhat taken aback, Pandit Shashadhar replies: "Why, sir, I simply explain the teachings of the ancient Hindu scriptures—including their philosophical technicalities and their prescribed rituals—because modern people need to receive such explanations." Floodgates of intensity open within the Paramahamsa, and he begins to speak with vigor, directness and delicate humor.

RAMAKRISHNA During this present Iron Age, this era of acceleration and disintegration which encompasses the entire world, the path of ecstatic love will be most effective. Where can contemporary people find the leisure or the concentration to fulfill the complex scriptural injunctions of an ancient way of life? The ancient medicinal remedies, concocted slowly after painstakingly gathering the appropriate roots and herbs, are no longer completely effective to combat modern diseases, which are like an extreme fever that needs immediate relief. By the time your elaborate traditional methods are learned, Pandit Shashadhar, the patient may have already died! Radical medicine is now necessary—not gradual, complicated treatments that few persons will have the discipline to undergo.

When encouraging seekers to practice certain disciplines, I always tell them to sever the head and the tail from the fish before cooking it. Cut away unnecessary ritual and solemn formality. Make spirituality directly accessible, joyous, easy to practice. I tell my friends to ignore the complex preparations and ceremonies prescribed by the Vedas and the Tantras, technical forms of worship that must be completed with perfect exactitude to be effective. I advise them to enter instead directly into the very heart of Divine Presence, with all the love and intensity of their being. I cannot enjoy performing endless rounds of *mantra* on prayer beads, or laboriously counting with my fingers, increasing the numbers day by day as some form of sacrifice or austerity. I enjoy only the continuous inward remembrance of God.

O Pandit, if you really insist on re-creating the sacred ceremonies of past ages—as if complexity or ancientness were somehow more pleasing to God—than at least do not require this exercise from everyone. Offer a direct, simple, powerful path for those who are sincere in their longing to reach the goal of human evolution in this very lifetime. As for your method of addressing vast crowds in lecture halls, it should be clearly recognized that even hearing hundreds of your eloquent presentations will make no deep impression on those who remain caught in ordinary perspectives and assumptions. Adding more religious conventions to their lives will not change their basic conventionality. Can one drive a nail into a stone wall? What use is there in striking the back of a thick-skinned alligator with a dull sword? The gourd-vessel of purifying Ganga water that belongs to a holy *sadhu* visits many sacred shrines but remains a bitter-tasting gourd nonetheless. Your lectures may cause some commotion among aesthetes and intellectuals, like milk frothing when it boils, but ponderous words delivered from podiums and printed in newspapers are incapable of creating genuine spiritual transformation.

You will recognize these facts gradually, my dear Pandit. Then you will awaken into maturity. The newborn calf cannot stand immediately on all four legs. Sometimes it manages to bring its front legs beneath its weight. Then they collapse, and it tries its back ones. Soon it learns to stand firmly on all four. Then it walks. Finally, it runs and leaps for joy.

Your present obstacle is that you cannot clearly distinguish the sensitive lovers of God from those persons who pursue merely a superficial interest in culture and religion. You are divinely called not to instruct society in general but to awaken and guide the lovers of Truth. Of course, in the initial rush of enthusiasm that your eloquent words may generate, it is difficult to discriminate accurately between real love and mere infatuation. When the onrushing storm is lashing the branches, how can you tell a tree that bears sweet mangoes from one that bears pungent tamarind? People are like cakes. Some have a sweet filling, while others have no ecstatic love awakened within them. Yet both may appear the same from the outside. Please find the authentic lovers. Encourage and guide them. Certainly they must be introduced to some sacramental practice, some ritual context within which to unify body, mind, heart, and soul. Only God-realization frees one completely from the necessity for sacraments and disciplines.

How will you know when ceremonial worship has become superfluous? When you shed profuse tears and feel currents of ecstasy flowing through your body while repeating one of the beautiful Names of God. When the fruit appears, the blossoms fall away. Ecstatic love for God—which is none other than God's own Love, powerfully focused through the human lover—is the precious fruit. Ritual worship and scriptural study are the blossoms. What use is a ceremony of remembrance for someone who is already remembering God day and night, someone who never forgets God even for an instant? To forget God is simply to fall into habitual moods that lack the joyous acceptance, moment by moment, of Mother's merciful Will.

When one of the daughters in an extended family becomes pregnant, everyone feels great happiness. Gradually, her daily chores are reduced and given to others. By the time she is ready to deliver, the young woman is doing practically nothing external. All her attention is focused inwardly, on the sacred life within her womb. When the child is finally born, she has no responsibility other than to play, to sing, to rock, and to nurse. Thus the complicated household duties of ceremonial worship and contemplative discipline are gradually lightened and condensed, finally to disappear entirely—beginning at the moment of God-realization—into pure love, sheer play.

The true yogi, the practitioner of inward union with God, traces the sacred sound of OM, the mystic seed-syllable that contains the immeasurable power of Pure Consciousness. Finally, after traveling the path of OM, the silent source is reached and the yogi becomes a realized sage, merged with the One Reality. Complex religious responsibilities disappear. Even the minimal external signs and expressions of spiritual knowledge come to an end. The mature sage can therefore seldom be recognized.

Repeating the phrase several times—"external signs and expressions come to an end"—our Master now enters deep absorption. The Pandit recoils slightly in amazement before the empty form seated like a crystal statue where the dynamic Paramahamsa was located just moments before. A beautiful smile still plays across Ramakrishna's expressive lips. Light and delight radiate from his body, where no breath is discernible. The spectacle is not shocking, yet the absolute absence in a human person of any individual being is difficult to face unless one has become accustomed to witnessing the state of *samadhi*. Even then it remains astonishing.

The ecstasy of the Great Swan continues to deepen, generating an amazed silence among the family members and their friends who have gathered to witness this encounter. At the suggestion of the Master's attendant, we all chant OM, loudly and repeatedly. This somehow draws the sage back toward the border of relative awareness. He murmurs: "I think I will take a glass of water and have a smoke." We know by this request that he is attempting to propel consciousness down into the subject-object world of space, time, substantiality, individuality.

Remaining in the borderland between the Absolute and the relative— the mysterious realm of Goddess Kali—Ramakrishna now addresses Her.

RAMAKRISHNA O Divine Mother of the Universe, I must descend two levels from Your Supreme Nature before I can even utter the sacred syllable OM. O blissful Mother, You introduced me to Pandit Vidyasagar, who has nearly reached the end of his evolution during this lifetime. Now You are showing me a younger *pandit,* one who is struggling to awaken. Please help him to deepen his spiritual awareness. May his consciousness soon be illumined!

After taking a few deep breaths, like a pearl-diver coming up for air, Ramakrishna enters a state of spiritual sobriety once more. He addresses Pandit Shashadhar with new tenderness, his voice resonating with a subtle motherly inflection.

RAMAKRISHNA My dear, please acquire a little more strength and

intensity. Perhaps retire into solitude for a few days to practice meditation. You have just begun to climb the tree, and already you are
expecting to encounter a rich cluster of fruit. The fruit is ripe only in
the highest branches, which are flooded with sunlight. You are undoubtedly a genuine servant. You are truly motivated by love for
humankind.

Ramakrishna becomes extremely moved. Tears come to his eyes, and he
prostrates before the younger man with his forehead on the carpet.
Shashadhar withdraws his feet in consternation. Remaining speechless, he
salutes the prostrating sage with joined palms. The Paramahamsa now
rises and modulates into a light, conversational tone.

RAMAKRISHNA When I first heard about your wide reputation as a
teacher, dear Pandit, I immediately inquired: "Is he just a clever scholar,
with talent for verbal expression, or is he a person who genuinely
discriminates between the surface and the depth? Does he renounce the
emotional and conceptual waves and plunge into the serene, harmonious deeps?" Someone who remains on or near the surface of human
existence cannot be called a *pandit,* a person of knowledge. One can
actually offer spiritual guidance, awakening the energy of transcendent
insight, only if one has received the Divine Command, the direct touch
of ecstasy. Otherwise one's teachings, no matter how eloquent and well
received, will remain on the surface of intellectual, cultural, and religious convention. One may love humankind, but one is not able truly
to benefit anyone.

A single ray of light from the Goddess in Her aspect as Saraswati—
supreme knowledge and heavenly harmony—can ignite a person's being
so completely that before this powerful fire of realization, even great
scholars withdraw like earthworms before the noonday sun.

When the oil lamp is lighted in the evening, moths of rare beauty
come to circle around its golden flame. They do not have to be
summoned or cajoled. The teacher who has received the Divine Command, who has been touched and ignited by holy ecstasy, need not
invite people to taste his nectarlike words. He does not announce
lectures in the newspaper. Divine Attraction is simply irresistible to
those who are pure in heart and who are therefore ready to receive
genuine spiritual transmission. These pure-hearted seekers come from
every corner of society. Laborers, merchants, aristocrats, artists, even

presidents and kings gather spontaneously around the person who has received the Divine Command to teach.

Devotees will address the God-filled teacher with profound respect: "Revered sage, please accept these ripe mangoes and fine sweets, this beautiful woolen shawl, these funds for a new temple. Please accept the humble offering of our entire being at your lotus feet." The awakened sage will cry out in response: "I have the Command of God. What else do I need? What offerings could be attractive to me when I live in ceaseless communion with the infinite Divine Attractiveness?" If any persons persist in attempting to manipulate the sage, he will shout and drive them away. Once a wealthy devotee offered me a trust fund of ten thousand rupees. I fainted right on the spot, shocked at this invasion by the energy of conventional society. Coming to, I cried out to the Calcutta gentleman: "If you ever make such a suggestion again, you must leave this place."

Dear Pandit, does the magnet call to the iron-filings, "please come and attach yourselves to me?" The enlightened sage may or may not possess formal learning but is constantly overflowing with Divine Wisdom, which manifests afresh for each aspirant, each situation. Knowledge of scriptures and esoteric ceremonies is completely insignificant when compared with the irresistible force of the Divine Command. No matter how many scriptural passages one has memorized or how many philosophical treatises one has studied, knowledge produced by the intellect is quickly exhausted. When illumined knowing flows directly from God, however, it is absolutely inexhaustible.

As a youth in my native village, I enjoyed watching the man who measures out grain. Beside him rises a golden mountain of this precious substance. Regardless of how many scoops the man takes to weigh on the scales for a customer, more grain rushes down. As an awakened sage engages in teaching, the Mother of the Universe supplies him inwardly from Her golden mountain of Divine Wisdom. After an entire morning, the heap of grain on the village threshing floor will be somewhat depleted. Divine Abundance, however, never diminishes— not even slightly. A single glance from the Goddess transmits enough spiritual illumination to teach for an entire lifetime.

Pandit Shashadhar, please answer frankly. Have you received that Divine Command, that burning gaze from the Mother's Eye of Wisdom?

The Pandit remains silent, eyes downturned. In a low but distinct tone, he finally speaks: "No, revered sir. I have not received any such Divine Command."

The host of what was supposed to be a genial tea party nervously interjects: "He may not have received this mysterious Command of which you speak, sir, but Pandit Shashadhar preaches out of a sound sense of religious duty, not from any motive of personal gain."

Our Master responds instantly and uncompromisingly, his brilliant eyes flashing.

RAMAKRISHNA No results of genuine and lasting spiritual value will be achieved by mere lectures, regardless of how well intentioned they may be. The fire of realization is necessary to ignite hearts. Without operating solely by the Divine Command, the limited intellect intersperses the true teachings of the scriptures with its own obviously or subtly erroneous interpretations. During the course of his sermon, a liberal Hindu preacher once remarked: "Ultimate Reality is abstract, dry, difficult to conceive." I immediately knew that this person, although entrusted with the guidance of souls, had never experienced the flame of ecstasy nor even so much as a drop of Divine Love or Divine Knowledge. Therefore I exhort you with all my heart, dear Pandit: plunge into the luminous ocean of God-consciousness!

Like a songbird, Ramakrishna bursts into poignant melody.

> Dive deep, O mind, and penetrate
> the fathomless Divine Beauty.
> There alone will you discover
> the pearl of ecstatic love.

Tenderly gazing at the Pandit with Mahakali's own Gaze, the Paramahamsa now visibly manifests as the Goddess. His gestures and entire ambiance become feminine.

RAMAKRISHNA I request and beg you: dive deep, here and now, into the ocean of infinite Being, infinite Awareness, infinite Joy. You will have no anxiety whatsoever about the effectiveness of your teachings once you disappear into *satchidananda,* once you realize God to be the only Reality. Yes, you will definitely receive the Divine Command! You will truly teach and transform people! You will!

The whole drawing room explodes with jubilation. The release of nervous tension is complete. Tea and abundant refreshments are served. The Paramahamsa is now bantering in a charming manner with the family members and invited guests, making them feel completely surrounded and accepted by Divine Love. The host is smiling broadly. The expression on the sensitive face of Pandit Shashadhar is one of exquisite contentment and transparency.

26
Ramakrishna Sings the Tantric Transmission

THOROUGHLY ILLUMINED and filled with enthusiastic devotion, the renowned Pandit Shashadhar is visiting our Master today at the Dakshineswar Garden—this miraculous place of pilgrimage, consecrated to the dynamic manifestation of Wisdom Goddess Kali. The family with which the Pandit is staying in Calcutta accompanies their respected teacher on his pilgrimage to the Temple Garden and to Ramakrishna, living temple of the Mother's Presence.

It has been only six days since the Paramahamsa opened the secret inward intensity of this scholar and sincere practitioner, reaching directly into the depths of his heart, taking him beyond scriptural study, beyond commitment to ancient religious ritual, beyond involvement with the popular renaissance of traditional Hindu culture. The Pandit now looks more like a young boy than the dignified lecturer he was only days ago. He is a clean, shining vessel for the Mother's radical Wisdom, which Her precocious child is beginning to pour into him. The Paramahamsa is simply the brimful pitcher of Her Bliss.

When his new friend arrives, Ramakrishna at once leads him by the left hand to an icon on the wall of his room—the impressive Kali-image of Kalighat in the modern world-city, Calcutta. This miraculously awakened image can trace the lineage of its empowerment back to an ancient tantric Buddhist Kingdom, the Pallava dynasty of Bengal. Facing the Mother, our Master places his right palm upon his heart center, folding his first, second, and third fingers. Thrice the blissful sage repeats the powerful mantra OM KALI, and then offers the younger man *prasad*—sanctified and sanctifying food from the shrine of Mahakali at Dakshineswar. In an open, childlike manner, he comments to the surprised Pandit: "At Kalighat, I once saw the Great Goddess as a girl of fourteen with brilliant black complexion. She was playing with some children and chasing a golden butterfly. Once Mother talked with me and played by cracking my fingers. For three days afterward, I wept continuously."

The two sit together intimately on Ramakrishna's bed and begin to discuss the path most favored by Pandit Shashadhar—the ancient Upanishadic teaching about *brahman*, the all-encompassing, all-constituting Reality. The Great Swan is elucidating the way of *jñana*, direct knowledge of Reality. He speaks out of his own realization, which confirms yet transcends the revealed scriptures and their venerable philosophical commentaries.

> RAMAKRISHNA *Nitya*, the timeless, unchanging expanse of pure peace, and *lila*, the ecstatic cosmic play as temporality, are one and the same Reality. They are not two levels of reality or two parallel dimensions. The *nitya* and the *lila* are simply not two. They are nondual. The indivisible expanse of Pure Consciousness blissfully manifests as innumerable forms of life. This is the *lila*, the evolutionary Divine Play. There is Consciousness and only Consciousness. Even the notion of oneness, or unity, is inapplicable. Where is oneness if there is no duality? Where is unity if there is no possible disunity? Reality is beyond oneness as well as beyond twoness.

The Great Swan is entering subtle *samadhis*—flashes of total loss of individual awareness—even as he eloquently presents these teachings. It is an astounding spectacle. The *nitya* and the *lila* are manifesting alternately in a mode swifter than the speed of thought. This is more than the Paramahamsa's virtuosity in accomplishing spiritual transitions. The *nitya* and the *lila* are being demonstrated as simultaneous.

> RAMAKRISHNA My dear Pandit Shashadhar, your contemplative concentration on *brahman* as motionless and creationless is correct, as far as it goes, but still remains rather philosophical. What you need is the fire of ecstasy that not only burns away philosophy but consumes the entire cosmos as we habitually perceive and conceive it. The silent, changeless Reality is revealed to be simultaneously engaged in ecstatic dance.

Through these words—spoken in the most charming manner, entirely free from any overtones of doctrinal teaching—the Mother's initiatory energy flows. Both master and advanced disciple are entering a drunken state of delight. We, too, can feel the whole world spin slightly.

The Paramahamsa now sings a glorious medley of mystic hymns to the Black Goddess, improvising new lines, never heard before in the history of the mystic quest. Everyone present in the bare, small, simple room of the sage feels that he or she has come to the spacious palace of revelation, the original fount where *nitya* and *lila* are simultaneous. Here, right before our eyes, shines the timeless play of the Universal Mother. Scriptures, religions, and entire universes are being born and are disappearing again into Her radiant Blackness. The voice, rising to a very high pitch while remaining sweet and clear, is distinctly feminine. The smile is Mahakali's own blissful Smile.

> Is there anyone in the universe,
> among heavenly or earthly beings,
> who can understand what Kali is?
> The systems of all traditions
> are powerless to describe Her.
> Is Mother a feminine being
> or greater than Being itself?
>
> Chanting Her transforming Name—
> OM KALI OM KALI OM KALI,
> empowers Lord Shiva,
> Who is transcendent Knowledge,
> to drink the negativity of all beings,
> turning His Throat dark blue.
> Without Her protection
> such poison would be deadly,
> even to the highest Divinity.
>
> More than Creator and creation,
> Mother is sheer Creativity
> beyond any notion of duality.
> Universe and Father-God
> are thrilling glances
> from Her seductive Eyes.
> Always pregnant with ecstasy,
> She gives birth to manifest Being

from Her Womb of primal Awareness,
nursing it tenderly at Her Breast,
then playfully consumes Her Child.
The world dissolves instantly
upon touching Her white Teeth,
attaining the realization
of Her brilliant Voidness.

The various Divine Forms
that manifest throughout history
take refuge at Her Lotus Feet.
The Essence of Divinity,
the Great Ground of Being,
lies in ecstatic absorption
beneath Her red-soled Feet.

Is Mother simply a Goddess?
Does She need a male consort
to protect or complete Her?
The cycle of birth and death
bows reverently before Her.
Is She simply naked
or is She naked Truth?
No veil can conceal Her.
Her naked radiance slays demons
not with weapons but with splendor.

If Mother is a conventional wife,
why is She dancing fiercely
on the breast of Shiva?
Her timeless play destroys
conventions and conceptions.
She is primal purity,
Her ecstatic lovers are purity.
Purity merges into purity
with no remainder.

I am totally inebriated
by Her wine of timeless bliss.

The wine cup is Her Name—
OM KALI OM KALI OM KALI.
Those drunk on ordinary wine
assume I am one of them.

Not everyone will encounter
the dazzling darkness
called Goddess Kali.
Not everyone can consciously receive
the infinite treasure of Her Nature.
The foolish mind refuses
to perceive and accept
that She alone exists.
Even the noble Lord Shiva,
most enlightened of beings,
can barely catch a glimpse
of Her flashing crimson Feet.

The wealth of world-emperors
and the richness of Paradise
are but abject poverty
to those who meditate on Her.
To swim in a single Glance
from Her three Cosmic Eyes
is to be immersed
in an ocean of ecstasy.

Not even Shiva, prince of yogis,
can focus upon Her dancing Feet
without falling into trance.
Yet the worthless lover
who sings this mad song
aspires to conscious union with Her
during waking, dream, and deep sleep.

This flood of rare teaching flows easily and naturally from the very essence of the Paramahamsa, who is not merely a conduit for Her Wisdom but is none other than the Wisdom Mother. The Pandit is swaying with spiritual inebriation, whose effect is the opposite of physical intoxication.

Kali's wine of Love clarifies the mind, liberating it from egocentricity, breaking through subtle barriers, and releasing the energy of compassion, free from any sense of competition or separation. Shashadhar is now completely lost in Her Divine Drunkenness. All his philosophical knowledge, gleaned from the ancient Upanishads and the traditional commentaries on them, as well as all the concentration he has gained through countless hours of ritual worship, is catching fire. This excellent mold is now being filled with molten gold.

The Pandit is a willing participant. After an extended silence—respite from the torrent of awakened energy carried by these hymns to Kali, an energy that extends far beyond verbal meaning—he humbly requests the Paramahamsa to sing some more. Immediately, as if just waiting for this invitation, Ramakrishna partially opens his eyes—eyelids trembling faintly, a luminous stream of tears flowing from the outer corners—and bursts into the most poignant raga, the melodic mode called *bhairavi* after the Warrior Goddess. Mahakali's inexpressible Wisdom-energy is subtly encoded within the musical notes themselves.

> Mother's mystic Lotus Feet
> are a vast and empty sky.
> Through this luminosity
> my mind soars like a kite.
> A downward blast of wind,
> the force of egocentricity,
> throws the kite into a dive,
> but I have glimpsed the secret.
> All is Mother's Play—
> wind, sky, kite, and cord.
> This is my meditation,
> my ecstasy, my life.
>
> From a land of sheer awareness,
> where there is neither night nor day,
> came an adept of Mother's Wisdom,
> revealing the secret of nonduality.
> Now I no longer
> distinguish night from day.
> Ritual and scripture drop away.
> I will never fall asleep again

into that strange condition
the world calls being awake.
Mine is the insomnia of yoga,
union with infinite awakeness.

In profound *samadhi*,
one with Mother Reality,
I appear to the uninitiated
to be sound asleep,
but I sing Wisdom's lullabye,
putting sleep to sleep forever.

I bow with respect before
the power of a world-emperor
and the release of *nirvana*,
desiring neither.
I know with every atom of awareness
that the Kali-energy called the universe
is the boundless expanse of essential peace.
I discard both sides
of every dichotomy.

All creation is the holy sport
of my mad Mother Mahakali.
By Her playfulness all worlds
are enchanted and enamored.
She is mad, Her Consort is mad,
Her human lovers are mad with bliss.
Who can describe Her Loveliness,
Her glorious Gestures and Moods?
Lord Shiva repeats Her Name,
though His throat is enflamed
by drinking deadly poison—
the negativity of all beings.

Mother Kali strikes Personal God
against Impersonal Reality,
breaking one stone with another

and leaving only nonduality.
She fulfills desires graciously
and destroys the sense of duty.
The singer of this strange song
floats on the sea of Her Mystery,
carried here and there
by unpredictable tides.

I have entirely given over
at the Lotus Feet of the Mother
every sense of individual existence.
From this radical action,
the river of fearlessness flows.
Death is just a dry branch
swept away by the current
of Mother's irresistible Wisdom.

My entire nervous-system
has become pure resonance—
OM KALI OM KALI OM KALI,
containing all *mantras*,
all scriptures, all worlds.
I have given back my mundane body
to the marketplace of convention,
and in its place remains
only the power of Her Name.

Deep within the heart of humanity
wakes the potent seed, OM KALI,
bringing forth a vast tree—
its timeless roots are heaven,
its fruitful branches the earthly plane.
This Mystic Tree fulfills all aspirations.
When Lord Yama, King of Death,
comes to call my soul away,
he will see this Tree of Life
spring forth miraculously
where my soul used to be.

The animosity and negativity
of the six atavistic urges
have entirely melted away,
leaving passion to function
as pure, liberating energy.
I am now sailing free
on the shoreless ocean of Reality,
crying: "To Mother, the victory!
To Mother alone belongs victory!"

Both *pandit* and *paramahamsa* are shedding copious tears as they smile and gaze deeply into each other's eyes. The close companions of our Master are also weeping freely with ineffable joy and awe. Even the casual visitors who, through their mysterious *karma*, have entered these mystic chambers for the first time today, are wiping their eyes with their wearing-cloths. These are gnostic tears, bearing no common emotional content, flowing from the outer corners of the eyes. As Ramakrishna often remarks: "People cry enough tears over their families and even their material possessions to fill large water jugs. Who sheds a single tear of longing to meet God and to become God?" The tears that are now flowing down the outside of our cheeks spring from infinite awareness, not from any finite thoughts or perceptions. They are expressions of the pure wisdom and pure love that are awakening in Pandit Shashadhar as the Great Swan continues to sing.

O longing mind,
dwell within the depth
of your own pure nature.
Do not seek your home elsewhere.
Do not confine your innate infinity
within the mansions of finitude.
Your naked awareness alone, O mind,
is the inexhaustible abundance
for which you long so desperately.

Mother will grant liberation
to every conscious being,
but Her own spiritual station,
pure love that is pure wisdom,

can seldom be attained.
The sage who manifests
Her intrinsic transparency
is adored by every being
and becomes a mystic guide
for the entire universe.

The companions in our Master's blessed presence are now praying inwardly, in secret unison: "May Divine Mother empower us to assimilate even a drop of the timeless nectar which flows from the lips and through every pore of this adorable being, this tender guide of the entire universe."

27

The Master's Terminal Illness

His Friendship with the Humanist, Dr. Sarkar

RAMAKRISHNA HAS unaccountably developed throat cancer. The disease has progressed rapidly, and the companions have rented a garden house where their beloved guide can receive regular medical attention and nursing. Certain immature persons theorize that this severe illness is merely an illusory sleight-of-hand that the Master is projecting in order to test their faith and loyalty. Some members of Ramakrishna's outer circle have lost confidence in the Divine Nature of Mother Kali's child, unable to accept the paradox of his total vulnerability. The fiery young Narendra stands powerfully against both these superficial trends of thinking, insisting upon Ramakrishna's full humanity as well as his full Divinity and refuting every emotional evasion of the sage's terminal illness.

The Western-educated homeopathic doctor who has honestly and courageously diagnosed this cancer as incurable has come to the sickbed again today, only to discover the usual country fair of mirth, music, and madness for God. Dr. Sarkar's medical warnings about extended conversation, singing, dancing, and ecstatic states have no effect upon the Paramahamsa, who constantly forgets his own desperate physical condition, even though it continues to generate excruciating pain. For months, Ramakrishna has not been able to eat, except for a few mouthfuls of farina pudding. Whether standing, sitting, or lying down, he finds no relief from an intense burning sensation throughout his body.

During this period of vicarious suffering—taking on the negativity of the entire world, like the Shiva of sacred history who drinks poison, turning his throat dark blue—the cheerfulness of the Great Swan has never diminished. He often remarks: "Let the body endure its inevitable ailments, but you, O mind, be immersed in the Divine Nature and enjoy unalloyed bliss." At other times, he ingenuously explains: "Within me are two persons—Divine Mother and Her child. The child has taken ill." He points at his throat, now almost perforated by the cancer, and exclaims: "Just something peculiar here. I am like a paper doll with a hole in it. What can be done?" Occasionally, Ramakrishna enters an intensely childlike mood and weeps with misery, calling out MA MA MA, but moments later he is passionately discussing the deepest wisdom or is lost in the most exalted hymns of mystic union.

As the Paramahamsa reveals, in the most humorous tone of voice: "Why should I lead a monotonous spiritual life? I enjoy every possible preparation of fish—curried, fried, pickled, plain. Sometimes I worship Divine Reality with ceremony, sometimes I repeat various Divine Names, sometimes I sing mystic hymns, sometimes I dance in ecstasy, sometimes I plunge into silent meditation." This life of brilliant Divine Communion simply continues undimmed by terminal illness. To suggestions that he seek spiritual healing, our selfless Master responds: "I seem to be unable to ask God to cure this disease. Once in a while, I used to say: 'O Mother, please mend a little this tattered sheath of the sword.' But such passing thoughts have become less frequent. I can no longer find enough provisional I-consciousness to make any prayer for healing. I encounter only Goddess Kali residing in and through this form now before you."

As Mother Sarada reports: "I recently experienced a vision of the Goddess as a beautiful black girl, seated with me on my bed. She was holding her head to one side. I inquired why and She replied: 'I have a sore in my throat.' Ramakrishna and Kali are one."

His face literally shining with heavenly joy, the Paramahamsa now addresses the doctor, who is at once a lover of God and a man of sobriety, restraint, and skepticism. It was Dr. Sarkar who examined the Paramahamsa with a stethoscope during *samadhi* and discovered no heartbeat, who touched his eyeballs and found no reflex.

RAMAKRISHNA Dearest doctor, please open your entire being. Why should one feel self-conscious about calling out the Divine Names with total abandon? Surely you have heard the wise proverb: "One who is subject to shame, hatred, or fear can never experience God." Consider carefully, doctor. You may be clinging unconsciously to some conventional notion, thinking: "I am an important, responsible man. How can I act the utter fool, dancing wildly and calling out to God like a child crying desperately for its mother? What will become of my reputation in the medical community? At best, they will pity me." Please renounce even the slightest trace of such reasoning. God simply cannot be realized through a mind that is steeped in conventional notions and habitual reactions. For sincere seekers of God, the constant companionship of those mature in the way of sanctity is absolutely necessary. Why? Because the disease of calculative thinking has become chronic. The spiritual physician prescribes a complete change of diet— that is, a transformation of thought-forms.

The practitioner of wisdom must transcend philosophical and religious knowledge, as well as scientific knowledge. Such information, no matter how subtle or sophisticated, amounts to mere ignorance, mere projection. One must discard the apparent dichotomy of knowledge and ignorance to awaken as Divine Reality. The reflection awakens as the original. The ray awakens as the sun. Within the unitive panorama of sheer awakeness, to know various subjects, to concentrate on various paradigms, is revealed to be ignorance. Obvious or subtle pride of scholarship is certainly ignorance, even if such scholarship includes familiarity with the great world religions. By contrast, true knowing, or *jñana*, is the unwavering awareness that God dwells within all living beings as the very principle of consciousness. An even richer, more intimate knowing or communion is called *vijñana*, nondual awareness. *Vijñana* is like tasting God directly. In fact, it is like God tasting God.

If a sharp thorn plunges into your bare foot, only by skillfully using a second thorn can you dislodge the first. When this operation is complete, both thorns can be discarded and cast into a blazing fire. The contemplative practitioner uses the thorn of philosophical or religious knowledge to remove the thorn of obsessive, habitual ignorance by which he has been wounded. Then both thorns, knowledge and ignorance, are burned up in the fire of true knowing. *Akhanda satchidananda*—indivisible Being, Awareness, and Bliss—does not manifest the conventional frontiers of knowledge and ignorance.

Noble Lakshmana once commented to his brother, the glorious King Rama: "Is it not strange and even astonishing that the sage Vasishta wept so bitterly at the death of his sons, even though he is a man of knowledge?" Lord Rama, the incarnation of Divine Wisdom, responded: "Beloved brother, someone who possesses knowledge also inevitably possesses ignorance."

The person who has knowledge of unity must also entertain a perception of diversity, through which he defines unity. The person who is aware of light must consciously or unconsciously be contrasting it with darkness. The ineffable Reality, dear Dr. Sarkar, is beyond unity and diversity, light and darkness, knowledge and ignorance, merit and demerit, propriety and impropriety. It is beyond the sacred and the profane.

Unable to lift his voice in song because of persistent pain, the Parama-hamsa recites a mystic hymn, its radical teaching tempered by his tender tone.

> When will you learn, O mind,
> to sleep in perfect comfort
> between the captivating lovers,
> holiness and defilement?
> Only when you can keep
> these two consorts peaceful
> beneath a single roof
> will you truly encounter
> the brilliance of the Goddess.

VISITOR Revered sir, what can possibly remain when one throws away both thorns, knowledge and ignorance?

RAMAKRISHNA The quintessence of timeless and transparent enlightenment—*nityashuddhabodharupa*. Yet how can I make the content of this term clear to you? Suppose someone from a distant culture inquires: "What is the taste of *ghee*?" Although the taste of this clarified butter is so delicious and familiar, could you really describe it, even by using any number of words? At the very most, you can say that *ghee* has a wonderful flavor. More accurately, all that one can really assert sounds like nonsense: "*Ghee* tastes like nothing other than *ghee*." There is no analogy for supreme Reality because nothing else exists. Suppose a very young girl innocently asks her older sister: "What sort of special pleasure do you enjoy with your husband?" The married woman can only reply: "My dear, you will experience this for yourself when you are mature and have a husband. I simply cannot explain it to you."

Certain scriptures teach that the Mother of the Universe manifests as sublime Uma, daughter of King Himalaya. She generously reveals to her noble father many Divine Forms by generating visionary states of consciousness. Then the king of holy mountains requests his beloved Uma to reveal the essence of awareness that is directly realized by the sages of the Upanishads. She replies: "Revered Father, for this experience you must practice transcendent insight after receiving transmission from an awakened knower of *brahman*. I cannot show it to you through any particular religious vision, no matter how sublime." What is termed *atman* or *brahman* by the exalted *rishis,* the ancients who awakened as limitless awareness, can never be visualized, described, or even indirectly indicated by words, no matter how forceful or eloquent they may be.

Every describable structure or event has been touched by the tongue of human beings and as a result has become commonplace. Conventional experience consists only of what has been used and reused, and therefore it cannot be presented to God as a fresh, undefiled offering. Only *atman,* the Principle of Awareness, which is *brahman,* the Ground of Being, remains essentially untouched, ever pristine. Even revealed scriptures—including the Vedas, Puranas, Sutras, Tantras, and their accompanying commentaries—have been used as mere commonplace, as religious and philosophical conventions. They have become like stale, leftover food. But Reality remains intrinsically pure, forever new. The Principle of Awareness can never be used, manipulated, or distorted by any limited form of thought or perception.

No teacher or scripture can actually describe or explain the supremely delightful play of Divine Reality as communion and union between lover and Beloved. Only one who has realized God can blissfully know Reality and its Play, without relying upon or becoming ensnared within any finite pattern of knowledge.

Respected doctor, please listen. You cannot experience the marvelous state of true knowing, no matter how firm and sincere your personal integrity may be, unless you are utterly free from egocentricity. Non-egocentricity is synonymous with liberation. I-ness and my-ness, the conventional structure of subject-object awareness, is simply spiritual ignorance, no matter how ethically or religiously refined its manifestations may be.

The ecstatic lover who with total abandon cries out continuously to the Beloved actually becomes the *Thou*, the Beloved. This true lover has discovered an effective antidote for egocentricity. Love's infinite cry is superior to philosophical analysis or dialectic, which permit the ego of the thinker subtly to persist. Nor is this cry some dualistic devotion of the earthly soul for its heavenly Lord. The all-consuming *Thou, Thou, Thou* of the ecstatic lover is true knowing.

The mystic who is profoundly mature in the way of Pure Love calls out: "O blissful Mother, You alone are the sole agent. All action springs only from You. What appears as an independent self is merely Your instrument. This apparent *I* performs only what You ordain. My limited personal possessions, no less than the limitless universes, belong directly and solely to You. This humble dwelling and this extended family are Yours alone, O Mother. There simply is no substantial I-consciousness to claim them for its own. What continues to appear as a separate self can function as Your servant only if You generate such activity."

People read one or two books on religion or philosophy and become insufferably arrogant. I once opened a conversation with Kalikrishna Tagore about Divine Reality. He actually proclaimed: "I already know about all that." I replied: "Does a well-educated person, familiar with the cultural centers of Delhi and Calcutta, brag about his knowledge before simple peasants in the countryside? Does a highly refined person go about claiming to be highly refined?"

VISITOR Master, if God alone is obviously or subtly performing every action, why is a person subject to the results of his negative thoughts and deeds?

RAMAKRISHNA My friend, you are talking obsessively, like a goldsmith weighing out grains of gold. You are permitting your mind to become pervaded by self-centered, self-serving calculation. O mind, why not wander through the mango orchard like a carefree child? Eat ripe mangoes and be immersed in bliss. What use is there in calculating how many hundreds of trees, how many thousands of branches, how many millions of shining green leaves? Why speculate on how much income the mangoes will produce in the village market? Why even investigate the process by which these golden fruits spontaneously spring forth? You have come to this planetary orchard to taste Divine Sweetness. Taste directly and be supremely content. You have taken birth in this beautiful human form to worship, experience, and eventually merge with Divine Reality. Taste God's Love. Kiss the fragrant Lotus Feet of the Lord. Do not become distracted by attempting to analyze Divine Mystery. Can you experience God by speculating about God? Will you ever know Truth by philosophizing? A few sips of the precious Wine of Love will thoroughly intoxicate you. Why leave the full glass untouched on the table while inquiring how the wine was produced or estimating how many gallons may exist in the infinite wine cellar?

Dr. Sarkar is becoming progressively more animated. His entire body and being are expressing agreement with our Master's inspired words, which have opened his secret heart, just as the right key instantly opens an ancient lock. "Yes! Yes!" he cries out drunkenly. "The wine in God's Tavern is beyond all measure, beyond all conception, beyond all description. There is no limit to it. Absolutely no limit!"

The doctor and all the companions of Divine Love are now enraptured. Ramakrishna asks ingenuously: "Does what I say during states of ecstasy really attract people?"

28

My Play Is Over

T HE HEAVY HEAT of afternoon is present in the sickroom. Straw screens hang over the windows to keep out some of its intensity. A handful of loyal companions are seated around the bed. Ramakrishna has become very impatient to see Dr. Sarkar, for whom he feels immense love and spiritual attraction. Sometimes the Paramahamsa enters *samadhi* simply at the sight of his new friend. The doctor embodies the best of the modern world. He is a rational humanist, a scientist, a man of compassion, and a lover of God. However, he rejects on principle the teaching of *avatara,* the descent of God into human form, because he considers this view to be a subtle dehumanization of Ramakrishna, for whom he feels profound friendship and respect. The doctor sometimes remains for six or seven hours in animated conversation with the precocious child of Mother Kali.

Dr. Sarkar has confided to us, with amazement, that he now spends most of his busy professional day thinking about the Paramahamsa. He even lies awake on rainy nights wondering whether the windows to the Master's room have been properly closed. Some of our companions cannot understand the intensity of this mutual attraction between a timeless, ecstatic being and a rational, Europeanized modern man who rejects their cherished traditional understanding of Ramakrishna as *avatara.* But the doctor never wavers in his basic appreciation, often exclaiming: "Ah, I see the Paramahamsa has again been able to extract the essence."

In his great restlessness to commune with Dr. Sarkar, the sage is continuing to sit up and lie down, even though every movement is unimaginably painful. Again and again, he inquires: "When is the doctor coming?" In the tone one uses with a child, the devoted companions reply that Dr. Sarkar is not expected until the cool of the evening. Ramakrishna is not placated. He questions repeatedly, "What time is it now?," as though he were an ecstatic maiden, a *gopi*, feeling pangs of separation from her beloved Krishna. As the blissful sage often teaches: "At first, the human seeker appears as a bee and God as a lotus. Finally, one realizes that God is the bee and humankind the lotus."

Suddenly, the Paramahamsa enters an exalted state. The very shape of his body changes. His movements and expression become distinctly feminine. He takes a pillow in his arms like an infant, caressing it and holding it tenderly to his breast. His motherly smile clears the room of shadows and fills our heavy hearts with heavenly radiance. He shifts his wearing-cloth as though it were a sari. With uncannily accurate gestures, he manifests as a breast-feeding mother. The disciples gathered around the bed, although we are intimate with the Master and somewhat accustomed to his spiritual moods, are staring with astonishment at this total transformation. The Mother of the Universe is appearing directly before our eyes.

Just as unexpectedly, the human emanation of the Divine Mother now regains consciousness of conventional space and time. He samples a birdlike portion of farina pudding and begins to whisper to us about his various mystical experiences. The painful throat cancer no longer permits him to converse in a normal tone. But as Lord Shiva, His throat on fire from consuming the poisonous negativity of all beings, continues to call Goddess Kali's Name, so our beloved Master makes great efforts to whisper loudly so we can hear and understand. That Ramakrishna speaks solely out of compassionate love for humanity is evident at this moment. Tears come to our eyes.

RAMAKRISHNA Do you know what I once encountered during ecstasy? There is a vast green meadow extending in every direction. Wandering freely through this ineffable expanse, I encounter a sixteen-year-old boy who has clearly attained realization. He is a *paramahamsa,* a *mahasiddha*—one who has transcended worldly and religious convention, one who is without fixed perspectives, parameters, paradigms. A gentle mist of Divine Bliss is arising from the meadow. We two sky-clad wanderers now travel together, simply as God through God. We run joyfully across the soft greenness, naked and totally unencumbered. The awakened young sage, who resembles our companion Purna, becomes thirsty. He drinks radiant water from a crystal tumbler and offers me what is left. I reply tenderly: "Dearest younger brother, how can I drink what is not new and untouched?" He laughs with appreciation, carefully washes the glass, and presents me with fresh water.

By reliving this vision, the God-intoxicated sage is thrown into *samadhi,* the unadulterated experience of the Divine at play with the Divine. Regaining a slight awareness of individuality, he greets the companions around his bed as Narayana, experiencing each one of us as a manifestation of God. Now he continues to form words—struggling to communicate, to adumbrate the Divine Mystery, which is impenetrable to the ordinary mind yet becomes strangely accessible through these whispered utterances. The sense of intimacy is intense. An indefinable thrill radiates through us.

RAMAKRISHNA My sensibility is undergoing a radical change. I no longer enjoy food that has been offered in any temple to any formal aspect of Divinity. The transcendent Reality and the profusion of manifestations of this One Reality are becoming absolutely equivalent. The sense of distinction necessary for even the most minimal ceremonial worship is no longer present. My play is coming to an end.

Do you know what I witnessed earlier this afternoon during the state of absorption? I experienced the Divine Mother as a young woman nine months pregnant. She gave birth to the manifest world, cradled and caressed it, nursed it at Her breast, and then began to swallow it. As the universe entered Her dark Mouth in the form of a radiant infant, it was immediately revealed to be void of any substantial or independent existence. I was shown that every possible being and event is void in precisely this way. The luminous, insubstantial form of the Cosmic Mother then cried out in a charming voice, laughing as She mimicked the words of a village magician: "Come, delusion! Come, confusion!" The Divine Magician alone is real. Her created magic is mere play and sleight-of-hand. In this new spiritual mood which is coming over me, the direct vision of Reality is continuous—during waking, dream, and dreamless sleep. All phenomena, including blissful Divine Forms, have become sheer transparency. There is nothing to hold on to, here or anywhere. My play is over.

29

The Master
Transforms Dr. Sarkar

THE PARAMAHAMSA, emaciated yet animated, is now deep in conversation with his dignified homeopathic doctor. Although so single-pointed about his professional responsibility—persistently reminding our Master that conversing and entering ecstasy may aggravate the disease—Dr. Sarkar has now forgotten the medical context entirely and is concentrated on burning questions, which are not merely intellectual but emerge from the very center of his being.

This excellent man, so impressed by the wisdom of the blissful sage, has brought his son, Amrita, to the sickroom, which he visits without fail every day. Whispering in powerful, condensed phrases, the Great Swan is offering precious instruction to the clear-eyed youth.

RAMAKRISHNA Do you know what authentic meditation feels like? The entire mind melts and becomes like rich oil—pouring perpetually, flowing freely without separating into drops. In this continuous flow, the only subject and the only object is God. Pure mind, or ecstatic mind, neither thinks nor perceives in a fragmentary manner. The faintest breath of air makes a candle flame waver. Mediation is like a candle burning in a windless place. If there is the slightest break in a telegraph wire, the message cannot be transmitted. Meditation must be continuous. Can a pearl be found in knee-deep water? You must dive deep.

Place milk in a quiet place to curdle and then, by rhythmic churning, extract the butter. After transforming the milk of the mind into the butter of spiritual knowledge, that transformed mind can float in the water of the world without becoming diluted.

When you retire at night, go to sleep on your back, visualizing the luminous form or the formless radiance of the Mother in your heart. You will have significant dreams. What intense mental labor is required to pass an examination—reading and memorizing night and day! Much greater intensity is necessary to realize God. Only when a person feels that life is absolutely unbearable without God-vision is Divine Reality revealed. God is simply transparent, timeless Consciousness.

Do not strain at meditation. It is not helpful to sit leaning forward or to hold the body rigidly straight. Make your meditation a continuous state of mind. A great worship is going on all the time, so nothing should be neglected or excluded from your constant meditative awareness. You should remain aware of God throughout the activity of daily life—thinking, perceiving, eating, walking, moving, talking, sitting, sleeping. Do not find fault with anyone, not even an insect. Pray fervently that your mind will become completely clear of habitual faultfinding. Simply flutter your wings and shake off these drops of water called the conventional world.

At dusk, put aside all sense of finite responsibility and plunge into prayerful contemplation, just as devout Muslims do five times every day. One is reminded of Divine Presence by the mysterious approach of evening, when one enters an entirely different mode of awareness than during daylight. Dark, overcast days are also conducive for meditation, for inwardness. Nangta, the naked sage who initiated me into the way of formless awareness, used to offer this instruction: "Everywhere is water. All regions and realms, above and below, are water. You are a great fish, swimming freely and joyously through this indivisible expanse. You are not confined within a bowl, a river, or even an ocean." One can meditate this way, with eyes open, even as one carries on conversation.

As hunger and thirst arise spontaneously, so does longing for God. It is simply a matter of time. Yearning for God-realization cannot arise until one has to some extent satisfied the desires of social existence or has seen through them and been freed from them. Do not renounce desire by pressuring or forcing the mind. If the blossoms of gourds or pumpkins are removed prematurely, the fruit will not ripen. But when the fruit ripens properly, the flowers will naturally fall away. Call out every evening with a longing heart and hold on to Truth. You will eventually see God. Living consciously within God, you will not be overwhelmed by the inevitable misery of the world.

Do you think everyone has to cook? Divine Mother has prepared this delicious meal for you. Have pure faith. Partake of these delicacies. You will be nourished and illumined!

Frank discussion now reveals that Amrita, following his modern father, has no confidence in the ancient teaching of *avatara,* the full descent of Divine Reality through a perfect human form.

RAMAKRISHNA Dr. Sarkar, imagine that! Your son also does not accept the avataric descent of God. But this is perfectly all right. It does not matter in the slightest whether Amrita believes in this exalted teaching. He is, in his very being, a spiritual man. And why not? Does a mango tree of the famous Bombay variety ever bear sour mangoes?

Everyone in the room bursts out laughing. We are amazed at the playfulness and vibrancy of the Paramahamsa, who is becoming weaker every day. Last night, we awoke long after midnight to discover the frail sage walking vigorously around our sleeping mats, repeating MA MA MA.

RAMAKRISHNA Doctor, I have examined, probed, and discovered that your son Amrita possesses an unshakable faith in Divine Reality. That conviction alone makes him a true human being—a vessel of the nectar of immortality, of *amrita.* Only that person is truly human whose mind dwells constantly and naturally on God—not intellectually or through cultural conditioning but because the subtle nervous system has been awakened. Gradually, the awareness of such a truly dignified and alert human being evolves and intensifies until it becomes ceaselessly clear—even during the distracting drama of daily events. Such an awareness eventually realizes that God is the sole Reality, that all conscious beings and all events are insubstantial mirror reflections of this Original Reality. At that point, what does it matter whether one espouses some doctrine of Divine Incarnation? Now there is only the Divine. Certain sages once greeted the Incarnation of God, Lord Rama, in this way: "Revered sir, we adore supreme Reality through the formless sound OM. We neither need nor desire any human manifestation of God." The God-man smiled, well pleased with their particular mode of adoration.

The sole factor necessary to initiate and sustain the process of becoming truly human is the conviction that Divine Reality is manifesting just a drop of its Power as this entire universe, filled to the brim with intensely conscious beings. There is the beautiful garden and the owner of that garden. We must sincerely strive to meet the Divine Owner, who knows so much more than the garden reveals. To anyone who lacks even this basic conviction, I suggest the following prayer: "I honestly do not know whether You exist or not, O Lord. You alone can resolve my doubt. Please unveil Your True Nature."

There are diverse teachings concerning the incarnation of God. Some scriptures affirm ten *avataras,* others twenty-four, while more radical scriptures reveal that there are innumerable emanations of Divine Reality. My usual attitude is this. If you perceive with purified mind, heart, and senses any particularly intense manifestation of power or beauty, you can be certain that God has incarnated through that form, to one degree or another. But there is an even more radical level of understanding, which recognizes that God alone has become every phenomenon one can encounter under every possible condition of experience. From this perspective, there is nothing but Divine Incarnation.

Reality is like a *bel* fruit, which includes shell, seeds, and pulp. The shell is the physical universe, the seeds are the living beings, the pulp is pure awareness. The Absolute manifests relatively as this universe, and the relative universe is always expressing and revealing the open, luminous expanse of the Absolute. Relativity permits spiritual evolution, which culminates in the conscious realization of the Absolute. But the realization of the Absolute—even if facilitated by negating the objectivity of relative phenomena—never cancels out the relative universe, any more than our enjoyment of the pulp cancels out the seeds and the shell. The whole fruit is necessary. The whole fruit is Reality. But as long as the limited, habitual awareness of I-ness and my-ness is in control, no person can awaken to Reality.

First comes knowledge of Reality. From this springs nondual or ecstatic love, which melts forever the division between subject and object. The ecstatic lover swims sometimes within the ocean of the Absolute, sometimes up the river of relativity—free from dry philosophical discrimination between the real and the unreal, free as well from one-sided devotional attitudes. Such is the teaching that emanates from this place. Not everyone can appreciate it. The key to this room must be turned in the opposite direction.

Dr. Sarkar appears delighted with these lucid, simple, yet startlingly profound words of the Paramahamsa, words that flow like an unbroken stream of fragrant, healing oil. But now the doctor becomes argumentative, expounding his modern views vehemently and abrasively: "What nonsense to bow abjectly before another human being, calling him the unique incarnation of God for this age! But if you regard someone as a particularly clear reflection of God's Light—respecting and loving him, but not worshiping him—that I can gladly accept."

The brilliant Bengali playwright Girish Gosh is present in the room. Dr. Sarkar, both as medical man and spiritual aspirant, has been impressed that during the course of his friendship with our Master, Girish has been liberated from his suicidal consumption of alcohol. Ramakrishna never forbade Girish to drink but subtly supplanted false physical intoxication with true spiritual inebriation. One night, at two or three in the morning, Girish arrived at Dakshineswar by carriage—drunk and abusive, coming directly from a house of prostitution in Calcutta. Ramakrishna was singing the Names of God. When Girish reeled into the room, the blissful sage leaped to his feet, tenderly grasping both hands of his companion, and they danced in rapture, crying MA MA MA.

Passionately convinced by personal experience that Ramakrishna is none other than Divine Reality in human form, Girish Babu now responds in a surprisingly mild manner to the inflammatory words of the doctor. "My brother, have you actually seen God's Light, so that you can speak knowledgeably about who or what may be a reflection of this ineffable Radiance?"

Dr. Sarkar carefully considers Girish's words, quite struck by them and by the confident smile with which they are delivered. Finally, he replies: "But you, too, Girish Gosh, are perceiving in the Paramahamsa only a reflection."

Girish now becomes adamant. The atmosphere of the room is suddenly intensified and elevated. "I see the Divine Light itself when I gaze upon the Master! If my foolish tongue is not able to prove this to you, I shall cut it out with a sharp blade!"

Laughing ecstatically, the Great Swan interrupts what he evidently regards as the play of puppies, growling and biting each other. Ramakrishna often encourages and even generates debate among disciples with different spiritual temperaments. Sometimes he cries out in delight: "Now, please argue this point in English!"

RAMAKRISHNA An ant crawls onto a mountain of sugar and with great difficulty returns home bearing a single grain. While struggling with the large crystal, it foolishly thinks: "Next time, I will bring back the entire mountain." Divine Mystery can never be exhausted by inquiry.

I saw you inwardly, Dr. Sarkar, while I was immersed in *samadhi*. You were revealed to be a gold mine of knowledge, but it is still dry knowledge. You have not yet drunk the nectar of Mother's Bliss. Beloved Girish, if this doctor ever tastes even a single grain of Divine Ecstasy, he will perceive all existence, above and below, as indivisible Consciousness and Bliss. He will no longer claim his personal ideas to be right and those of others to be wrong. He will no longer argue with sharp, cutting words. At the time when a person's conventional concepts are being destroyed, there is a great commotion in his mind, which occasionally issues from his lips. Wood crackles as it burns, particularly its dry outer bark. But when the fire has reduced the fuel to red coals, there is warmth and silence.

The discussion of doctrine is useless verbiage. To reason about the mystery of *avatara* is like the raving of a delirious typhoid patient, who cries out: "I will consume an entire pot of rice. I will drink a whole lake of water." The compassionate doctor humors the patient, speaking in soothing tones: "Certainly you will. You can enjoy whatever you wish, but only when you have recovered from your illness." The sense of separation from God is the illness from which one must recover.

These words of the Great Swan are like an afternoon rainshower. All the uncomfortable heat of argument disappears into refreshing coolness and fragrance.

RAMAKRISHNA Precise signs are manifest when mature knowledge of God dawns within a person. One sure indication is that doctrinal reasoning and divisive argumentation come spontaneously to an end. Butter sizzles in the frying pan unless it has first been thoroughly boiled.

DR. SARKAR But can anyone retain this silent state of knowledge permanently? You claim there is absolutely nothing other than God, and yet you have taken up this profession of being a holy man, with all sorts of people attending on you. If there is only God, why is all this verbal teaching necessary? Why not just keep silence?

Shock waves spread from these words, so ferociously delivered. Yet everyone knows the doctor to be a scrupulously honest man and a sincere lover of our Master. Ramakrishna smiles broadly, free from the slightest trace of tension or reaction.

RAMAKRISHNA Dearest Dr. Sarkar, water remains water, whether it stands still or breaks into waves. Divine Reality remains exactly the same when one is silent and when one speaks. Relax your mind a moment and consider this parable. A guru teaches his disciple that every being and event is simply God. The ardent disciple, while walking home meditating on this truth, encounters a mad elephant. The elephant-driver, who has completely lost control of the animal, shouts to all who are in the way, warning them to run. But the stubborn disciple refuses to deviate from his path. He continues his contemplative exercise, regarding himself as God and the elephant as God. The crazed beast picks up this foolish man with its trunk and dashes him to the earth. The guru, famous for his healing powers, is called to revive the unconscious victim. After certain prayers are recited and holy water is sprinkled, the young man regains consciousness. He is surprised to find his guru gazing at him. When asked why he did not run from such evident danger, he replies: "Why should I run? My guru, you teach that all beings and events are God. I have implicit faith in your inspired words." The venerable master then addresses his immature disciple: "But my child, why did you fail to heed the inspired words of the elephant-driver, who is also God?"

The room sparkles with laughter. We have heard this tale many times before, but today its subtle irony highlights the stubborness of Dr. Sarkar and releases our reactive energy. The intonation of the Paramahamsa, imitating the dogmatic young disciple and the amused elderly guru, somehow becomes irresistably hilarious. We receive, in this blessed moment of mirth, what no amount of solemn doctrinal recapitulation can convey—the perfectly natural, balanced experience that Divine Reality alone exists. Cosmic ignorance, this mad, death-dealing elephant, is God. The human heart, sincerely yet naively seeking Truth, is God. The elephant-driver, the practical intelligence that warns us, is God. The guru, the pure mind that tenderly revives our consciousness and teaches us, is God. The peaceful, smiling Paramahamsa is God. The fiery Dr. Sarkar is God. The devoted Girish is God. The singing birds and the bright gardens are manifesting God and only God. Shell, seeds, pulp—all is God.

RAMAKRISHNA It is Mahakali who manifests through everyone, both as pure mind and as practical intelligence. The personal ego is simply the instrumentation—Divine Mother is the sole owner, agent, and operator. The conventional sense of I-ness is the house, while She is the one who actually dwells there. Mother alone is speaking through every voice, from the gentle words of the guru to the excited cry of the elephant-driver.

DR. SARKAR Beloved Paramahamsa, allow me to pose a frank question. If all is God, why do you request me to treat your illness?

RAMAKRISHNA I importune you like a child—"Please heal me! Please heal me!"—only when I am conscious of the jar. Divine Reality is a limitless ocean of Consciousness and individual awareness is a jar. This vessel does not simply bear a finite amount of awareness but is totally immersed in the ocean of Consciousness and Bliss. There is water both inside and surrounding the jar. Yet until the jar is broken or dissolves, there remains a slight sense of distinction between inside and outside. Divine Mother keeps this jar of ego together for Her Play, Her Theater.

DR. SARKAR What is really implied by such teaching? Is God deceiving humanity by keeping us confined to a conventional ego? Surely, that would be absurd.

GIRISH Dear sir, how do you know that God is not playfully deceiving you, particularly about what you so confidently judge to be absurd?

RAMAKRISHNA It is the Goddess alone who keeps this jar of body and mind intact. This is Her Divine Play. The sultan has four small sons, each a royal prince. When they play together, however, one takes the role of a general, another of a police officer, another of a lion-tamer. The youngest acts the parts of lion, prisoner, and soldier. This is the theater of the world.

Dear doctor, when you realize *satchidananda*, the infinite ocean of Reality, Consciousness, and Bliss in which we are constantly immersed, you will perceive the meaning of this talk about jars and theatrical roles. After the clear vision of Divine Reality, every possible doubt dissolves. No sense of absurdity or incompleteness can remain.

DR. SARKAR But is it realistically possible to resolve all doubts?

RAMAKRISHNA A significant portion of your doubt can be cleared by talking together this way, if you approach to learn and are honestly receptive. You should not hold the attitude: "Listen to me, listen to me!" Why should anyone listen to you, Dr. Sarkar? You are under the control of conventionality and egocentricity. You are not free. Subtle self-infatuation is like the *peepal* tree. Cut it down today and you find a new shoot springing up tomorrow.

However, if you really yearn to attain the complete resolution of doubt—*jñana*, or perfect knowing—you must pray fervently to God in silence and solitude for at least a few days. Ask God why only God exists.

The child of the house can greet a beggar at the door and offer him a small measure of rice and lentils. But if the beggar requests substantial train fare to return home from his pilgrimage, then the lady of the house must be called. You are that destitute pilgrim, Dr. Sarkar, I am the child, and Mother Kali is the lady of the house.

At this profound point in the conversation, the doctor finally remains silent. All the companions in the Master's sickroom, including young Amrita, are plunged into a mysterious inner solitude and silence, each soul crying for total illumination, supplicating the Wisdom Mother for the train fare home. Noting the receptive mood of Dr. Sarkar, the Paramahamsa continues to speak in a clearly audible whisper.

RAMAKRISHNA Well, doctor, since you are so fond of rational thinking, let us reason together on the highest possible plane of thought. For the knower of Truth there is no isolated event of Divine Incarnation. Krishna remarks to his devoted companion, Arjuna: "You always insist upon speaking about me as an Incarnation of God. Come along, I want to show you something." The ardent devotee follows his beloved Lord until they see a gigantic tree in the distance. "What precisely do you observe, Arjuna?" "Precious Lord, I perceive a tree more vast than anyone could imagine. Its branches are bursting with large berries, dark blue in color." The noble Krishna rather sternly replies: "These are not the ordinary fruits you assume them to be. Move closer." As Arjuna approaches supreme Reality more intimately, he discovers that these are not berries but billions of dark blue Krishnas, growing in clusters. Then Lord Krishna reveals: "Divine Incarnations without number appear and disappear on the Tree of Pure Consciousness."

The more profoundly one approaches God, dear doctor, the fewer the veils, the fewer the Divine Forms. A devoted worshiper may enjoy his first vision of Divine Reality as the august ten-armed aspect of the Universal Mother, bearing various esoteric weapons, riding a ferocious lion. When the practitioner becomes more mature, concentration intensifies and a more intimate, loving vision of the six-armed Goddess appears. Further evolution occurs and the devoted lover encounters the blissful four-armed or two-armed aspect of the Goddess. Perhaps even the playful Baby Krishna appears. Then, as love and knowledge intensify to the highest possible degree, Divine Forms dissolve and worshiper becomes meditator, communing with the formless Divine Light. Beyond that is the radiant darkness, the union of Absolute and relative, sometimes called the play of Mahakala and Mahakali. The secret is to come closer and closer. Never permit the slightest sense of distance to remain.

Listen to the Vedantic teaching. An adept magician is displaying his magic to the king. He moves some distance away from the royal party and suddenly appears as a warrior on horseback, bearing various weapons. The king is a practitioner of Vedanta and so reasons with his companions: "How could this armor, this horse, and these weapons be real? Surely, only the one who is appearing as the rider is truly present." Only *atman*, original awareness, is real. All manifestations are simply its magic. It is source, mirror, and reflection. Please think carefully about this, my dear friend.

DR. SARKAR I have no objection whatsoever to such reasoning.

RAMAKRISHNA You may have no objection, doctor, but actually to rid oneself of this persistent illusion—the mounted warrior with gleaming armor and terrible weapons—is extremely difficult. A faint sense of anxiety or apprehensiveness remains until the dawning of supreme knowledge. If someone dreams vividly of a tiger, his heart continues to palpitate for some time, even after he wakes up.

Some intruders enter a field at night. They encounter a straw figure designed to resemble a fearfully large man in the dim light. The most courageous one approaches nearer and then reports back to his companions: "There is nothing to fear. It is merely straw." But hearts are still palpitating. The mysterious figure in the distance appears to move slightly. The leader of the group is obliged to return and bring the straw man down, shouting: "It is nothing! Nothing at all!" This is the courageous practice of *neti, neti*—the negation of relative appearances, which continue to appear but remain completely insubstantial.

"These are eloquent words," Dr. Sarkar affirms with exhilaration, awakened by the Vedantic dialectic to which the Master playfully yet effectively alludes. "What kind of words?" the Master asks, not yet entirely satisfied with the doctor's level of assimilation. "Excellent words!" the medical man replies, humbly and fervently.

"Then give me a *thank-you*." The Paramahamsa enunciates the English phrase, *thank you*, with a hilarious British accent, repeating it several times. Tears of laughter flow from our eyes. Dr. Sarkar becomes sensitive, imagining that Ramakrishna may be mocking him or misunderstanding his intention. With near anguish of spirit, which is the sign of true longing, the doctor cries: "Are you not aware of what is really in my mind? I am on fire with your teachings. Why else would I go to endless trouble to visit this remote neighborhood every day?"

The Master nods sweetly to his physician and requests the companions to serve special refreshments, for today is Vijaya Day, the feast of spiritual victory.

RAMAKRISHNA You feel genuine love for this form before you, doctor. You have told me that you love me. This will be sufficient. You will be victorious. The lover of Truth must have a firm understanding that cannot be shaken under any condition, like the anvil in the blacksmith's shop.

30

Ramakrishna and Lord Buddha

ARENDRA HAS JUST returned to the feet of our beloved Master from the first formal pilgrimage of his young life. He traveled to Bodhgaya, the luminous site of Lord Buddha's world-transforming Enlightenment beneath the Bodhi Tree. Narendra is destined to become a revolutionary sage as well, Swami Vivekananda by name, who will travel in 1893 to the Parliament of Religions in Chicago, helping to unify Western and Eastern cultures with the mysterious power of Ramakrishna that so abundantly flows through him.

Viveka is the sword of penetrating, clarifying insight. *Ananda* is the bliss that streams from supreme knowledge—beyond subject and object, free from the limited pattern of knower and known. At the age of thirty-nine, this Vivekananda will make the last formal pilgrimage of his short life, traveling once again to Bodhgaya to sit beneath the graceful, spreading branches of the Tree of Enlightenment, passing away from this visible world soon afterward.

As a young boy, engaged in contemplative discipline without the guidance of a teacher, Narendra encountered in waking vision a golden person whom he regarded as a manifestation of Lord Buddha. The connection between Gautama Buddha and Narendra is intimate indeed. Ramakrishna requested his companions several times for an icon of Lord Buddha to place in his room at Dakshineswar. Strangely enough, this request was never fulfilled, leaving Narendra to function as a living Buddha-image for the Paramahamsa, who will transmit the entire reservoir of his sacred power to this uncompromising young sage.

We are seated around the sickbed, placed in the reception hall on the second floor of this garden house rented by the Master's wealthy disciples so that the young men can nurse our beloved guide day and night. Here the intimate lovers are given free access to the Great Swan, who claims nothing, demands nothing, expects nothing. The cramped room of Mother Sarada is located under the slant of the roof. She is the only attendant who always remains present. Operating from a rare state of dynamic contemplative union, her service is silent, invisible, perfect. She is a chalice of Goddess-energy for the emerging planetary civilization.

It is a sultry evening and Mahendra, who is destined to record the conversations of Ramakrishna, is fanning this emaciated yet radiant form. Every few moments, he dips the sandalwood fan into a bowl of cool water. The sage reclines delicately against a round bolster. He is light as a feather, floating on the brink of invisibility. Using few words because of the agonizing perforation of his throat, the Paramahamsa now requests Mahendra—largely with humorous gestures—to purchase for him a plain upper cloth and a pair of ordinary slippers, setting a strict limit to the price Mahendra should pay in the bazaar. Melancholy as we are, we cannot resist laughing at this hilarious pantomime through which Ramakrishna plays with his most earnest disciple.

Our master is indeed most precise and practical. His modest personal effects are always kept in impeccable order, so he can find any object immediately, even in the dark. When he was first brought to this garden house, although weak from illness, he inspected the kitchen storeroom, discovering that the earthenware pots did not have coil stands or proper lids. He instantly sent someone to the market to purchase these items. For the thirty years he lived at Dakshineswar, the sage never neglected to collect his regular salary as a temple priest, although the amount was minimal. If the administrators of the Temple Garden ever forgot to pay him, the Master carefully and humbly reminded them.

With a most affectionate gesture, Ramakrishna now invites Narendra to massage his feet, using precious breath to inquire whether the young man has taken his evening meal. Narendra prostrates before the Paramahamsa. Ramakrishna tenderly reaches out and wipes the dust from the noble forehead, ruffling the young man's hair, complaining about its being so neatly combed. These two souls visibly manifest communion and union. The blissful sage suddenly smiles and proclaims in a loud whisper, with a subtle blend of humor and delight, "Naren went there!," referring to Narendra's pilgrimage to Bodhgaya. Mahendra, still fanning as gently as possible, asks the intense young man to describe the essence of Buddha's teaching. Naren replies passionately.

NARENDRA Lord Buddha's realization beneath the Bodhi Tree was of sheer ineffability, absolutely inexpressible through words and concepts. This Enlightenment shone forth spontaneously from great inner heat—an ever-rising, all-consuming flame, cultivated during six years of ceaseless longing and concentration. Since Gautama Buddha refused to compromise by using any conventional religious terminology, undiscerning persons call him atheistic or even nihilistic.

Totally ignoring physical pain, the Paramahamsa sits straight up and whispers loudly, with great intensity.

RAMAKRISHNA Lord Buddha was not an atheist or a nihilist! He was simply beyond speech and mind. Do you know what Buddhahood is? To realize one's true nature as *bodha*—sheer awakeness, expressed through selfless compassion.

NARENDRA True indeed, revered sir. There are three levels of Buddhist realization. The *arhat* achieves his own individual liberation from any form of manifest existence. The *bodhisattva,* after realizing universal transparency, identifies completely with both the suffering and the aspiration of all living beings, consciously taking rebirth to serve and to elevate every form of life within the countless realms of manifestation. The *bodhisattvas* of the Mahayana, the Great Vehicle, are reborn not from karmic compulsion but from universal compassion. Vajrayana, the Diamond Vehicle, opens direct access to Buddhahood—an infinite spirituality, capable of transforming relative existence into mysterious Pure Lands, where living beings are miraculously accelerated along the path to Enlightenment.

RAMAKRISHNA All these approaches are simply the free play of the One Reality—unthinkably deep, never repeating. Lord Buddha clearly recognized that our own true nature, or sheer awakeness, cannot be contained within the mental categories of Being or nonbeing. Naive realists are attached to Being, while nihilists espouse nonbeing. Gautama Buddha was not ensnared within either of these abstract positions, nor within any limited, one-sided view whatsoever.

NARENDRA Precisely so, revered sir. The Buddha's realization transcends opposites and fuses them. Brother Mahendra, you know from chemistry that a combination of hydrogen and oxygen can produce either flame or water. The Buddha's Enlightenment generates both intensive action and blissful nonaction. Through Enlightenment alone is absolutely selfless activity possible. The comprehensive experience of a living Buddha is far beyond the conceptual opposites of existence and nonexistence and therefore beyond all possible description by speech or mind.

RAMAKRISHNA Existence and nonexistence are attributes of relativity. Supreme Reality contains and transcends both.

A fruitful silence now pervades this mysteriously boundless room where the Paramahamsa is manifesting the painful process of physical dying. The spaciousness and delight of the Dakshineswar Garden, the freshness and peace of the sacred Ganges, the radiance of the Kali Temple—all this is fully present to our senses, minds, and hearts, even in this place of sickness and sadness. The timeless wisdom being discussed here is not abstract but palpable, like a ripe fruit resting easily on the palm of the hand. We are in the presence of fully realized Buddhahood. We are surrounded by the Pure Land of a living Buddha, experiencing together the mystical elevation and acceleration of *ramakrishnaloka*, the Realm of Ramakrishna, where indivisible Reality, Awareness, and Bliss remain constantly unveiled.

Immensely enjoying this conversation with his beloved companion and spiritual heir, Ramakrishna asks: "How did Lord Buddha instruct the seekers of Truth?" Naren responds, easily and intelligently, while continuing to massage our Master's feet.

NARENDRA Gautama Buddha did not entertain or encourage any speculation about Reality, but consistently upheld the principles of inconceivability and indescribability, while demonstrating selfless love for all conscious beings. During five hundred consecutive lifetimes, the future Buddha prepared his mind-stream for full awakening by acts of self-renouncing generosity. During one of these incarnations, the future Buddha observed a hawk swoop down upon a helpless songbird. He instantly intervened, satisfying the predator with some of his own flesh. What spontaneous renunciation of instinctive self-interest he developed!

Though Gautama was a prince destined to inherit an entire kingdom, which under his leadership would have become a world-empire, he renounced his conventional destiny, walking away from the palace late one night and retiring into the wilderness to intensify his quest for Truth. After manifesting Buddhahood six years later—while abiding in the timeless, unconditional wisdom called *nirvana*—he returned to his father's palace to teach his wife and son and to invite the entire kingdom to embrace the Middle Way. How flawless was Lord Buddha's renunciation of the conventional world! He was neither attracted nor repelled.

Ramakrishna becomes increasingly silent and concentrated as his beloved Naren's enthusiasm reaches higher and higher pitch, gazing with great tenderness upon this young man he often calls "the unsheathed sword of wisdom."

NARENDRA Buddha would not compromise. He would not live inside the suffocating, habitual structures of self and society. Neither was he confined by the assumptions of conventional religion. The traditional gods and goddesses did not concern him in the slightest. When he established his meditation seat beneath the Bodhi Tree, he took this adamantine vow: "Let my body disintegrate here, but I will not arise until fully awakening to Truth." What dispassion! What willpower! This limited body and mind are the only real obstacles. The body-mind must be disciplined, chastened, attenuated.

The Great Swan breaks his mysterious silence by asking Narendra whether, on this pilgrimage, he perceived a radiant tuft of hair on the Buddha's forehead. Narendra replies in the negative.

RAMAKRISHNA And what about his eyes? What spiritual mood do they convey?

NARENDRA Revered sir, the eyes of the great statue in the stupa at Bodhgaya indicate that Lord Buddha is immersed in *nirvikalpa samadhi,* total absorption in supreme Reality.

Ramakrishna again plunges deep into silence, as if communing directly with the ancient realization of the Buddha, attained over two thousand years ago—testing, probing, exploring, and making it new. Suddenly a brilliant smile flashes across his emaciated face. Narenda stops massaging and Mahendra suspends his fanning, both breathless with expectation. What has the Paramahamsa discovered?

RAMAKRISHNA Well, dear Naren. Here in this human form before you is found every possible spiritual modality—from rare and exalted delicacies to ordinary red lentils spiced with sharp tamarind. What do you think of the present manifestation?

NARENDRA Beloved Paramahamsa, you have penetrated, experienced, and thoroughly established your awareness in the most refined states recorded by the ancient scriptures. You have even transcended the scriptures, and are opening new possibilities for expressing indivisible consciousness and bliss in the most earthly human context—red lentils, spiced with tamarind.

RAMAKRISHNA Indeed, some Divine Force seems to have held my awareness to this earthly plane for a precise purpose. Look at the fan you are holding, Mahendra. Scrutinize it in detail from both sides, opened and closed. In a mode even more vivid and direct, I have gazed at Divine Reality from various perspectives, as well as panoramically and also nonperspectively. Dearest Naren, can you understand what I am really saying?

NARENDRA Revered sir, I have understood.

RAMAKRISHNA Then tell me.

NARENDRA I am not sure it can be expressed in words.

RAMAKRISHNA I have seen directly and known without the slightest uncertainty that supreme Reality and the mysterious presence that dwells within this subtle nervous system are precisely the same. But not in your impersonal Vedantic sense, Naren. They are one infinite, inconceivable Mother.

NARENDRA Yes, revered sir. Yes.

RAMAKRISHNA Only a transparent boundary, like a thin line of light, appears to divide these two dimensions called supreme Reality and Ramakrishna. This insubstantial boundary permits me to enjoy the bliss of conversing and playing with the lovers of Truth and with the eternal companions of God.

Astonishment and silence flood our entire conscious being. Suddenly, there is no temporality. We are actually seeing through the eyes of the blissful sage. At last, Narendra speaks, his rich voice full of gratitude.

NARENDRA Ah, brother Mahendra! Do you see how these great-souled ones, even though completely liberated from the illusion of finitude, retain a provisional ego and accept the pleasures and pains of physical existence in order to delight and console other souls, guiding and maturing them on the radical way of liberation? Out of Great Compassion alone, they become like humble laborers in the market-place of this world, bearing our burdens, suffering vicariously to accelerate our spiritual evolution. Their labor here is selfless and free from the slightest compulsion, whereas we labor bound by finite motivation. The living Buddhas pursue their labor of love as sheer play, sheer bliss, sheer awareness.

Again, timeless silence blossoms. The Paramahamsa is experiencing an ecstatic vision. His glowing dark eyes slowly sweep the space before him.

RAMAKRISHNA O inseparable friends, behold. Here! Now! The roof is clearly visible! Yet it is extremely difficult to reach.

NARENDRA True indeed, sir.

RAMAKRISHNA If someone who has reached the roof of timeless awareness knows how to let down a rope, others who are sufficiently agile can climb up directly. Here is the rope, right before your eyes!

Each of the companions of Divine Love now enjoys a unique experi-ence, ascending this mystic rope of Ramakrishna's realization, which he has compassionately provided for us and for all living beings.

RAMAKRISHNA Once a wandering sage from the Himalayas arrived at the Temple Garden. He observed me carefully for a few days and finally exclaimed: "How amazing! I can perceive five entirely distinct modes of *samadhi* manifest through you." The graceful and infinitely powerful current of Divine Energy, or Mother Kundalini, sometimes plays through this nervous system like monkeys swing through the trees, traveling swiftly without ever touching the ground. This *maha-vayu*, or great energy-wind, moves sometimes like minnows darting through the shallows and other times like huge ocean fish gliding majestically through the deeps.

Like a tiny ant climbing a giant banyan tree, this evolutionary energy arises in a spiral from the root of awareness. Then it becomes like a powerful serpent, moving up the trunk in wavelike patterns and then like a small, brilliantly colored bird, hopping precisely yet unpredictably from lower to higher branches. Finally, this Divine Energy manifests as a great golden warrior-bird, the noble Garuda, soaring in spirals into the empty blue sky. When Mother Kundalini reaches the thousand-petaled lotus, which is the golden sun far above the subtle body, the individual mind-stream disappears into the shoreless ocean.

Our Master now enters that ocean right before our eyes. Some companions actually submerge with him; others sit gazing across the open expanse. Reemerging from union, Ramakrishna fixes Naren with the most intense, yet tender gaze: "You have enough power to establish all thirty-six basic religious ideals—the entire spectrum of spiritual possibility. You will be able to overturn the ordinary world completely."

31

The Mood of Formlessness
The Master Gives Away His Treasures

D URING THIS terrible terminal illness of our Master, his concern for
the spiritual advancement of the companions intensifies. When the
beggars finished their noon meal at the Temple Garden, the Master loved
to clear away the used leaf-plates, touching them to his lips and carrying
them on his head, for he was directly serving the Divine Mother of the
Universe, manifest as the poor and the helpless. How much more did he
humbly and tenderly care for us during these last days, regardless of his
constant suffering. If the coachman whipped the horses while the Paramahamsa was riding in a carriage, he would cry out: "He is beating me!"
How much more did Ramakrishna identify with our spiritual struggles
during these last radiant days. A woman once came to the Great Swan,
weeping: "I have no one in this world!" He danced with her in ecstatic
joy, singing: "Whosoever has no one else has only God." The woman
returned home with peace prevailing in her heart. How much more did
Ramakrishna flood his companions with God-vision during the last days
of his physical manifestation.

As one of the most mature companions remarks: "The Master loves us
very much. It is the amazing depth of this love—much deeper even than
the purest parental love—that draws us to him and unifies us with him
eternally." Even now, when he can barely speak because of searing pain, if
no one arrives seeking spiritual instruction, Ramakrishna weeps: "O
Mother, what has happened? No friends have come for discussion today."
On the very last afternoon of his physical existence, the Paramahamsa will
speak patiently for two hours on the practice of yoga to a Calcutta
gentleman visiting him for the first time.

The God-conscious sage has been giving away with abandon all his rare treasures of initiatory energy. One afternoon, Ramakrishna pours so much indescribable wealth into the body, mind, heart, and soul of Narendra that he exclaims in a loud whisper: "Now I have nothing—like the *faqir*, the wandering Muslim sage who practices perfect poverty." The Paramahamsa is like a farmer whose orchards bear abundant fruit, which he carefully transports to the market, bargaining with each customer to establish a fair price. But as evening approaches, his price becomes more favorable, and at dusk the precious fruit is given away to everyone who asks. Recently, the Great Swan remarked: "If this present form were to be preserved a few days longer, many persons would receive spiritual awakening and even illumination. But such is not Mother's Will. She will not preserve this body, for I am simple and foolish. I will give away all Her Secrets."

During these radiant final days, the companions of Divine Love are witnessing for the first time some of our Master's wonderful powers, which before were kept largely concealed. Ramakrishna's prophetic statements are also now being confirmed. Often, during our years of friendship together, he would laughingly remark: "When large numbers of persons chatter with excitement about the significance of this body, this vessel of *shakti*, then Mother will draw it back into Her Womb of the Unmanifest, Her dazzling Darkness, more intense than Divine Light." Through the efforts of Keshab Sen and Ramchandra Datta—two of the most enthusiastic proponents of the Master's mission of universal regeneration—many people in the metropolis of Calcutta have now become fascinated by Ramakrishna. He is dissolving and disappearing before this public gaze.

This morning the outpouring of Mother's Grace through Her child's emaciated form reaches a new level of intensity. He is revealing openly the high stature of his young disciples. With great, loving respect he proclaims to Niranjan, "You are my father," and then sits on the young man's lap, transmitting such a current of spiritual energy that all of us in the room can feel it tingle through the mystical body of the community. Turning to Kalipada, Ramakrishna lightly touches the center of this young disciple's chest, uttering the powerful words: "May your consciousness be awakened to its very essence!" Kalipada immediately enters *samadhi*, absorption in Mother Reality. Playfully and affectionately caressing the youth's chin to return him to relative awareness, the sage stammers in ecstasy: "Whoever practices daily devotions with great faith and whoever has even once called with utmost sincerity upon God—however the Higher Power may be understood—will encounter the One who dwells now in this form as Ramakrishna."

Two women disciples approach for blessing. Our Master, deep in rapture, places both feet upon their heart centers. This is a rare gesture from the sage, who never encourages people to touch his feet, often reverently touching the feet of his visitors instead. Both women immediately enter profound ecstasy, shedding tears of pure love. Lost in bliss, again and again they are repeating: "Revered Paramahamsa, you are so kind, so kind."

Ramakrishna now turns to another young disciple and proclaims: "There is Latu, sitting with his head resting on his hand. I can clearly see that he is Divine Reality, sitting with its Divine Head upon its Divine Hand." Affectionately gazing at Nistarini and holding his right hand lightly on her head, the sage remarks: "Mother Nistarini, you have seen, fed, and served this form. The thousand-petaled lotus of the seventh plane of awareness will certainly blossom for you at the moment of death. This Ramakrishna-form will appear before your inner vision, granting you liberation and enlightenment." To the astonished companions in the room, the Master proclaims about his disciple: "She is a sublime soul—an emanation of one of the ten aspects of the Great Mother." We are all in a state of rapture now.

Ramakrishna begins to call out the names of certain intimate companions who are not present here this morning, longing to transmit their destined spiritual inheritance. These persons are sent for, wherever they may live in Calcutta or its environs. Divine Love is overflowing all imaginable boundaries. This rich drama of transmission continues from early morning to dusk. Finally, the Great Swan asks for incense to be lit and enters his indrawn mood, contemplating the transcendent aspect of the Universal Mother. We sit together for more than an hour in vast silence, without the slightest consciousness of passing time.

Earthenware lamps are lit. The darkness itself seems radiant. Our Master is in ecstasy, sitting cross-legged, his forehead resting on a round bolster in front of him. He raises his head slowly, eyes glistening. In a whisper, he begins to communicate verbally once more, revealing some of the secrets that he has already silently and directly transmitted to our souls.

RAMAKRISHNA Beloved friends, the appearance of my teaching others is coming to an end. I am losing the sensibility that can perceive students or seekers of Truth, that can perceive any conscious being who is separate or in any way incomplete. At this moment, I am seeing everyone here simply as Lord Rama. Just *Ram, Ram, Ram.* I laugh when I wonder: "Who is there to be taught? Who is there to present the teachings? What is there to teach?"

I have never posted a sign or advertised in a newspaper, yet a tremendous variety of sincere seekers and adept practitioners have come. But I can no longer perceive anyone as a separate individual. There is no one who is a beginner on the spiritual path and no one who is advanced.

The awakened sage falls silent again. Within a few minutes, this silence intensifies into *samadhi.* His human form is ignited, as if touched by an infinite flame. Every pore of his skin streams with subtle radiance and power. An elusive smile, playing across sensitive lips, is the only remaining life sign. The oil lamps burn steadily, without wavering. Just as mysteriously, the Paramahamsa regains awareness of relativity and manifests again as focused human consciousness, rather than as the shoreless sea of sheer awareness.

RAMAKRISHNA I am perceiving simultaneously all manifestation, on every plane of being, flowing dynamically from form into formlessness. I am shown the subtle meanings of structures and events the moment their intrinsic formlessness is revealed. I would enjoy sharing these wonderful revelations with you, but they are simply not expressible in language.

Well, friends, this new tendency of my mind toward essential formlessness may be a sign of impending disappearance. Do you think so? Even now as I speak, I continue to perceive the same primordial essence that is unveiled in the most profound state of *samadhi.* I am perceiving your human forms as perfectly transparent to this formless, essenceless essence. I have always attempted to contain and conceal the intensity of this particular spiritual mood—this Clear Light of Reality—but now it has become absolutely overwhelming.

32

Universal Victory
The Passing Away of Ramakrishna

EXPERIENCING A heightened sense of community, we gather every night at the garden house, where some thirty companions visit regularly, providing care for this precious organic form. We know full well that Mother Kali alone is manifest through this lithe body, hypersensitive and subtle in every respect. More and more often, our Master points to his physical frame and remarks: "Only a pillowcase." The younger disciples, relatively free from family responsibility, spend the night together here, meditating outside around an open fire, taking turns nursing the Paramahamsa, who is at once mother, father, sibling, friend, child, lover, and guide, but who is experienced most intimately as our own primordial awareness. Here at the Cossipore garden house, the lovers are being fused into one mystical body.

Such confident cheerfulness and radiance are flowing from Ramakrishna during these last days that were it not for his emaciated appearance and the excruciating pain he suffers, we would forget entirely about his illness and the imminent embrace of Goddess Kali called death. Often the sage murmurs: "Let this body and its pain befriend each other. You, O mind, remain immersed in Divine Bliss." Recently, a disciple entered the sickroom as the Paramahamsa was lying on his bed, alone, writhing slightly with agony, his throat now totally perforated by an advanced stage of cancer. The young man touched the feverish, trembling body gently and felt such a powerful current of bliss that he cried out involuntarily and jumped back. Ramakrishna turned his head and commented humorously: "Ah, you rascal! You have discovered my secret." Beneath the surface of his physical pain, which is nonetheless terribly real, flows a vast river of spiritual delight. Our Master lives entirely immersed in Divine Bliss, under every condition of consciousness.

One afternoon, earlier in the illness, the Great Swan was feeling stronger than usual and went for a stroll on the grounds of the garden house— some five acres of fruit trees and flowering plants. It was a holiday, so most of the companions of Divine Love were gathered. We were seated beneath an ancient tree beside a lotus pond, delighting in song and conversation. Some were enjoying a quiet smoke. The God-intoxicated sage approached his loyal lovers and cried out to Girish Gosh: "O beloved Girish, what do you think of the present manifestation?" This great rebel intellectual, whose faith in our Master's Divine Nature is the most passionate among the companions, eloquently testified to his experience of Ramakrishna as Divine Reality incarnate. Then he fell, weeping, in full-length prostration, his forehead resting on the God-man's feet.

The explosive devotion of Girish brings down all barriers. The scene becomes electrifying. Mother Reality manifests like a lightning bolt, coursing steadily through the sage's emaciated form—not visibly so much as tangibly. The Paramahamsa's right hand is lifted high, palm forward, thumb holding down second and third fingers. His left hand, palm inward, spreads open like a rare blossom at the level of the heart. The infinite current of Divine Energy flows back and forth between these two blessed hands, ascending and descending simultaneously. Some lovers run to the surrounding trees, pluck blossoms, and offer them at Ramakrishna's feet or simply throw them into the air while dancing or whirling in rapture. A miraculous rain of flower petals descends from the empty blue sky. A circle of almost one hundred ecstatic lovers is now whirling around the transparent form of the sage.

The Paramahamsa, wearing a beautiful green cap, moves swiftly like a flame, igniting the devotees. He places his radiant hands upon us, praying: "May your consciousness be illumined!" To a few pesons, he whispers tenderly: "You must wait a while longer." Everyone our Master touches now encounters the fullest experience, according to his or her particular line of spiritual discipline and predilection.

Beneath spreading branches in this primeval glade of revelation, each lover receives the sage's revolutionizing touch at a different level of the spiritual body—heart chakra, throat chakra, forehead chakra, crown chakra, or some combination of the four. Each experiences what he or she most longs to experience, from visions of Kali, Krishna, Buddha, Jesus, or

Muhammad to peaceful immersion in the formless sea of *satchidananda*. Certain fortunate persons recognize the astonishing stature of Rama- krishna as an *avatara* who contains and transmits all possible spiritual ideals. Some are weeping, others laughing, while still others fall in full prostration or enter profound trance, standing or sitting.

During his residence at the Dakshineswar Temple Garden, whenever Ramakrishna blessed any person, a very distinct joy was perceptible in mind and body for three or four days. But the God-man's blessing on this historic occasion was a new manifestation. Niranjan, after being touched on the forehead, could not close his eyes for three days and three nights because of the continuous blaze of Divine Light. Tarak reports that the moment Ramakrishna pushed aside his shawl and touched his bare chest on that mysterious day, he realized his own nature as *atman*—primordial awareness, timeless and free. The experience did not fade. Tarak realized as well, at the moment of this tender touch, that Ramakrishna is Divine Reality, fully manifest as a human being. Since this awakening, Tarak has known without any doubt that the purpose of his own existence is to serve this complete manifestation of Truth. He is destined to become Swami Shivananda, leader of the Ramakrishna Order of holy monks.

This mystic day upon which our aspirations were so richly and unex- pectedly fulfilled occurred on the first of January, the beginning of the new year according to the European calendar. We regard this bright winter day in 1886 as the inauguration of the New Dispensation.

The circle of lovers at the Cossipore garden house this evening is rather small. The Paramahamsa is resting his slight body against the large back of Sashi, who will later become the bedrock of the Ramakrishna Order, the great Swami Ramakrishnananda. He will receive the very name of the Master because of the tremendous service he offered his guru—both during Ramakrishna's last illness and after his death, for Sashi will conduct the daily worship of the Paramahamsa's sacred relics, thereby sending subtle waves of blessing far and wide.

It is an uncomfortably warm night in the middle of August. The sage's feverish body is being cooled by Latu and several others, who are fanning in unison, with a gentle rhythm. Narendra is lightly stroking our Master's blessed feet. Vast peace is descending.

Ramakrishna has clarified the situation by unequivocally stating: "I have taken upon this body the suffering of the whole world." He has asked again and again if we are willing to release his physical form, which, as he explains, is being kept together now only by the love and longing of his intimate disciples, those who cannot bear to lose the visible presence of their guide. We have reiterated our willingness to release him, although our unconscious attachment must be very strong because he is still with us, bound by the threads of our love. Tonight, however, the Master seems satisfied with the authenticity of our response, when he humbly asks our permission to leave. He remarks casually: "This vessel in which I am floating on the Ocean of Bliss is almost completely filled with water and is about to sink." This afternoon the sage consulted the astrological almanac and established that tomorrow is an auspicious day to begin a journey. He is able to eat more than usual.

Ramakrishna's charming smile and the fresh white cloth around his waist shine in the flickering lamplight. His honey-colored skin, dulled by illness, seems to regain its extraodinary luster. The rest of the room remains in mysterious darkness. Our Master now places his right hand upon his heart: "I see clearly that Mother and I are one. All phenomena emanate from here."

His smile becomes more intense, more blissful. The Paramahamsa gradually becomes all smile. His body disappears into Divine Delight as a thrill runs through his limbs, subtle tremors of which we can feel in our own bodies. A startling sound rings out three times: OM SRI KALI MA, OM SRI KALI MA, OM SRI KALI MA. Although in his present condition it is barely possible even to whisper, we know these powerful tones are emanating from Ramakrishna. We have never before heard the Parama-hamsa repeating aloud this way the complete *mantra* of his Chosen Deity, even during the countless moods of ecstasy we have witnessed. Though the rich tenor voice is distinctively his, there is also an unearthly quality to this sound, quite unlike the melodious hymns of mystic union which our Master is so fond of singing. Could this be the primordial sound of Goddess Kali? The original wave from which scriptures, hymns, souls, and universes are constantly taking form?

As we awaken from our state of astonishment at this cry of wisdom and glance at the Paramahamsa, he is supine, submerged in *samadhi*. His entire being is Divine Smile. His utterly still body radiates Divine Light. It is around midnight, the most auspicious hour for the worship of Mahakali. A full moon is illuminating the gardens. The *samadhi* deepens further, moment by moment. It becomes intuitively evident that we are witnessing *mahasamadhi,* the final absorption of the differentiated awareness and the dissolution of the physical form. The room is being filled with light. Or is it our own minds and senses that are flooded with the formless radiance of the Wisdom Goddess? It is like a lightning flash, prolonged for several minutes. The pressure is unbearable.

Some of us begin chanting—HARI OM TAT SAT, HARI OM RAMA-KRISHNA—hoping to bring his awareness down once more to the mental conventions of substance, space, time, causality, individuality. This method of chanting has worked so many times in the past, but the present situation appears entirely unprecedented. This is already the new manifestation of Ramakrishna, no longer centered in his physical form.

Some companions are weeping, not with a sense of ordinary loss but with a sense of new vastness, new sublimity, new responsibility. Rather than lack or absence, this is a sense of *purna,* completeness. There is certainly great physical shock, as if we have suddenly lost a major part of our own body. There is also a vast emotional void, for the brilliant sun of our reason for being has just disappeared behind the horizon. But on the spiritual plane we sense only boundless space, filled with clear guidance that will unfold spontaneously during the hours, years, and centuries ahead. Our own physical death is also mysteriously contained here, and we will each return to this light-filled room, with familiarity and confidence, at the moment of our last breath.

Checking the bodily points of yogic concentration, Narendra finds the crown of the head and the spinal column still distinctively warm. The body is still glowing with Divine Life, although it is no longer a form of biological existence. Some companions are leaving the room to communicate the news of this immense transition. Some are not yet able to accept the fact and are sending for Dr. Sarkar. Certain companions of Divine Love have become lost in meditation. Others are gazing with tear-filled eyes upon this incomparable image of God, which must now be ceremonially immersed in flames.

As the Great Swan often sings: "Why should I go to Kashi or to other places of pilgrimage, as long as I can cry the Name of Kali with my final breath?"

This is the supreme Vijaya Day, the return of the reflected image to its original. August 15—a day of complete spiritual victory for humanity.

33

Divine Communion

S URROUNDED BY swirling energy at the Master's bed, I close my eyes
for what seems just a moment. A lucid waking-dream unfolds. I am
with my beloved guide again at the Dakshineswar Temple Garden. Every
leaf shines, translucent. Every petal emits intense color and fragrance.
Every ripple on the Ganges reflects the red western sun, producing a
shimmering path composed from millions of setting suns, each one
coming into being and passing away every second. This sun-path is
manifest Being.

Ramakrishna is standing on the circular porch of his room, gazing out
across the sacred river which he reveres as a manifestation of the Great
Mother, even entering its holy waters very humbly and deferentially when
taking his morning bath. Softly and melodiously, he is now chanting,
"*Gita, ganga, gayatri.*" His beautifully proportioned body, moving in
dance, is only a small dimension of his radiant being, which shines like
millions of rising suns. He is the perpetual dawn of Divine Love and
Divine Wisdom.

Gradually, I realize that what lies before my contemplative gaze is not
the earthly Dakshineswar, where Ramakrishna experienced thirty years of
ceaseless rapture from 1855 to 1885. This is the timeless play, the Divine
Theater of Dakshineswar, incomparably more real than these gardens,
temples, and persons as they reflect in the insubstantial mirror of space
and time. I am with the Paramahamsa in the realmless realm of his
samadhi. I am surrounded by *ramakrishnaloka,* his Pure Land. I am within
the transcendent dimension of *kathamrita,* the Ocean of Nectar, a few
drops of which manifest as Ramakrishna's temporal existence.

The blissful sage turns now and greets me, palms joined at his heart. I
am communicating more vividly and directly with his entire being than is
possible on the level of fragmentary, historical consciousness. With com-

plete surprise, I realize that my entire communion with the Master—my experience of contemporaneousness with his charming person, both at the Temple Garden and at various households in and around Calcutta—has been unfolding entirely upon this plane of timeless *lila,* insubstantial play. My physical form is located in the Western world, a hundred years into the future. Perhaps as the Paramahamsa gazes into the setting sun over the waters of his beloved Mother Ganga, he can envision the wave of souls who will manifest his enlightening energy around the planet—some privately and intimately, as he did, others publicly to large numbers of seekers and practitioners of Truth, following the rays of light Ramakrishna emanates as Mother Sarada and Swami Vivekananda.

All these waves of manifestation are simply the play of Divine Light. The very principle of manifestation is Light and the nature of manifest Being is Light. Luminous forms are merging constantly into formless radiance.

The Ramakrishna of Light, eyes filled with indescribable tenderness, now affectionately touches my cheek. Laughing, he remarks: "Beings and events appear and disappear through the Will of Kali alone." The Wisdom Mother's perpetual stream of illumination now flows directly from mind to mind, heart to heart. There is no separation between master and disciple. There are no imaginary veils of substantiality. As we commune wordlessly, the sun sets and twilight slips through our fingers. The God-intoxicated sage often explains: "You no longer need to perform ceremonial worship when ecstasy becomes so intense that the handful of water you are attempting to offer slips through your fingers."

Mother Sarada has prepared a delicious supper—thick *chapatis* and *chana dal.* Plantain leaf-plates are set out at dusk on the southeastern veranda of the Master's room. We sit here on grass mats in full view of the hundred-foot, nine-domed Kali Temple. Its impressive white stone structure—begun to be built when Ramakrishna was still a boy of eleven, and destined to become his mysterious abode on earth when he reached nineteen—rises like a giant night-blooming flower filled with rare fragrance. This is the perfume of Mother Shyama, the beautiful Dark Goddess.

Ramakrishna is lost in ecstasy, weeping and praying, voice charged with an immense emotion that I can feel within my own body. "Mother, Mother, Mother! May those who sincerely approach You have their desires fulfilled on every level." So deep in rapture that he is barely able to form words, the Paramahamsa begins to sing.

> The black bee of my mind
> is drawn in drunken delight
> to the dark blue lotus,
> Goddess Shyama.
> Tasteless to this mystic bee
> are common blossoms of desire.
> Mother's Lotus Feet are black,
> jet-black the honey bee—
> black merges into blackness,
> the rest impenetrable mystery.

During the disappearing twilight, we watch a temple priest move purposefully, like a bee, from each of the twelve small Shiva shrines to the next, ringing a bell with his left hand and bearing a sacred five-pointed oil lamp in his right, accompanied by an attendant ringing a gong. As the evening raga from the southern music pavilion builds to its crescendo, the memory arises of Rani Rasmani, the courageous, dedicated woman who designed and endowed this Temple Garden. On her official stationery was emblazoned: "Rani Rasmani, who longs only to attain the mystic Feet of Kali." By acting exclusively through the guidance of the Goddess, the Rani re-created in temporality the transcendent realm of Kali. Here, the essentially timeless presence we call Ramakrishna Paramahamsa fully enters the flow of time, accompanied by his entire *mandala* of extraordinary male and female beings. Here, Divine Reality weeps, sings, and dances with its companions by the hallowed banks of the Ganges, among graceful gardens pervaded by the fragrance of gardenia, jasmine, oleander, rose, and the rare perfume of the seven lotus centers, fully blossoming.

Who or what is Ramakrishna? The words of the realized tantric practitioner and scholar Pandit Gauri come vividly to mind. When asked by our Master, "What do you think of me?"—a question that Ramakrishna addresses innocently to every sensitive soul who enters his ambiance—the adept replied: "I am convinced that you are the original fountainhead of spiritual power, only a particle of which manifests on earth from age to age as a Divine Incarnation." Rapturous laughter was the Paramahamsa's instantaneous response. Then he commented simply: "It is Mother alone who causes people to see and to understand Her Reality in different ways."

The sage's reply to any affirmation about his spiritual stature is always elusive. His responses are often surprisingly concise.

VISITOR Sir, you are God.

RAMAKRISHNA What can you possibly mean? The wave belongs to the river. Can one ever say that the river belongs to the wave?

VISITOR Sir, you are liberated from passions.

RAMAKRISHNA How do you come to suppose that? Just this afternoon I advanced a carriage driver some money and he failed to come. I became very angry with him. He caused me inconvenience and suffering.

VISITOR Sir, who are you?

RAMAKRISHNA My dear, I try to find the personal *I* but can never discover it.

VISITOR Sir, what is our responsibility?

RAMAKRISHNA To remain united with God.

VISITOR Sir, if the world is unreal, then so are my various indiscretions unreal.

RAMAKRISHNA I spit on your bogus spiritual knowledge! It is mere fantasy and abstraction.

VISITOR Sir, is the world unreal?

RAMAKRISHNA Nothing is unreal. What you are asking is merely a subject for vain philosophical discussion.

VISITOR Sir, what happens when the soul leaves the body?

RAMAKRISHNA To bother about what happens after death! How silly! You are born as a human being only to experience pure love.

VISITOR Sir, you have blessed me.

RAMAKRISHNA If you sincerely believe this, what can I say? I am simply one who eats rice and greens and chants the beautiful Names of God night and day. I am less significant than one of the hairs in your beard.

After finishing our evening meal with the intimate companions of Divine Love, we sit together all night in the radiance of the full moon, listening to our Master teach. This is not an unusual occurrence. For the Goddess-worshiping sage, night shines brighter than day.

RAMAKRISHNA You may hiss like the king cobra at negative or dangerous persons to prevent them from harming others. But never strike and inject venom. Never actually injure anyone, even to the slightest degree. Mother does not permit me to engage in criticism of any being—not even a worm. Never perceive faults in others. Discover the faults in your own attitude. Never address harsh words to anyone or make any remark simply to cause pain to another person.

Yet it is not possible to express true nonviolence without first merging into God. Mystic union is the great secret, which can never be reasoned about or penetrated by analysis. Listen to a song.

> How foolishly you try, O mind,
> to know the nature of Reality.
> You are searching in vain,
> as a mad person seeks treasure
> in a pitch-black, empty room.
> God is known by ecstatic love,
> there is no other adequate mode.
>
> Truth is only experienced
> by recognizing all as God,
> never by discriminating *neti, neti:*
> "This is not God. That is not God."
> Nor is God encountered
> through Vedas, Tantras,
> or any system of philosophy.
>
> The elixir of pure love
> delights Divine Reality,
> who dwells secretly and joyously
> in this chamber of the human body.
> For a single drop of pure love,
> yogis meditate for ages.
> When ecstatic love awakens,
> Reality absorbs the soul.

God can be seen and conversed with more intimately than I am seeing and conversing with you. And God has the nature of an innocent child. Follow these two guidelines fully and you will live in the perpetual monsoon of newly awakened love. You will become a *siddha* among *siddhas*—one who is more mature even than those who are spiritually mature. Awaken your subtle love-body and commune directly with God, who is none other than Pure Love. Do not seek to disappear into Divine Reality, for there is a level of realization much more advanced than that. One sees God absolutely everywhere when one loves with Divine Love.

I once asked Narendra his spiritual ideal. When he replied, "To merge in *nirvikalpa samadhi* for three or four days at a time, coming down only to take nourishment," I exclaimed: "What a narrow-minded person! There is a much greater experience than that! You are the one who sings the Sufi hymn by Jafar."

The Master now turns to Narendra and asks him to sing this hymn, so highly renowned among lovers. The unsheathed sword of wisdom responds instantly, great eyes shining with joy.

> I have united my heart with You.
> O Lord, You alone exist.
> Wherever I look, I find only You,
> Beloved, for all beings exist
> only through Your Being.
> You abide fully within every heart,
> whether Hindu or Muslim,
> manifesting every form of devotion,
> for You are all that exists.
>
> Whether entering Paradise
> or making pilgrimage to the Kaaba,
> Your Presence alone is found.
> All beings prostrate before You,
> for You alone pervade every world,
> from earth to highest heaven.
> There is nothing comparable to You,
> sings Jafar to his Beloved,
> for You are the Only One.

RAMAKRISHNA I received initiation and instruction from the Sufi Master Govinda Rai. He transmitted to my heart the beautiful Divine Name Allah, which I then repeated with every breath. I visited the small mosque behind the Temple Garden, learning to make the Call to

Prayer and to perform *namaz,* the graceful cycles of prostration and praise offered by devout Muslims five times every day. My practice of Islam was crowned by a vision of the noble Prophet Muhammad—a robed, dignified, bearded figure of supreme sanctity—who merged intimately with my being, pervading my body with rose fragrance and lifting my awareness into union with him and then into mystic union with Allah Most High. It was precisely the same profound *samadhi* attained along the paths of Veda and Tantra. Muslims call it *fana.*

During this brief but intense period of Islamic *sadhana,* I enjoyed Muslim dishes and wore Muslim clothes. I removed the pictures of Hindu deities from my room and constantly chanted verses in Arabic from the Holy Quran. One afternoon, while returning from a visit to Mother Kali at Kalighat, the carriage was moving slowly through the crowd before the Grand Mosque at Geratala. Through the open courtyard I glimpsed a Muslim sage crying out with palms upraised: "O Allah, O Supreme Beloved, please come! Please come!" I leaped from the moving vehicle, raced madly into the mosque, and tearfully greeted this noble Sufi. We held each other in a long embrace.

The Sufis follow the way of *prema,* a love so intense that it melts and dissolves the entire being. I was once shown a Persian book which explained the spiritual essence of the human body—inside the flesh is bone, inside the bone is marrow, inside the marrow are more subtle substances, but the innermost is *prema.* At the core is pure love.

> How soon will dawn the timeless day
> when I plunge into the ocean of *prema,*
> enjoying the delight of Paradise
> during this very earthly life?

Beloved companions, please take this mystic hymn most seriously. This present life can become Paradise. God is never *there* but *here.* A person is ignorant when he assumes that God is far above. He has knowledge only when he perceives all creation filled with Divine Consciousness.

> Face shining with Divine Light,
> chant the beautiful Names of God
> until your secret heart overflows
> with the nectar of *prema.*

> Drink this elixir ceaselessly
> and offer it to all humanity.

You are each destined to share with your generation this drink of timeless bliss. Become intoxicated with the sound and energy of any beautiful Name of God, and Divine Grace will arise directly from within your heart. You will become a spring of the Holy Name—bubbling up ceaselessly, providing refreshment for humankind.

A sudden vision or a flash of intuitive understanding is not realization. You must bring Divine Reality into your own room. You must converse intimately with God. Some have glimpsed the king at a distance, no doubt, or even visited him at the royal palace. But how few have brought the king home and entertained him? How few have danced with him?

I used to ascend every night to the roof of the *kuthi*, the palatial residence of Rani Rasmani, where I lived for sixteen years before moving to this room nearer Mother Ganga. Desperately and drunkenly, I would call out: "Where are you, my beloved companions? Please come to me!" I waited for more than twenty years before my intimate inner circle began to arrive. I would low like a cow, udder full of milk, who is searching for her calf. When you each came, one by one, I greeted you: *"namo narayana*—salutations to God." My whole life is immersed in the *naralila*, the beautiful and mysterious play of God as the human being. Each of you is a clear ray from Divine Reality.

Tears flowing from his eyes as he gazes for a long time at each one of us, the Master continues.

RAMAKRISHNA Yes, one should courageously follow many sacred paths—practicing every authentic religious discipline, receiving every powerful initiation, enjoying every mystical attitude. Yet how few are ready to plunge into the ocean of supreme knowledge. They learn a few phrases and immediately begin delivering lectures. Why? Because Mother's Delight is in continuing the game. She does not liberate all the players. The playful Goddess instructs the human mind: "Go forth and experience every possible aspect of manifestation." Can one blame the mind? Awareness can be disentangled from conventional, habitual experience only when the Wisdom Mother, through Her ineffable Grace and Attraction, inspires the mind to investigate its own intrinsic nature, which is Her Reality.

Unfortunately, having scored more than a hundred points, I am out of Her Game. I can no longer thoroughly participate. Some of you have scored ten points, some six, others five. Through you, Her Play can go on. How wonderful! If you ceaselessly hold to the highest Truth, there is nothing wrong with being immersed in Mother's cosmic manifestation. Simply consider it all as Her sublime Mystery, never as a mundane, self-centered world, never as a substantial, solid universe. The key point is to attain transparency of mind. Worldly bondage and spiritual liberation are simply contrasting attitudes of mind. The essence of mind, primordial awareness, is beyond both these limited notions—beyond imagined imprisonment or release from such empty imagination. If you truly think you are boundless awareness—ever-free, ever-pure, never touched by the dreams of bondage and liberation— then, quite simply, you are that. Mind is a white cloth, just washed in the river. It will take whatever color you wish. Or you can simply leave the mind as clear light.

The colorless brilliance of primal awareness is what I call pure love. I do not desire any of Mother's variegated dyes. Constantly I pray: "O Mother, please remove from my heart both virtue and viciousness, both knowledge and ignorance. Grant me simply pure love for You." It is a great help to withdraw from the social world for just three days and sincerely weep for God. Weep for the sake of pure love. Tears stream from the eyes of human beings for so many reasons. Who weeps for God-realization? But one cannot realize God without being guileless and liberal-minded, that is, without being free from worldly conventions and calculations.

Never become self-important or sanctimonious. Never plan obsessively for the future. Never become one-sided in your approach. One-sidedness is the greatest obstacle to spiritual progress. Follow my simple attitude. I eat, drink, and live happily every day. The rest only my blissful Mother knows. I do not care for all these philosophical and religious complexities. Mother and I. Mother and I. That is all. Nothing else.

Perfect freedom dawns when a person genuinely feels that Divine Reality is the only knower, the only agent, the only action. You continue to suffer because you insist that you know and that you act. People become obsessed either with advancing themselves or with doing good for the world. But who is really acting through every action, be it narrow-minded or broad-minded? Divine Presence alone. So cease to be conscious of doing and thinking. Then only will you become a genuine blessing to humankind.

Consider the case of Rani Rasmani. She lovingly prepared an elaborate pilgrimage to Kashi in order to visit Divine Mother in Her Aspect as Annapurna. This devoted and wealthy widow assembled a convoy of twenty-four large boats, filled with enough provisions for six months. She generously invited her entire extended family. There were seven boats simply for food and other supplies. One boat bore four cows and another boat carried their fodder.

The night before the Rani and her vast entourage were to sail up the sacred river from Calcutta on this auspicious adventure, the matriarch had a dream of her Chosen Ideal, Mahakali. The Goddess of Wisdom told her not to make pilgrimage to Kashi but to create instead a holy place of pilgrimage right here on the banks of Mother Ganga. The complex plans were immediately canceled, the provisions distributed among the poor, and the substantial wealth set aside for this epic journey was used instead to purchase the Dakshineswar Garden from an Englishman and to construct the various shrines and temples here.

How often we sing that song: "Why should I go to Kashi or to other places of pilgrimage, as long as I can cry the Name of Kali with my final breath?" Rani Rasmani experienced the radical truth of Mother's omnipresence. Goddess Kali built this Temple Garden through the Rani's noble heart, mind, and hands. But one must adopt the heroic attitude: "I have chanted the all-powerful Name of Kali. How can I be a limited, powerless being any longer?" The true devotee of Kali is a *jivanmukta*—one who is liberated while still living on earth, liberated by tasting the nectar of Mother's timeless Bliss.

Liberation occurs instantly if you can experience Kali as your own real Mother, not merely godmother or stepmother. You can force authentic demands on your Divine Mother. She abides within your most intimate inwardness. Is it an artificial or formal relationship? Demand illumination from Her now! The busy mother does not come to the child as long as it sucks its red toy. But when it throws the toy away and screams, she comes running with the rice pot from the hearth. The red toy is the conventional world of honor, leadership, scholarship, refined comforts, giving publicly in charity, and exercising the eight occult powers. Cast all this away and just cry! Be mad with love for

God! Let people know that you have simply gone crazy and cannot handle mundane responsibility any longer. Then no one will come to you for advice or suffocate you with adulation. Throw aside ceremonial religious duty as well. You cannot attain spiritual intensity by moving at a slow pace. You need to renounce conventionality completely.

Part of the present Dakshineswar Garden was an ancient Islamic cemetery. The holy tomb of a Sufi saint situated here was visited daily by devout pilgrims, both Muslims and Hindus. The blessed soul of this exalted Muslim *pir* appeared to Rani Rasmani in a dream and agreed to the presence of the proposed Kali Temple as long as his tomb was kept sacred by lighting an oil lamp and reciting certain Islamic prayers there each evening. The Rani wrote this request into the constitution of the Temple Garden. She knew how to respect and accept the Divine Command, from whatever unexpected direction it may come. I greet this living Muslim saint with extreme reverence every time I pass his sacred tomb on the way to the main Temple Gate. It was through the subtle presence and blessing of this great soul that I received Sufi initiation and pursued the Islamic way. No one can assert with finality that God manifests only one way and not another. You are experiencing the same room whether you look at it from different sides or from the center. The same substance manifests in its solid form as ice, its liquid form as water and formlessly as vapor. Mother manifests according to the level of the aspirant.

You can think of Divine Reality provisionally as a shoreless sea of indivisible Being, Consciousness and Bliss. Through powerful effects produced by intense yearning, this ocean of awareness mysteriously crystallizes, at certain places, into beautiful forms of ice, which melt again beneath the brilliant sun of *jñana,* perfect knowing. What remains then is sheer indescribability. Just as there is nothing other than gold which can really compare with gold, so Divine Reality is absolutely incomparable. Since nothing other than God exists, how can there even be any process of comparison at all? Who can formulate any description, when even the crystal of I-consciousness has melted? As long as your individuality remains crystallized, so long will the universe manifest as solid and describable. God will continue to be revealed through Divine Forms or Attributes. This crystallization of sheer radiance is real, not merely illusory. Its existence is simply not permanent or substantial. The *jñani* witnesses the evaporation of form.

When the mind is enmeshed in the conceptuality and emotionality called worldliness, it is confined to the lower three planes of awareness, the lower three *chakras* in the subtle nervous system. When one reaches the fourth plane of awareness, the mind enters the heart *chakra* with a burst of unimaginable light, which is actually gnostic love. Whatever direction or dimension one gazes into is then filled with illumination. The fifth plane is attained at the mystic throat *chakra,* where one cannot speak or hear any partial or provisional doctrine. One can then enjoy only God or Truth. None of these *chakras* is located within the physical body. They are focal points in the ascending-spiral energy currents of the subtle body which, when experienced directly, irradiate the visible human form.

The sixth plane manifests at the forehead *chakra.* This ineffable plane of awareness exists two distinct levels above all-pervading illumination. Who can speak of it? Here one intuits Divine Reality directly through myriad transcendent forms and energies. Yet these sixth-plane manifestations are like transparent glass. One cannot actually touch and merge with the ultimate Radiance behind them. One becomes like a master burglar, separated from a vast treasure by an impassible glass wall. One cannot sleep or rest, even for a moment, but ceaselessly gazes at the treasure and considers how to pass through this final barrier.

The seventh plane manifests when the upward-flowing current of awareness, the *kundalini,* finally enters the crown *chakra,* the thousand-petaled lotus, the sole and supreme Consciousness. Upon reaching the seventh plane, a yogi who is not miraculously sustained by the Divine Will drops away the physical body, like a dry leaf, within twenty-one days of earthly time. I once spent six months exclusively merged in the seventh plane of awareness. A master yogi who happened to be visiting the Temple Garden sustained this body on milk, not simply through force-feeding but through his advanced yogic knowledge and power. He was a visible manifestation of Mother's Will. She returned my awareness into the dynamic play of the fourth, fifth, and sixth planes. She requested me never to abandon suffering beings, but to bring them all with me. She taught me to race back and forth, like a sailboat, between the sixth and seventh planes.

Deeply moved at the thought of suffering beings and those who are advancing spiritually in order to benefit them, the Paramahamsa—his very countenance an image of humility—reverently bows low, touching his forehead repeatedly to the stone floor, as he calls out: "I prostrate at the feet of the lovers who seek God through Divine Forms, and I prostrate at the feet of those who seek the formless Divine Reality. I salute the knowers of Truth from ancient times as well as those of today, wherever they may be found, inside or outside religious traditions." Much to our consternation, the God-filled sage now bows before each companion who is present.

Lamenting the condition of those persons who refuse the Divine Call to awaken—who suppress and deny the longing for Truth which arises spontaneously within them—Ramakrishna explains: "Like the silkworm, they could certainly come forth from the cocoon of their conventional worldly existence, but they cannot bear to leave behind the soft, silvery web which they have spun with such great effort. So they die there."

"Please chant the precious name of Baby Krishna," the Paramahamsa supplicates, suddenly becoming like an impatient child. If no intimate companions are present, he requests one of the temple guards to chant certain Divine Names for him in the middle of the night, then feeds the fortunate man delicacies from the shrines of Goddess Kali or Radha-Krishna. Sometimes he visits the Sikh soldiers who guard the government armory north of the Temple Garden. They chant the Divine Name together while sitting in the barracks, and the Master clears their doubts on various subjects. He keeps the pictures of Guru Nanak and the other Sikh gurus on the wall of his room, bowing reverently before them every morning and evening, remembering the first words the noble Nanak uttered after his full illumination: "There is no Hindu. There is no Muslim."

For almost an hour, we vigorously sing for our Master the tender names of the youthful Krishna, Gopala and Govinda. Ramakrishna is floating in ecstasy and so are we. Whenever we chant this way with the God-intoxicated sage, we feel blissful for several days. His spinal column becomes slightly swollen with the flow of Divine Energy. His face, eyes, chest, and even palms are reddened with the uprush of holy emotion.

It is about two in the morning. Among extended silences and captivating discourses, an entire evening has passed. Suddenly, the Paramahamsa leaps to his feet. With hypersensitive perception, he discerns the tide rushing up the Ganges, still far south of the Temple Garden. For him, this natural event is a vivid image of Divine Manifestation—the ocean of the Absolute rushing mysteriously up the river of the relative. Emitting an ecstatic cry and throwing aside his wearing-cloth with the words "What a nuisance! Who needs it!" the Swan of Bliss rushes naked through the deserted temple courtyard to the stone embankment of the sacred river. Quite often Ramakrishna runs or strides powerfully through the Temple Garden late at night, overflowing with Divine Energy, appearing exactly like Goddess Kali, lost in Her perpetual Ecstasy. When the companions of Divine Love see him in this mood, their hair sometimes stands on end.

Tonight the companions are somewhat drowsy. We arise slowly, carefully tightening our cloths around our waists and strolling in a leisurely manner to the bathing *ghat* at the edge of the Ganges. The tidal bore has already passed by, with its exhilarating roar and wall of white water. Our Master is bent over with laughter: "Will the Divine Tide wait for you to don your conventional dress and move at your conventional pace? God manifests the spontaneous nature of a child. You must become childlike to encounter Divine Reality." We feel an unimaginable sense of freedom welling up within us in the company of this supremely happy and precocious child and emanation of Goddess Kali.

The naked sage now returns to his room, murmuring in an ecstatic mood: "A person becomes fully liberated during this present lifetime only by realizing that Mother is the Doer of all actions." Through bright moonlight, we walk side by side with the God-man, offering him support as he reels slightly with Divine Inebriation. We are swimming through the balmy, fragrant night air. We are moving through the radiant darkness of Mahakali.

The nectar of teaching continues to flow through Her child from the sublime Wisdom Mother, punctuated by rich silences and the lilting melodies of mystic hymns, their poetry of intensity catching our souls on fire. Sleep has simply fled. Still naked, the Paramahamsa is now sitting on his bed.

RAMAKRISHNA Is it possible to form even a faint conception of Divine Action or Divine Motivation? Mother creates, preserves, and dissolves countless finite forms, countless worlds. Can we even begin to imagine why? I always pray to Goddess Kali: "O Mother of the Universe! I feel absolutely no desire to reason or to understand. Please destroy with Your Diamond Thunderbolt the slightest impulse to discriminate or analyze, and grant me ecstatic love for Your beautiful Feet." Dear friends, do not enter Her sacred Temple and meditate before Her living Presence with eyes closed. Would you return to your native village and sit before your mother without looking at her? Open your eyes every moment to the mystery of Kali!

The Master picks up a jasmine garland that is resting beside him on a dark green plaintain leaf. He places it upon his own shoulders, as though he were a priest carefully decorating a sacred image. With his left hand, he now touches in descending succession the *chakras* of his subtle body—crown, forehead, throat, heart, and navel. We can distinctly feel this wisdom-energy flooding down into our own bodies, which are not essentially separate from his. We enter dynamic silence. The Master's sweet voice emerges from that silence, one with it.

RAMAKRISHNA Remain patient, beloved friends of God. One does not reach maturity immediately. Nothing can be achieved except at the appropriate time. If an abcess is lanced before it is soft, the result is not good. A sore bleeds if you remove the scab too soon. When the dry branches of a coconut palm drop to the ground, a mark is left on the trunk, indicating that once there was a branch at that level. The branches of worldly convention must dry up naturally and fall away of themselves, leaving only a mark—a mere semblance of ego, personality, individuality. No amount of pulling can remove a green palm branch. To be green or unripe is to identify the timeless awareness at the core of every experience with the functioning of your particular body and mind.

God is realized simply by following the path of Truth. Never remain satisfied with anything less than Truth. The commitment to what is true deteriorates subtly as one becomes a slave to social and religious conventions. Spit on public opinion! Orient solely to Divine Reality and attempt to please Mother alone. No doubt, one needs to make precise spiritual efforts, and for this purpose traditional practices are useful. One uses a sandalwood fan to generate a fragrant breeze on a sultry night, perhaps even dipping it in water for greater coolness. Thus we fast and keep vigil, repeating the glorious Divine Names—counting them with prayer beads or on our fingers, singing them to the accompaniment of drums and cymbals. We also practice simplification of desires and occasionally retire into seclusion to make room for selfless love, just as the expert fisherman throws spiced bait into a deep lake to attract the larger fish. But the manmade fan is joyfully set aside when the strong, cool southern breeze blows from the ocean, bearing the delicious perfume of many flowers. Every sense of personal effort then comes to an end.

You must not just listen with respect but actually assimilate such instruction. Experience the southern breeze! Do not just imagine how it might feel. The image that falls on a specially prepared photographic plate is retained. Thousands of images are reflected from a bare piece of glass, but not one of them becomes a photograph. This preparation, this film, is ecstatic love.

No amount of telling your beads can generate this transforming love. I once tore Hazra's rosary from his hand and threw it out the window. Whoever comes sincerely into this company of ecstatic lovers will have his consciousness awakened and illumined all at once, without bothering much about repeating *mantras* on prayer beads. This is why I often inscribe a *mantra* with my finger directly on the seeker's tongue—the repetition of the sacred syllables should be spontaneous and internal, not mechanical and external. Go to Calcutta and you will notice thousands of people telling their beads. Even the prostitutes are repeating *mantras* as they ply their trade. What good does it do? I complain to Mother about Hazra: "O blissful Kali, what an insensitive person he is! He lives in Your tangible, visible Presence here at the Temple Garden, yet still focuses attention entirely on rosary and *mantra,* meditating with eyes tightly closed."

The mind soaked in worldliness, filled with denial and indifference, is like a wet matchstick. Strike it even a thousand times and it will never burst into the flame of genuine comprehension. God will simply not appear within the heart of any person who acts like the sovereign master of his own world or the world of others. Mother cannot be realized without guilelessness and innocence. This is why some *paramahamsas* or *mahasiddhas* enjoy keeping five or ten children around them. This is why I cavort and run through the temple grounds with the young boys—climbing trees, swinging on vines, playing leap-frog.

Once, lost entirely in this childlike mood, I was chasing crows from the trees of the Panchavati with a small bow and arrow. It reminded me of Rama's magical arrow, which chased an arrogant crow everywhere, through every dimension of heaven and earth. The crow finally becomes humble and flies back to Lord Rama to seek refuge from His arrow. This powerful Divine Incarnation immediately seizes the bird and swallows it. The terrified creature slowly opens its eyes. It is sitting comfortably on its own nest, realizing at last that the entire universe exists inside God, deep within the heart of Rama.

As I was playing this way, a rather conservative companion arrived. I could see he was aghast to find me shooting at crows. I threw down the bow and ran like a child to embrace my friend, crying: "I want to visit the zoological garden to observe the lions. Mother, in Her majestic Aspect as Goddess Durga, rides on a ferocious lion. I entered *samadhi* just seeing the stone lions outside the Asiatic Museum. I have never encountered a living lion." My friend hired a carriage and we left immediately for Calcutta. It is good to take direct action under all circumstances. When you do anything, do it wholeheartedly. One should perspire profusely while dancing and singing the beautiful Names of God, just as humble laborers sweat to earn their daily wage.

DISCIPLE Beloved Paramahamsa, what is the real function of image-worship?

RAMAKRISHNA The moment you glance at a portrait of your father and mother who have passed away from the visible world, you suddenly remember being in their presence. It is an experience of complete recall—sounds, fragrances, colors, tastes, tender words, embraces, teachings, scoldings. When one engages with an icon of God through the intensity of ceremonial worship, the nature of Divine Reality is revealed in a similar flash of total Presence. It is this flash, which may be calmly intuitive or intensely ecstatic, that permits the worshiper to know that his worship has been successful or, in other terms, has been accepted by God.

True worship is not an automatic mechanism. One must be prayerful and attentive, selfless and free from limited concerns. Some adepts experience the flash of Divine Acceptance as rays of light, streaming from the eyes of the sacred *murti*—luminous tendrils, like living flames, that touch the food offerings as well as the various *chakras* in the subtle body of the worshiper. Other advanced practitioners encounter this mysterious Divine Response simply as a profound state of tranquillity or transcendence. The spiritual experience of each conscious being is unique, but each one is communing with precisely the same Divine Reality. Jealousy and malice need never exist among sincere seekers and lovers of Truth.

Do you know what Divine Forms and formless Divine Attributes are like? They resemble transparent bubbles rising in an infinite expanse of clear water. The water is so pure that it seems like open space. The *avatara* is the most impressive of these bubbles. The primordial power of Pure Consciousness plays freely through the teaching, the daily life, and even the slightest movements of an *avatara,* who is really a bubble as large as the entire ocean. Yet the Divine Incarnation appears humbly and moves gracefully, remaining in harmony with the deepest values of a particular religious tradition.

One approaches God most intimately not by worship but by investigating directly who or what this I-consciousness really is. The instinctive *I am* could be considered the primary image or icon of Divine Reality. But Mother must give you eyes of Divine Love before you can behold the Divine Face. The most fruitful approach is not philosophical analysis or contemplative introspection but passionate love of God, love for the sweet sake of love alone, not wishing for any reward apart from the supreme joy and fulfillment of loving. You should not even desire beatific visions of Divinity or high states of concentration and absorption. Simply be a child of the Mother.

One never knows who may be truly advanced in the Way of Love. I have witnessed a prostitute dying in the holy Ganga, retaining her clear and prayerful consciousness to the very last breath. Many dedicated worshipers who lead upright lives will not be able to attain such a sublime state at the crucial moment of death.

DISCIPLE Revered Master, what is the true role of the guru?

RAMAKRISHNA The mystic guide is one's very best friend, not an authoritarian superior. This feeling of intimacy is mutual between master and disciple. It is a beautiful relationship, a providential meeting, the intertwining and merging of two souls as one. The guru is the matchmaker who arranges the marriage between the soul and its Supreme Beloved. When beatific vision dawns for the disciple and his chosen aspect of Divine Reality is about to manifest, the guru appears— in physical, visionary, or intuitive form—and lovingly introduces the aspirant to God. After this gracious introduction, the form or subtle presence of the guru disappears into the aspect of Divinity which is being realized. You will then discover, to your great amazement, that the guru was none other than Divine Reality, reaching out to you palpably with helpful instruction and tender encouragement. Your gratitude will be infinite.

Remain dedicated to the guide and spiritual friend you genuinely respect and adore, enjoying full knowledge that this human person is simply the liberative art of the Divine Power. The particular aspect of Divinity you are approaching under the patient guidance of the guru is, in turn, simply the liberative art of nondual Reality. The guru is the golden thread which, followed carefully through the complex tapestry of your life, leads to God, the Weaver of this tapestry. Before accepting him, observe and test the guru by day and by night. Then, once you are satisfied, take the firm attitude: "Even if my guru spends all day in the tavern drinking wine, he remains for me the boundless reservoir of Divine Bliss."

You know I cannot bear to be addressed with this solemn title, *guru*. *Akhanda satchidananda*—indivisible Reality, Awareness, and Joy—is the only guru, the only teacher. I have no disciples. Please do not call me *baba*, either. I am an eternal child of the Mother. How could I be anyone's spiritual father?

Persons with a tendency toward pride often inquire whether a guru is really necessary for spiritual development. I respond: "It takes a full day to travel up the Ganga to Chinsurah by country boat, but only a few hours by steamer. Were you to ply the powerful current yourself in a small bark, without much knowledge gained from direct experience, you might never reach Chinsurah. The humble, worthy, qualified guide is a country boat. The God-realized sage is a great steamer."

The somatic, moral, and spiritual disciplines to which the aspirant voluntarily and joyously submits are the daily work of guru and disciple together. These instructions and the energy to sustain their practice need to be renewed when the disciple becomes forgetful. This transmission must be clarified and intensified as the disciple reaches higher levels of understanding and experience. A principal concern of the guide is to help the aspirant remove from his mind even the slightest attachment to any results of these concentrated efforts. The mind can never become pure while it is projecting some particular outcome or is distracted by some dogmatic presupposition.

This process of guidance is like curing a disease under the strict regimen of a skilled physician. Medicine is carefully prescribed and conscientiously taken at precise times during the day and night. The prescription is changed as the cure progresses. But medicine is not designed to remain in the system permanently. When the body is healthy again, it sustains and balances itself. In this way, religious disciplines and suppositions eventually disappear into natural spiritual balance and spontaneity. The guru retains the regular practice of certain disciplines only to be able to prescribe and demonstrate them to others who need medicine.

One may ask: "Why are we not just instantly released by the mercy of God from the suffering of the world?" This is a grave misunderstanding. The present realm of embodiment is actually a compassionate place for healing, filled with experiences rich in spiritual meaning. Mother will liberate the soul from any sense of existing in a separate world, as a separate body and a separate mind, when the cure has been completed, when the addiction to egocentric existence has been overcome. Once a person consciously registers his name in this hospital, he can no longer run away. Wherever he runs, he is still inside this miraculous institution. The doctors are the realized masters—known and unknown, visible and invisible. No compassionate doctor will sign the release papers of a patient who is still infected by disease.

But why speculate so much about the nature of human existence? Such speculation easily becomes obsession. It is more than sufficient for genuine advancement to love the Mother of the Universe, humbly and joyfully acknowledging all existence as Her impenetrable Mercy and Mystery. Too much reasoning and analysis throws the mind into confusion. Books are knots. We cannot be nourished by abstractions. We must drink clear water, drawing it carefully from the surface of the spring. If, becoming too eager, you reach into the spring clumsily with your vessel and stir up silt from the bottom, the water becomes muddy and undrinkable. When one approaches Divine Reality with unalloyed devotion, one does not become clumsy in this way. Pray to Mother for pure love alone, for transparency of mind, for delicacy and subtlety of spirit.

DISCIPLE Blessed Master, why practice ceremonial worship and other formal religious disciplines?

RAMAKRISHNA Devotion expressed through traditional ceremonies and disciplines is like traveling to a nearby village in a roundabout way along a winding river. During the monsoon season, when ceaseless rain has flooded the streams and they inundate the countryside, one no longer needs to follow the ancient, winding course of the river. One can travel by small boat directly to whichever village one wishes. *Prema,* ecstatic love, is the monsoon. Then you will not only love Mother as your nearest and dearest, you will experience Divine Reality to be closer than your own most intimate, inward being. You will become unable to engage regularly in ceremonies and disciplines.

When entering *samadhi,* or absorption in God-consciousness, one feels like a fish released from a small jar into the vast, powerful current of Mother Ganga. One swims everywhere with perfect freedom and spontaneity. There are no partitions, no boundaries. This sense of release is experienced constantly by the ecstatic lover. But no one should speak glibly about attaining *prema.* This love is so overwhelming that you will lose consciousness of the conventional world. You will not be able to entertain the slightest feeling of personal ownership, not even toward the body, which is the most precious and jealously guarded possession of most persons. There will no longer be any instinctive notion that the body or the mind constitutes your being. To awaken *prema,* one must humbly seek out those who have become entirely sanctified by love. First taste a drop of this nondual love, subjectless and objectless. Later on you can practice some formal prayer and meditation. Such is the teaching that emanates from this place—*prema, prema, prema.*

Our Master places his hand on his heart. Tears of joy flow from the outer corners of his eyes. Ecstatic love streams from his very pores. We are being drenched by this monsoon. Every cell of our body and strand of our awareness is soaked with his pure love. Ramakrishna has informed us that wandering spirits—confused beings, haunting the earthly plane— often cry out to him: "Please go away! We are being scorched by the blazing light of your purity."

RAMAKRISHNA *I* and *mine*—that alone is spiritual ignorance. It ignores Reality in favor of personal and collective ego. Right now, invoke your most penetrating insight! If only for a moment, you will realize what you call I-consciousness to be fundamentally none other than limitless, timeless awareness. Look clearly! Are you really this body? Are you really this culturally conditioned mind? If you are uncompromising, you will inevitably recognize that you are none of these habitual structures. You will sense spontaneously that you have never been the originator or the performer of any action whatsoever. You are sheer awareness, free from routines, free from both faults and virtues. You cannot be essentially characterized as righteous or unright-eous, as liberated or bound.

It is only from the perspective of spiritual ignorance that any person calculates: "This is gold of a certain purity and that is mere brass." The person of radical insight joyously affirms: "It is all gold—Pure Consciousness, absolutely unalloyed." Listen to a song.

> The beauty of your face,
> beloved Lord Chaitanya,
> glows brighter than gold.
> A smile from your lips
> illuminates the universe.
> When you shine in the heart,
> who will care to contemplate
> even a million full moons
> gathered in the autumn sky?

Precious companions, Divine Reality alone exists, graciously manifest as all we experience, including the experiencer. It is through the completely unveiled human being, however, that one encounters the fullest manifestation of Divinity. God is directly and expressively present through the heart of an awakened lover who laughs, cries, dances, and sings with Divine Ecstasy.

Our stay in the conventional world of space and time is equivalent to a brief, three-day visit. O companions, be like a troupe of wandering minstrels who appear unexpectedly, play their music passionately, and disappear without a trace. What do I care if this world accepts or respects me? I consider myself a mere speck of dust on the feet of the true lovers.

The Paramahamsa rises and bows low before each of us, one by one, placing his head at our feet as Jesus washed the feet of his companions, illuminating their minds with his humility and love. Ramakrishna has confided to his inner circle: "The Divine Reality which manifested perfectly through Jesus and Chaitanya manifests as well through the form now before you." Years ago, our Master became an avid admirer of the holy life and teachings of Lord Jesus. Once, while a liberal-minded Hindu gentleman was reading to him from the Christian Gospel, the eyes of the blissful sage became fixed upon a European painting of the Virgin Mother. The Divine Child came forth from the icon as a ray of light that penetrated the heart center of Ramakrishna. For three days he could not even enter the Kali Temple, so immersed he remained in the Christ-power. On the third day, while wandering through the wilderness region of the Temple Garden, the child of the Mother encountered the child of the Father— beautiful large eyes shining, countenance serene, complexion fair. The Great Swan immediately heard these words resound from the depth of his being: "Behold the Christ! While remaining in timeless union with the Father, he shed his life's blood for the redemption of the world. Behold Jesus! He is Divine Love incarnate." The two transparent images, Jesus and Ramakrishna, merged into one, and then dissolved into imageless Reality. Since this experience, which elevated our Master into the same union with Divine Reality which culminates both Vedic and Tantric paths, Ramakrishna has bowed his head at the very mention of the beautiful Name of Jesus. Two of his young disciples, Sashi and Sarat, were revealed to him in transcendental vision as among the historical companions of Jesus.

A Christian monk visited the Temple Garden. Years before, he had clearly perceived the face of Ramakrishna during prayerful meditation. This monk patiently searched the *ashramas* of India for this unforgettable face until he arrived at the retreat of the famous Pavhari Baba of Ghazipur, who keeps a photograph of Ramakrishna. The devoted Christian lover immediately recognized the holy face from his vision and set out for Dakshineswar. When he arrived, he recounted his experience to our Master and removed his ordinary outer garments to reveal the ocher robe of renunciation which he wore secretly. The Great Swan stood up in ecstasy, tears rolling down his cheeks, and entered *samadhi*. The humble monk knelt before him with palms joined—weeping, trembling, and gazing intently at the smiling, bearded countenance. Later this profound Christian, born within an Indian brahmin family, reported to the astonished companions of Divine Love: "Today I have seen the one to whom I have prayed during so many years of wandering, solitary life. In the blessed form of Ramakrishna Paramahamsa, I have directly perceived Lord Jesus of Nazareth."

RAMAKRISHNA Naren once asked me: "Why do you bow and offer your salutations before the modern temple of the Brahmo Samaj? The intensity of spiritual practice there is weak and consequently the power of Divine Presence is lacking." I answered him instantaneously, without the slightest forethought: "Please do not speak this way! People worship God according to their levels and temperaments. The sight of Keshab's temple invokes God in my mind. The fire of God-consciousness then breaks out and I bow in ecstatic adoration. God is present, not partially but fully, wherever people sincerely speak or even think about Divine Reality, whether or not they worship intensely. At that consecrated place, no matter how insignificant it may appear, the power and radiance of all holy sites of pilgrimage are subtly manifest. It becomes a living focal point for ultimate human aspiration. Every grand or humble place of worship has this effect upon a spiritually sensitive person."

One must become mad with love. True disciples cherish such devotion for their qualified guide that even the sight of the guru's secular neighbors throws them into ecstasy. Through their master's outward form, they enter intimate communion with Divine Love. One must catch on fire! I once plunged into *samadhi* just watching an umbrella being folded. Why? Because it reminded me of the withdrawal and concentration of awareness within the heart. I once became absorbed in God-consciousness simply by watching a master drummer playing his *tablas,* entirely one with the music.

A lover of Krishna noticed some *babla* trees and was drawn into ecstasy by suddenly recalling the *babla*-wood handles of the spades used in the garden of the Krishna Temple. Krishna-consciousness, or sheer Divine Love, would flood the body and mind of Krishna's consort, the supremely passionate Radha, at the mere sight of a dark thundercloud or a deep blue sari. Before her eyes would flash the vision of her Lord— sapphire in color, with radiant smile. She would then become inconsolable in her longing for union and cry out like a mad person: "Krishna, Krishna! Where is my beloved? Krishna is my breath, my life, my heart, my mind, my soul."

VISITOR But, sir, is such madness a desirable state?

RAMAKRISHNA What absurdity are you suggesting? Is the magnificent, ecstatic madness of Radha, who is the very embodiment of Divine Love, to be compared with the insanity of unbalanced minds or with the ordinary madness that worldly people exhibit in their relentless pursuit of self-centered pleasure and power? The madness that you call being sensible is indeed an undesirable state. Have you never heard mention of the love-madness and knowledge-madness displayed by the saints?

Ah, but one cannot even be confident of the existence of Divine Reality unless the heart becomes pure. Many who think they believe in

God are engaged in mere talk. They have heard vaguely from someone that Divinity exists or that every event occurs only through Divine Will. But this is not their inner conviction, based on direct experience. It is like children swearing by God when they play. They have overheard their elderly aunts and uncles using God's Name while quarreling or gossiping. Therefore, never accept my words without your own personal experience and conviction. That would amount to mere hypocrisy.

The person who defines himself and everything around him in terms of habitual, conventional categories may even feel an occasional yearning for God or Truth. But this mood is momentary. It lasts about as long as a drop of water on a red-hot iron pan. The water is what we need to irrigate the garden of the heart. The hot pan is egocentric desire, conventional understanding, habitual perception. Dearest companions, you must actually perceive the golden peacock feather in Lord Krishna's crown, shining like a lightning flash within a dark blue thunderhead. You must become the peacock of ecstasy, dancing in Krishna's holy presence, spreading its brilliant tailfeathers in the rapture of limitless joy. Radha used to cry aloud: "Please inscribe upon my body and my heart only Krishna's precious Name."

Repeating Radha's cry of love, the Paramahamsa leaps to his feet in ecstasy. He tears away the shirt we put on him against the predawn chill. His body hairs are standing on end as if electrified. We gaze up at his dynamic figure in astonishment. He is fully manifesting Krishna-consciousness as the ecstatic Radha, clearly demonstrating the full intensity of love-madness and knowledge-madness, both fused within a single form. In the most captivating tones we have ever experienced, Ramakrishna sings. Tremors pass through our limbs.

> Krishna, my sole Beloved!
> Where have You gone with my life?
> O friends, O companions of Love,
> bring my tender Krishna to me!
> Then alone will you be friends.
> Or take my inert form to Him,
> and I will be your eternal slave.

The God-man takes his seat again, chest glistening, wet with tears. We place a cloth around his naked shoulders. He is still drunk with the wine of Love, stammering over and over: "O Mother, what people call living beings are only pillowcases, manifesting various colors and patterns. Nothing but pillowcases, filled with the consciousness which is Yours alone." Gradually, the sage returns to spiritual sobriety.

RAMAKRISHNA Whether you remain caught in conventionality or unveil your innate freedom depends solely upon Mother's inscrutable Will. She is the gold in all, although gold is often hidden under deep layers of clay. Her Power alone keeps various minds under various conditions. When She calls someone to Herself, according to Her own sweet Will, this person becomes totally liberated, even while still living on earth. It is like the mother who calls her children home at mealtime from playing tag in the village lanes and fields. They have absolutely no choice but to return. If they are dusty or muddy, she washes them.

Mother causes certain fortunate persons to become unbearably restless to meet God directly. This is nothing like ordinary religious obsession, which is bound by doctrinal abstractions and one-sided devotion. It is sheer, naked longing for Truth. One feels like a person whose head is being held underwater, struggling desperately to rise for a breath of air. It is like the desperation of a clerk who has lost his job and has a large family to support. He makes his rounds of the various offices every day, ready to accept any opportunity. He would never consider resting, even for a single afternoon, nor can he become complacent, even for a moment. He has difficulty sleeping at night and wakes up spontaneously before dawn. When a comparable humility and restless desperation arise in the center of your being, you have become a genuine seeker of God, a *sadhaka*.

Can the fashionably dressed person, seated comfortably, one leg casually crossed over the other, chewing betel leaf and gazing into the sky, twirling his moustache—can such a person attain God-consciousness? But the fact is that one cannot always tell from looking at external appearances how spiritually advanced someone may be. All plain cakes look alike when displayed together in the market, but some have fillings of rich cream.

Every possible confusion and misjudgment comes to an end once one authentically realizes that Mother alone is manifesting as atheist, agnostic, believer, *sadhaka*, and sage. God alone is manifest as whatever appears to be good and whatever appears to be bad, as both the real and whatever is discriminated to be unreal. God alone is present during the states of waking, dreaming, and dreamless sleep. Divine Reality constitutes all phenomena, and Divine Reality is beyond all possible conditions of experience and categories of existence as well.

One cannot attain even a drop of spiritual awakening through rationalization or procrastination. Nor can anyone advance in contemplation who calculates or speculates obsessively about any subject whatsoever. Persons who are intoxicated and even suffocated by limited forms of enjoyment become very philosophical about spiritual progress. While doing nothing, they proclaim: "Everything unfolds at the proper time. One cannot rush or force the realization of God." But true *sadhakas* even become angry with Divine Reality. They cry out passionately: "O great Mother, You have created me, so You must reveal Yourself to me!"

Spiritually unawakened persons are like certain poor villagers who live in windowless clay huts. There is scant natural light inside, and they can barely see outside at all, as a curtain covers the doorway. But *mahasiddhas*, those persons who move through the universe after victoriously attaining supreme knowledge, are living in a vast mansion of crystal. For them, there is nothing but light, inside and outside. Every experience whatsoever then becomes an experience of Divine Bliss.

One cannot even begin to establish the mind in God-consciousness without developing the contemplative art of entering silence and abiding peacefully there, even when surrounded by complicated family affairs or the busy marketplace. Yet during the early stages, one certainly must retire into solitude for two or three days at a time. The goldsmith melts gold in order to make ornaments. But this process must be uninterrupted, or else the gold hardens again. Your heart must become molten gold. Conventional people needlessly yet habitually dissipate the mental power by which the gold is melted. They do not notice how spiritually anemic and debilitated they have become. A person possessed by a wandering spirit cries out: "I am perfectly all right." A drunken man insists: "I am more sober than you are."

Initially, the regular practice of contemplative disciplines to renew the subtle energy and to purify and strengthen the subtle nervous system is absolutely necessary. God exists like butter in milk, which can only be tasted by patiently churning the milk after letting it sit quietly before sunrise. Later, one can keep the butter afloat in the water of the world without the slightest danger that God-realization will be dissipated.

One should humbly receive instruction and guidance from an adept. The doctor does not prescribe medicine at the patient's dictation. Be open to the compassionate words of the guide. I advise certain companions to meditate completely naked at midnight. God exists like the stars, which cannot be perceived during daylight hours but only appear when night falls. To see God, one must enter a state of consciousness very different from daily routine. Later, one will be able to commune with Divine Reality in every context.

When certain persons come to this room entangled in limited passions, I tell them to increase their passion infinitely. To others, I recommend simply the discipline of Truth—speak only what you truly think and know. Still others I remind that *adyashakti*, the Primordial Power, emanates in a special sense through the female form. Their practice is to contemplate and worship the Goddess in every woman. I request other seekers to meditate this way: "O Lord, You are the lotus of Divine Love and I am the bee. You are the ocean of Divine Delight and I am the fish." Men or women with a particularly devotional temperament should cry out: "O Lord, You are the Sultan and I am Your most beloved dancing maiden. I am Your umbrella, Your prayer carpet. O Krishna, I am Your anklet, Your flute."

Even the simplest action can become a powerful discipline. When you partake of food, for instance, you should experience the Divine Energy, focused at your heart, accepting and transforming this sacred offering. Just to recite a traditional prayer before the meal is not enough. If you dwell even slightly on the primitive sense that you are taking food for personal survival, then you are spiritually weakened rather than nourished.

The ultimate purpose of all such practices is that the mind recognize its own essential silence, unity, and peace, no matter how active or dispersed it may become under any given circumstances. All the subtle energies of one's being come into spontaneous alignment when the mind unveils the diamond of its intrinsic nature. The *paramahamsa*—the Great Swan, the unveiled human being—clearly perceives that Mother Kali alone gives the mind its negative as well as positive tendencies. God has created both the mango tree, which yields exquisitely sweet fruit, and the hog plum, which produces terribly sour fruit. The *paramahamsa* joyously realizes that all fruits—sweet or sour, positive or negative, real or unreal—are the glorious radiance of *mahamaya*, the Mother Power that projects and veils. This is the truly profound teaching. No one can ever establish a sect, an organization, or a system upon this basis.

Too much study of religious doctrine, even too much reading of the sublime ancient scriptures, can do more harm than good. The secret key of spiritual practice is the ability to keep the essence of the scriptures constantly in mind. Then one can dive deep into the ocean of this essence, without being distracted by yet another philosophical treatise, yet another scriptural commentary. Sounding the depths of the perennial teaching, day and night, one then actually realizes God-consciousness. A *sadhu* once wandered into the Temple Garden carrying a large book. Opening the pages and smiling, he showed me that they were filled with a single phrase—OM RAMA, OM RAMA, OM RAMA. When one repeats the glorious Divine Name Rama just once, with profound emotion, one receives the results of ten million scriptural recitations. The astrological almanac forecasts rainfall for the entire year, but you can squeeze the pages with all your strength and not get a single drop of water.

The sublime Kali, Goddess of Transcendent Insight, revealed to me the essence of the abstruse teaching of Vedanta: "*Brahman* alone is real. There is only supreme Reality. Apart from *brahman*, nothing actually exists—either partially real or merely illusory." The essence of the *Bhagavad Gita* can be discovered by repeating the term *gita* ten times. The word one begins to hear is *tyagi*, which signifies renunciation—radically divesting the mind of all cultural and personal assumptions by dwelling in nondual Reality alone. Mother also unveiled to me the essence of the tantric path: "Renounce conceptual limits and strive for ultimate realization. Experience your body, mind, and innermost awareness as God alone."

O beloved companions, allow me to reassure you that realization is possible for every human being without exception. Accept no teaching of exclusivity. Impose no limits whatsoever upon humankind, for the human being is ultimately God, transparently at play. But the milk of knowledge and realization comes through the udder. The *avatara* is that udder. Who can understand the mystery of complete Divine Incarnation? Can a one-gallon jug hold ten gallons? Inquire intensively about God like the calf that bumps the udder with its nose; then simply drink. Arise and meditate joyously during the middle of the night—at three or so, around the time it is now—and again at dawn and once more during the final mystic moments of dusk. This will be sufficient.

"And come here!" Smiling, the blissful sage holds his right hand, palm upward, at the center of his chest. "Visit this place, so that every doubt may be resolved. Any person who comes here for God-realization, for direct knowledge of Reality, will have his desire fulfilled. Let me repeat it very clearly. These men and women will definitely have their exalted desire fulfilled."

A tremendous joy and confidence wells up in me at this moment, precisely at the center of my chest, at the same level where Ramakrishna is still holding his open hand. Spontaneously, I prostrate before the Great Swan, offering my secret *mantra* and my rosary of *rudraksha* seeds. My forehead and the strand of one hundred eight beads are resting upon his beautifully shaped feet. As I rise to a kneeling position before the bed, Ramakrishna enters ecstasy and places his right foot on my head and his left foot on my chest. His touch tingles yet soothes. He cries out in a tender voice: "O Mother, let him have illumination! Let him become continuously aware of his own true nature!" I lose outward consciousness in a blaze of light. Inwardly, I am perceiving most clearly, without visualizing any form, that Ramakrishna Paramahamsa embraces all aspects of Divine Reality. Coming forth from mystic union, I am spontaneously repeating *shanti, shanti, shanti.* The Master is now feeding me sweets with his own hands and whispering into my right ear.

RAMAKRISHNA You have learned to fly. You will not have to practice many more formal disciplines. Just visit Dakshineswar whenever you can, bearing a small offering. Your life will be to serve the lovers of God in every way. To behold an ecstatic lover is equivalent to a vision of the Supreme Beloved. Offer whoever comes to you sanctified food and cool water. This service of humankind will be equal in spiritual power to repeating the Divine Name while fasting and keeping vigil. It will be sufficient to meditate now and then upon this form here before you. Whatever aspect of Divine Reality that may appeal to anyone can be found inside this transparent case. If you meditate sincerely upon a certain ideal, you will actually acquire its particular nature. Meditate on me and attain universality.

Before you came to the Temple Garden, you did not know who you really are. Now you will know. The One Divine Presence, through the transparent form of the guide, alone can make you know. You still have impurities. They will gradually be cleared away. Do not become ensnared in religious obsession or self-concern of any kind. Mother tells me She will make you perform some teaching work for Her. She can create great teachers from mere straws, you know.

After an extended silence, Mahendra asks earnestly: "Blessed Master, how can we possibly hope to realize God? As you always say, even if a single fiber remains unaligned, the thread cannot pass through the eye of the needle."

Ramakrishna laughs aloud and replies to his cherished disciple, the recorder of his conversations for the modern world: "Yes, if you find even a single hair in the food you are chewing, you spit out the entire mouthful." All of us are laughing now, healing various forms of hesitation and doubt. Our laughter pours into the empty temple courtyard, illuminated by the light of the setting moon. Mahendra continues to reveal his doubts, presenting his symptoms to this great physician of souls. "Beloved Paramahamsa, perhaps as a result of my European education, I simply cannot accept the doctrine of reincarnation, although I understand it intellectually." Laughing once again, sweetly and tenderly, the Great Swan responds with a stream of enlightening words that transmit not only mental clarity but evolutionary energy.

RAMAKRISHNA It makes absolutely no difference, my dear, what doctrines you accept or reject. It is sufficient to know that absolutely any structure, any process, any event is possible in this mysterious Divine Creation. Practitioners who hold specific doctrinal views are often lacking in the true openness that accepts every Divine Possibility. Never allow the thought to cross your mind that your ideas are the only true ones and the ideas of other persons are false. This openmindedness will be much more difficult to sustain than some particular notion of reincarnation. When you have attained this selfless openness, the Wisdom Goddess will clarify the career of the soul by opening your inward wisdom-eye.

What can human beings understand of Divine Activity? Reincarnation represents only one point of view, whereas the facets and dimensions of Mother's creativity are infinite. My attitude is simply this. Never attempt to describe or to circumscribe God in any way, through any notion whatsoever. I do not give a single thought to any structure or procedure of the universe but meditate on the Source of the Universe.

Once Goddess Kali unveiled in transcendental vision the reservoir in my boyhood village. I saw a beautiful man, shining with sanctity, push back the thin film of green algae, fill his transparent vessel, and drink. The water was clear as crystal. Mother then explained to me that the crystal clarity and intrinsic luminosity of *akhanda satchidananda*— indivisible Reality, Awareness, and Bliss—remains concealed from ordinary eyes by a fine covering of *maya,* which is like algae. Simply remove this insubstantial film and experience Pure Consciousness. However, even if you throw a large brick into a pond covered with algae, though you catch a glimpse of clear water, very soon the green growth comes dancing back and covers the surface once more.

For me there is no covering, no veiling, no *maya.* I have seen with my own eyes that the brilliant luminosity of *satchidananda* is manifest as the very physical body, including its sexual organs. I can clearly perceive the Divine Energy at play everywhere—even through the sexual intercourse of the stray dogs that haunt the jungles of the Temple Garden. There is neither high nor low, clean nor unclean.

Sentient beings are conscious only through Divine Consciousness. I can contemplate Mother's infinite Consciousness at play even through schools of minnows, glinting as they turn in the morning sunlight. I experience intimately that the entire universe, including inanimate existence, is saturated with Consciousness, just as the soil becomes totally soaked during the rainy season. Although there is this ceaseless vision and exalted realization, I never feel proud. I can tell you with complete honesty that I never feel even a trace of vanity or specialness. Lord Krishna said to his beloved companion, Arjuna: "Friend, if you find anyone who has acquired even one of the eight occult powers, know for certain he will not be able to realize God in this lifetime." Why? Because the exercise of miraculous power produces subtle pride, and God-realization is not possible as long as there is even the faintest suggestion of self-importance. I used to clean the public bathrooms at the Temple Garden with my long hair, praying fervently: "O Mother, please remove from my mind any pride of being born into the priestly caste."

Dwell in Truth alone, dear friends, and you will realize panoramic God-consciousness. Success is assured if you really plunge. Only Mother exists, you know. Whenever any description of God is attempted, no matter how subtle, the result is a false sense of duality.

The nearer you come to God, the more you will realize that Divine Reality possesses neither name nor form nor attribute. It is simply inconceivable and indescribable. Whatever one encounters in this universe is the mystic union of *purusha,* the essential stillness of Consciousness, with *prakriti,* the omnidynamic power of Consciousness, which both projects and dissolves. The very universe is therefore in the state of union or God-realization.

As for abstract, philosophical reasoning—I spit on it! Why should I become dry as driftwood through engaging in rote dialectical thinking, in theoretical discrimination between the Real and what is imagined to be unreal? Why should anything be regarded as unreal? All is my blissful Mother. May this mind be flooded with pure love for the Lotus Feet of Kali! May She pursue Her beautiful Play as *I* and *Thou* within this heart eternally! Sometimes I call out to Mother: "You are truly none other than I. I am truly none other than You." But then She takes me higher and I can only cry: "You are You alone. You alone are You." Within that exalted atmosphere, there is no trace of any I-consciousness.

Pleasure and pain, as well as joy and sorrow, are inevitable when the soul accepts embodiment. This is true for sages no less than for unawakened persons. But no matter how intensely the mature lover experiences the rising and falling waves of human existence, he always retains nondual awareness and enjoys immediate access to the ecstasy of Divine Love. God-consciousness neither comes nor goes, neither increases nor diminishes. Simply awaken and embrace the God-consciousness that belongs to you naturally. You will experience precisely the same ineffable delight that I am experiencing right now. Boundless Divine Bliss lies below the surface of your being—like a vein of pure gold in the bedrock beneath your house, like an underground stream of pure water beneath forbidding desert sands. What covers or obscures this natural bliss-consciousness is simply the projecting and veiling power of Reality—the Divine Maya, the Play of the Great Mother, Her Cosmic Magic that sparkles as countless evolving worlds.

The person of knowledge, the *jñani,* recognizes the universe as unreal in the sense of being totally insubstantial. This is like the yogi living in the Himalayas who experiences Mother Ganga flowing in one direction only. But the mature among the mature—the *vijñani,* the nondualistic lover—is like someone who lives near the ocean. Here the holy river flows in both directions, manifesting both ebb tide and flood tide. Supreme Reality is real and the insubstantial universe as well is real. These mysterious tidal surges, as Absolute and relative, are the ebb and flow of Divine Ecstasy. This play is not the product of egocentric desire. The enlightened lover swims joyfully in this bidirectional river of God-consciousness—sometimes being swept by the ebb tide into the open ocean of the Absolute, other times sailing upstream with the flood tide of the relative. Sometimes the ecstatic lover sounds the deeps and other times plays like a child on the surface. The way of knowledge is full of brilliance. The path of love is drenched with sweetness. The *vijñani* embraces both simultaneously. This is the radical teaching of my blissful Mother.

The *jñani* contemplates the fact that fire exists potentially in wood, and through great effort succeeds in kindling the fire of knowledge. The *vijñani* effortlessly boils water over that fire, cooks rice, and distributes nourishment to humankind. To experience the Absolute directly is spiritual maturity, but the mature among the mature intimately converse and play with *satchidananda*—miraculously enjoying Absolute Being, Absolute Consciousness, and Absolute Bliss as Divine Child, Divine Friend, Divine Beloved. The last word in maturity is Mother-worship. There is not the slightest duality in this childlike play with Mother Reality. It is God meeting and enjoying God, not just transcendentally but through living beings on earth.

Supreme Reality alone exists—as *brahman,* the Pure Consciousness within and beyond all finite forms of consciousness, and as *shakti,* the primordial, evolutionary Divine Energy. They are not two. *Brahman* and *shakti* are like the snake and its smoothly flowing motion, like milk and its whiteness, like water and its wetness. When considering water, one inevitably thinks of its wetness. When contemplating the wetness of water, one inevitably thinks of the water itself. Precisely the same is true of the Absolute and the relative, which are indifferentiable in essence. The Absolute is inevitably expressed by the relative, and the relative is inevitably contained by the Absolute. *Shakti* is the creative Mother-Father God, the fount of revelation. *Brahman* is the inconceivable, indescribable nature of Reality. Through these lips, Goddess Kali now teaches that *brahman* and *shakti* are one.

Whatever you may think, hear or see—during common awareness or during meditative states of consciousness—is simply Mother Mahamaya, or Divine Creativity. Your very sense experience is therefore already pure worship. Where is the harm, then, in chewing betel leaf, eating fish, enjoying a smoke, rubbing the body with fragrant oil, or tasting the sweet experience of conjugal delight? What will one achieve be renouncing simple, legitimate pleasures and becoming a stern, proud, argumentative ascetic? The essential practice is to renounce, moment by moment, any sense of separation from God—any sense of the personal, the private, the uniquely individual, the separate, the superior. One is then living solely within the Mother—not within the abstract, manmade categories called *world* and *self.*

Men and women are beautiful masks. Behind them all is the same Divine Power, Mother Kundalini, who rises up gradually through the six subtle centers of this precious human body, giving each person a unique flavor and intensity, unveiling through each living being a unique degree of Divine Manifestation.

DISCIPLE O Ramakrishna Paramahamsa, please bestow your Grace upon us.

RAMAKRISHNA Please never say such a thing! I am only Mother's child. Address God with a guileless heart: "O Mother, reveal Yourself to me, here and now!" Weep and dive deep. How can anyone discover the mystic pearl while merely swimming on the surface of the ocean? You absolutely must dive. Then you will be able to experience the unimaginable abundance of Divine Grace that is always present.

The less people know about your contemplative practices, the better. Make your plunge in inwardness and solitude, even when surrounded by the busy world. Meditate on your bed, inside the mosquito net— people will assume that you are sleeping comfortably. If you develop enough confidence in the infinite power of God's name, you will not need to travel anywhere on pilgrimage. The distinction between those on the periphery and those in the center of my *mandala* is simply this: members of the inner circle are intensely receptive to Divine Grace, whereas members of the outer circle manifest a slight spiritual ego by thinking that realization can occur only through their own stern efforts and formal practices. It is the usual attitude of beginners in religion to worship the Divine Presence out of fear or with an obsessive sense of sinfulness and unworthiness. This is not your way. Please sing constantly about God-realization. Express Divine Joy alone through this human form.

The process of God-realization is greatly accelerated if you accept sincerely what every sacred tradition reveals and teaches about God or Truth. The cow that carefully selects only certain grasses does not give an abundance of milk, whereas the milk of the cow that grazes on every kind of grass and plant comes in torrents, although it may have a strange odor and need to be boiled. Such is the case with the adept practitioner, or *sadhaka,* who enthusiastically accepts the holy words and sacraments of all religions. The abundantly flowing milk of his realization must be boiled over the fire of unitive knowledge.

Beware of becoming just a scholar of religions. Regardless of enormous amounts of important information, your mind will remain subtly fixated on fulfilling the conventional goals of social life. The mind of the true lover is concentrated, not upon convention, but on the Lotus Feet of the Lord, on radical intimacy with the Beloved. A knowledgeable scholar often speaks one way and lives another. Not so the person who has actually given his body and mind entirely to God. The egocentric scholar is like the vulture who soars to impressive altitudes, but keeps its sharp eyes focused on the earth, scanning for dead and dying creatures.

The naked Paramahamsa now drops the shawl from his shoulders, stands, and playfully demonstrates the way a dry scholar walks, speaks, and moves his hands. We laugh until tears come, recognizing the pompous formality, the basic uneasiness and uncertainty of such a person—the arrogance masked as scholarly objectivity, the awkwardness and ineptitude covered over by self-importance. But the brilliant mimicry of the Master remains compassionate, not in the least sardonic or superior. We recognize our own foibles as the sage now imitates each of us, one by one. The intensity of healing laughter increases.

Ramakrishna shifts ground. He is now demonstrating the gestures and moods of the *paramahamsa* or *mahasiddha*—a totally free and illumined being. Each motion and expression is selfless, graceful, and joyful. Each step is accurate and truly humble, each breath is powerful, each glance melts the heart with love. The tone of voice is that of an earnest child, punctuated by ecstatic laughter. The body is totally relaxed, eyes shining with unshed tears. We are filled with highly charged emotion as our Master now reveals dimensions of his own being which are usually kept concealed. Suddenly, the Divine Theater is over, as unexpectedly as it began.

DISCIPLE What wonderful relief one must feel when this mere pillowcase of a body finally falls away in death.

RAMAKRISHNA Why such a gloomy view? Certainly the world of convention can be looked upon as a form of imprisonment, as both obvious and subtle suffering, even as empty illusion. But if your consciousness truly awakens, the very same field of experience becomes a country fair of delicate humor and mystic delight. Let this blessed human body remain functional. Go and enjoy! Why not? Transform your experience totally into Divine Bliss, here and now! Granted there exist the eight strands of worldly bondage—primitive passions which are like bonds attached into the very muscles of the back. But these fetters, terrible as they may be, can drop away in a flash through the transforming illumination of Divine Grace. You have watched a village magician at work. He ties eight strong knots in a cord and invites his audience to test them. No one can untie a single knot. Thereupon the adept shakes the cord once, twice, thrice—all the knots unravel by themselves and disappear. The Mother of the Universe is not just a village magician. She is infinitely powerful. Do not attempt to analyze Her Actions. Shiva appears to the dying person and says: "Look! Here is My role in the drama of *mahamaya*. I assume this Divine Form because of the expectation of My lovers. Now look again! I am merging into the formless ocean of *satchidananda*. Come with Me!" This is Mother's Cosmic Magic.

Pretentious minds calculate this way: "Precisely so much of God has manifested as the universe, and the rest remains transcendent." Others speculate: "Twelve out of the full sixteen measures of Divine Energy have descended as this particular *avatara*, this Incarnation of God." I experience a severe headache the moment I hear such discussion. I once swooned and fell to the earth when Mahendra drew diagrams of the solar system in the dust of the Panchavati to illustrate the conventional European understanding of an eclipse. I also faint when hearing complicated plans that extend years into the future. Calculative mind must become ecstatic mind.

I only know that I know absolutely nothing. I do not even attempt to think about God, much less speculate about the creation. I simply call out MA, MA, MA. Newborn kittens, eyes not completely open, always remain exactly where the mother cat places them, crying only *mew, mew, mew*. Let my blissful Mother Kali do whatever She wants and place me wherever She wants. Whenever She wishes me to understand a small mote of Her Mystery, I grasp the point instantaneously. Whenever She wishes to keep me in a state of mystic unknowing, I joyfully accept. A young child cannot possibly know how much wealth or knowledge its mother possesses, and it does not care to know. The child simply cherishes its mother and lives with one fundamental conviction: "I have a mother." Basking in the presence of its mother, how can this child become anxious or worried in any way? But the searing pain that one experiences when clearly aware of separation from the Divine Mother—the separateness caused by egocentricity and conventionality—is so intense that it radiates heat from the body that can even scorch the green plants where one is sitting. During my *sadhana,* I experienced this.

The Great Swan turns and directly engages Mahendra's attention. Placing his open palm upright at the center of his chest, fingers spread open like petals, Ramakrishna stammers in a charming manner: "Well, Mahendra, there is apparently some Divine Presence here. What do you think?" As usual, this reticent disciple keeps silent. Our Master enters ecstasy. As he begins to disappear into the mysterious Presence that radiates from his heart center, the God-intoxicated sage speaks to us slowly, barely able to form words: "I can still perceive you, but I feel that we have been sitting here together eternally. I do not recall when we came or where we are." Now the Paramahamsa plunges through a subtle frontier and begins to converse fluently with the Mother of the Universe.

RAMAKRISHNA O blissful Goddess! O mystic embodiment of OM! O tender Mother! Countless assertions about Your Nature are made by poets, scholars, and foolish persons. I do not understand or accept any such opinions. I know nothing about Your Essence, O Mother most sublime. I only know how to cry MA MA MA. I place one constant, fervent prayer before You. Grant me pure love—love that seeks absolutely no reward, no response, no miraculous sign. O Mother, please do not conceal Yourself from this child by the glorious radiance of Your Cosmic Magic, Your Universal Manifestation that captivates every living being. I seek refuge in You alone, O Mother, and receive protection only from You. You are the only Consciousness, awakening through every form of consciousness. Every dimension of being and awareness is simply You.

O companions, the contemplative experiences God as an infinite lotus and himself as a bee, humming with the resonance of the Divine Names while sipping nectar from this ineffable blossom. But just as this lover cannot live, even for a moment, without being consciously immersed in the Divine Beloved, so God, who is none other than Pure Love, cannot bear separation from the human lover. As you become mature, you will experience yourself as the lotus and God as the ecstatic black bee. Finally, you will see that *brahman,* the transparent Ground of Being, has become both God and the lovers of God in order to taste its own Sweetness, to experience its own Bliss. This alone is the meaning of Radha and Krishna—the mystic play of Divine Lover and Divine Beloved.

At the beginning of the spiritual path, when you are like the bee buzzing through the jungle in search of the lotus, you adopt certain formal practices, such as wearing a string of prayer beads and traveling on pilgrimage. But outward ceremonial behavior gradually diminishes and finally ceases. Why? Because you discover yourself already enfolded in the fragrance of an infinite lotus, tasting the delicate nectar of timelessness. Like a bee settled deep within a blossom, you still hum faintly, experiencing in ecstasy that there is no separation or distinction between Divine Reality and Its revealed Names. But even this melodious humming sound ceases entirely when you enter mystic union.

Every manifestation of devotion will become essentialized by this inward silence. A pile of pennies equivalent to sixteen silver coins looks rather impressive, but when you actually exchange them for silver, these coins fit into a small purse. When you exchange the silver for gold, you have only a single coin that can be held easily in the palm of the hand. When you exchange that goldpiece for diamond, the stone is so small that no one notices it. Thus the spiritual wealth of the awakened sage, which is so immense, is barely visible. The *paramahamsa* exchanges every religious expression and even every ecstatic experience for the incomparable diamond of nondual awareness. Supreme Reality is neither material nor mental but is the very principle, the diamond essence, of sheer awareness. The final realization is invisible to the eyes of the world. This awakening comes as a sudden flash, like striking a match in complete darkness. Instead of remaining momentary and partial, the flash prolongs and intensifies. Rather than startling the nervous system, this continuous flash calms, heals, and integrates. There are no limits to this wonderful illumination, called *atman* or *brahman* by the original Indian sages.

I have always considered religious one-sidedness to be the major obstacle to such awakening. Therefore, I have sought and received countless sacred teachings. In holy Vrindavan I was initiated as a Vaishnava monk, wearing traditional robes, imbibing and entirely assimilating that particular mystic atmosphere. At the Temple Garden in Dakshineswar I was initiated into the mystery of Rama worship, painting my forehead with sandalwood paste and wearing a diamond amulet around my neck. In both instances, after three days these outer expressions no longer seemed appropriate, as the inner power of the initiation had fully blossomed. With the same wholehearted spirit, I practiced the ways of Christianity and Islam, each for a period of three days of total intensity, during which these particular mystic ideals came to full and permanent fruition in my being. No genuine initiation ever disappears. But now I have become a vat that can dye cloth whatever primary color or subtle hue anyone may desire. All the most advanced spiritual experiences from human history are contained in the form now before you, as in a transparent case. I swear to you that I know nothing but God!

An adept female practitioner, an unconventional yogini of great stature, once looked carefully at me and exclaimed: "You have definitely experienced inner realization." She turned to everyone and cried out in ecstasy: "Inside this man is the real diamond." Watching me partake of the noon meal prepared by Mother Sarada, the yogini inquired playfully: "Revered sage, are you eating, or are you feeding Divine Reality?" But all this remains invisible to most observers.

You are heroic practitioners. Why should any of you be afraid of the world? The radical sage, Vasishta, master of nonduality, proclaimed to his student, Prince Rama, who was Divinity incarnate: "Beloved Rama, why should you reject or flee the world? Is your earthly kingdom some separate existence, outside or below the infinite Divine Existence? If absolutely nothing but God truly exists, what is there to reject or to accept? Awaken instead as that One True Existence, which manifests both as God and as God's radiant creation." It does no good merely to express this notion of nonduality in words. Renounce immediately whatever false assumptions are standing in your way. You should not postpone this renunciation even for an instant. All obstacles are simply some form of conventionality or egocentricity.

For this grand renunciation, however, initiatory energy is necessary. Vasishta's words transmitted this liberating energy, and Lord Rama possessed a remarkable capacity to receive. Thus it is between every true master and true disciple. This drama of transmission—free from the slightest sense of hierarchy or duality—is replicated from generation to generation, from age to age. It is occurring at this very moment. After experiencing Divine Bliss, one will regard the habitual, obsessional world as mere crow droppings. Our life and our intelligence are simply Divine Life and Divine Intelligence. God is transmitting to God. God is awakening as God. My friends, be like the boatman who has penetrated through the breaking waves with great effort, who has rowed vigorously against the current and who now encounters a favorable wind. He unfurls the sail, keeps a light touch on the rudder, and enjoys a quiet smoke.

Ramakrishna once again turns toward Mahendra, engaging his eyes directly: "What do you think of me?" This time the Master's amanuensis overcomes his reticence and replies, quietly but with great intensity: "You are simple yet totally profound. It is difficult, perhaps impossible, to understand you." The Paramahamsa laughs for several minutes. The sound is like a crystal cascade. Ecstatically, he stammers: "Those who I think of as my own are part of me, are emanations from me. People visit a well-known holy man once or twice at the most, perhaps because they expect some external miracle. But all of you come here so often. It is only because of love. Could you do this if you were not part of my inner circle?" Gradually the Paramahamsa's state of intoxication subsides somewhat, and the steady stream of Divine Wisdom continues to flow, expressed in the most charming, surprising, playful manner.

RAMAKRISHNA Always speak truth. This is the central discipline. The person who tenaciously holds to truth will eventually realize God-consciousness, because God is the living Truth. By even slightly disregarding the practice of truth-speaking, a person gradually and unconsciously loses spiritual integrity. If I declare that I am going to the pine grove to answer the call of nature, even if I no longer feel that necessity, I still go there. Why? Because I said I would. If I tell the host that I will not take any more refreshments, even if I become hungry again later, I cannot eat. The way of truth-speaking should be this intense, including even the smallest details of daily life. It must cease to be simply a vow and become instead an instinctive response. I have discarded every possible attachment on the path to God-consciousness—attraction to virtues as well as to vices, involvement with knowledge as well as with ignorance—but I can never and will never discard my passionate commitment to Truth, which is both the way and the goal.

Advancing along the path, one develops authentic *bhakti,* which is not mere emotion but a love for God just as deep and real as the affection experienced between intimate friends. Then comes the development of *bhava,* the dawning of mystic union, which is like intense conjugal delight. One becomes utterly speechless, or else utters words in a drunken state of astonishment. The energy currents in the subtle nervous system are stilled and realigned. One experiences suspension of breath. The final step is *prema*—becoming Divine Love alone. There is no more gross, subtle, or causal body. There is no more universe, soul, or God. Just *prema, prema, prema.* Pure Love is an extremely rare state of realization, even among sages.

Many religious *pandits,* devoid of even a drop of Divine Love, speak inaccurately about God, regardless of their voluminous scriptural knowledge. During a lecture, Pandit Samadyayi once remarked: "Ultimate Reality is abstract and dry." Imagine such absurdity! To describe as abstract and dry what the Vedic wisdom authentically witnesses to be the essence of bliss! How many religious teachers exist who do not know what Divine Reality actually is! Look around you. There is only one infinitely blissful Consciousness everywhere. There are differences in the degree of its manifestation, no doubt, but both animate and inanimate existence are embodiments of sheer Divine Bliss.

DISCIPLE Master, is this world unreal?

RAMAKRISHNA Certainly it is unreal, as long as you still imagine it to be a separate, substantial world. But when you have awakened into God-consciousness, every being, every event, every process is sublimely real—the blissful play of Mother. After knowing the Mother Reality directly and intimately, one is no longer living in an impermanent, deceptive world. One is living in the Divine and as the Divine. When you feed your child, you will clearly perceive that it is God feeding God. When you serve your aged mother or father, it is God serving God. At this level of realization, the greatest imaginable joy is communion with the awakened lovers of God—through discussion, play, worship, service, silence.

Immature practitioners cannot easily recognize fully awakened souls—*paramahamsas*, who move through the world mysteriously in various disguises. I once pointed out such a fully awakened one to my nephew Hriday, who then made the mistake of pestering this liberated sage for instruction. The strange wanderer replied in stern tones: "When you see no difference in sanctity between the waters of the Ganga and an open sewer, then you will have realized Truth." When pressed for further explanation, the man ran away. Hriday pursued him. The unconventional master turned and threw a brick. Hriday ducked to the ground. When he stood again and began to search, he could find no trace of the illumined *mahasiddha*.

Such realized beings are usually not drawn to taste the pleasures of common sexuality. They are plunged instead in the Divine Ecstasy, for which every pore of the skin becomes like a sexual organ, experiencing sheer delight. In every moment, these holy beings are consciously surrendering body, mind, and innermost awareness to God alone. They do not use or manipulate persons in any way, but adore and worship them as embodiments of Divinity. The gestures and speech of these surprising sages are not limited to ordinary forms of communication. Their very tones are blissful, sweet as honey. Or they can appear fierce and frightening. Their presence, no matter how unconventional, is always healing and illuminating. They are constantly engaged, inwardly or outwardly, in the humble service of all creatures, whom they experience as transparent and beautiful vessels of the one Presence. In their holy company, the longing to know and to merge with Truth arises and intensifies naturally. They are the Wish-fulfilling Tree, which bears four varieties of fruit in abundance—righteousness, wealth, delight, and mystic freedom—each one an expression of selflessness. After experiencing the nectar of these fruits, egocentric enjoyment and ambition taste bitter in comparison. After experiencing the profound attraction of an illumined sage, who can still care for worldly success or even for Paradise?

Two of the companions of Divine Love have fallen asleep at the feet of our Master, just as predawn light is beginning to manifest, birds are beginning to sing, and the temple cooks, priests, and gardeners are beginning to stir. The Paramahamsa smiles and gazes tenderly at these peaceful sleepers, gesturing to us not to disturb them in any way.

RAMAKRISHNA Anglicized intellectuals—the Hindus I call *Englishmen*, who whistle European tunes and climb stairs two at a time, wearing leather riding boots—are always insisting that one should first engage in scientific study of the universe and then, on that basis, think about God. But Mother comes first, then the manifestation of Divine Radiance which they call the universe. After attaining God-consciousness, all phenomenal structures become transparent. Then alone can deep scientific study begin. One can only know the universe truly by first knowing God, thereby discovering the astonishing fact that it is timeless, spaceless Divine Reality which appears as a universe in space and time. One must meet Mother Mahamaya, who projects this universal appearance for the education and delight of souls, who are themselves simply rays of Her Light. By knowing the Mother Reality first, the mind does not become obsessed or veiled by partial forms of knowing—whether through the senses or by various methods of reasoning. The mind thus becomes free to conduct true research, which is the unveiling of Oneness—on every level, in every direction or dimension. By knowing Divine Oneness, you know the ground for every possible manifestation, the origin and the harmony of all phenomena. If you inscribe fifty zeros after the numeral one, you are indicating a very large number, but if you erase the numeral one, nothing remains. First write the numeral one—first realize God-consciousness—then inscribe however many zeros you may wish. People with no real spiritual, mental, or even physical stamina proclaim: "There is no God." They collapse, completely winded, on the first few steps of the steep staircase of realization. These are your atheistic or agnostic Calcutta gentlemen.

The contemplative must develop burning faith in the words of perennial wisdom that flow through the lips of the realized teacher. God-consciousness cannot be attained by a mind that is hesitant, hypocritical, evasive, calculating, argumentative, reactionary, partial, tricky, or twisted in any way. Your experience must become comparable to the intense yearning of a small child for its mother. The child knows when its mother is away. You may try to distract its attention by placing candy in its hand, but it refuses to be consoled, repeating forcefully: "I want to go to my mother!" How restless the child feels for its mother's special, tender presence! To the lover of God, the candy of limited enjoyment is tasteless. This authentic lover is consumed by the pangs of separation from God. It is like being kept awake all night by a throbbing toothache. To the intensity of this love, Divine Mother comes running. Restlessness and yearning are what is essential, no matter what path you follow. Mother is the active inner guidance of all conscious beings, so it makes no difference if you take a wrong turn sincerely. Your very sincerity will attract Mother Kali to establish you upon a more fruitful way.

There are distortions and wrong turns in every religious community, in every society. Each community assumes that its own clock is completely accurate, but in actual fact, no manmade reasoning tells the absolute Truth. This partial blindness, which is inevitable, does not impede genuine progress on the path so long as one feels intense longing for Truth. Continuous yearning will inevitably bring one into the blessed company of reliable truth-speakers—holy persons who have renounced conditional, egocentric viewpoints, who have given their whole lives to Truth and who have become Truth.

The Paramahamsa, completely fresh after so many hours of animated discourse, indicates the light of dawn with a subtle gesture, opening both hands. The sacred work of the Temple Garden is fully under way. The Master intones, OM OM OM OM OM OM KALI MA, harmonizing with the sounds of the dawn service now emerging from the Kali Temple. Sounds of activity can be heard as well from the gardens and the kitchens.

RAMAKRISHNA At the approach of dawn, the eastern horizon becomes red. One knows with certainty that the brilliant orb of the sun will soon appear. If you see a person profoundly restless for God-realization, you can be certain that the golden face of the Beloved will soon rise over the horizon of limited perception. Only the person for whom living without God becomes unbearable will actually encounter God. The mother bird does not break the shell of the egg until she hears the baby bird pecking vigorously from within. How long do girls play with dolls? After marriage, they pack their dolls away in a box and pray for the blessing of motherhood. What need is there for an icon of God when the Divine Presence becomes palpable?

Unexpectedly and with great power, our Master cries out: "Why should I live like a bird, imprisoned in a cage? Absurd! Totally absurd!" The moment these words are spoken, the body of the Paramahamsa becomes motionless as a statue in the dawn light. Tears are streaming down his cheeks and onto his bare chest. Gradually he descends from absolute identity to the mysterious realm of Divine Communion.

RAMAKRISHNA O Mother, make me like the noble Queen Sita— completely forgetful of her royal kingdom, unconscious of her beautiful hands and feet, withdrawn from her limited organs of action and perception, merged only in the single longing: *Where is Rama? Where is Rama?*

This body is like a glass bowl, O Mother. Pure mind is the clear water that fills the bowl. The sunlight of *satchidananda*—Being, Consciousness, and Bliss—is what illuminates the water. Meditating on this luminous water, one attains the vision of the universal sun, the single source of radiance on all planes of awareness. This supreme awakening comes through Your Grace alone, O blissful Kali. I am just a dry leaf, blown away by the storm of longing. What do I care for sophisticated philosophical arguments about the irreality of the world? You alone are manifest through all phenomena, O Mother. Even Shiva, sheer transcendent Knowledge, when awakening from the peaceful trance of Great Yoga, arises and dances powerfully, crying KALI KALI KALI. He does not sit passively, arguing that the world is unreal.

Suddenly, the Master enters a state of crystal-clear attention to the relative plane of awareness. His gaze seems to reach through our eyes directly into our heart. We trust him implicitly and would not feel the slightest hesitation to tell him any of our innermost secrets.

RAMAKRISHNA A person understands in one mode by hearing, reasoning about, and contemplating such teachings. But the ecstatic lovers understand in an entirely different mode when Mother Kali demonstrates Truth directly. This immediate knowing, this communion with the Wisdom Goddess, is now yours, my precious friends. You will never be confined within mere words or concepts, nor will you be limited to historical religions, contemplative practices, or meditative states.

One must become Sita to understand Rama. Reasoning and even meditation are indirect, whereas the nondual love shared by lover and beloved is direct. I once encountered the sublime Lady Sita in a transcendental vision. Lord Rama had filled to overflowing with radiant

Divine Presence every dimension of her life and being. Without repeating the beautiful Name Rama, she simply could not remain alive. Not even for a moment.

One must become mad with love in order to realize God-consciousness, which is ten million times more blissful than sexual experience. I used to walk about the Temple Garden carrying a small metal image of the child Rama cradled in my arms. I bathed him in the holy river, prepared food and cajoled him to eat, put him down for sleep, and played with him. We ran through the open fields together. I became mad with love for the Divine Child. This total love is what kindles *samadhi*, conditionless awareness. The ecstatic love of the milkmaids for the captivating dark blue Krishna is the master key to realizing God as the consciousness of all beings and as one's own innermost awareness. The *gopis*, the spiritually feminine companions of Lord Krishna, whether they are embodied in male or female form, receive the knowledge of supreme Reality, radical *brahmajñana*, without seeking or even desiring it. Sometimes God acts as an infinitely powerful magnet and countless lovers of God are instantly magnetized, like needles. At other times the lovers are the magnet and God is drawn to them like a needle. How astonishing! God, although infinite in power, cannot resist the attraction of pure love, even flowing from a single human heart.

It is merely the notion of separateness, and the conscious or unconscious desire to maintain the sense of separation, that prevents the mind from entering the state of *samadhi*, which is perfectly natural to it. It would be very easy for me to give up this body, here and now, in *mahasamadhi*, but Mother has placed in my heart an insatiable longing to enjoy the love of God in the companionship of pure-hearted lovers. This thread alone keeps me connected with the physical body.

The highest *samadhi* is not momentary or reversible in any way. It is not a separate trance state but continues to blossom subtly throughout all possible conditions of awareness—waking, dreaming, and dreamless sleep. Lesser meditative states resemble the situation of a mongoose with a brick tied to its tail by cruel village boys. Every time this poor animal attempts to retreat into its hole high in the stone wall, it has to come out again because of the weight of the brick. This weight is the brooding attachment to limited goals that makes certain yogis stray from the path of perfect union.

Various practitioners can experience forms of momentary *samadhi*, or partial absorption. Their minds, however, are like lotuses that open in direct sunlight yet close again the moment the sun goes behind a cloud. Night and day, the *paramahamsa* is always blossoming.

Intense love is like moonlight and intense knowledge like sunlight. The light of the moon—so delicate and healing to gaze upon—is simply sunlight in another form. In the infinite sky of consciousness, you can always clearly observe sun and moon. The *paramahamsa* constantly embraces both—ecstatic love and supreme knowledge. Knowledge is the flower, love its fragrance.

VISITOR Revered sir, precisely what is Divine Grace?

RAMAKRISHNA Lazy persons are always speculating about God's Grace. Of course, such Grace can and must be received. But is this process easy or automatic? A begger may get a penny from you immediately upon asking, but what if he requests first-class train fare from the north to the south of India? There is butter in milk, but one must patiently churn the milk to release it. There is oil in mustard seed, but one must gather the seeds and place them under great pressure to extract this nourishing and delicious substance. Immense fish live in the depths of a large lake, but to glimpse them you must throw spiced bait into the water. Although Divine Grace is omnipresent, to receive this Grace takes more effort and skill than churning butter, pressing oil, or catching carp.

Miraculously, whenever one actually makes the effort by raising the sail, the wind of Divine Grace is always blowing. Honest, well-guided spiritual efforts are always fruitful. Why? Because Mother alone exists. The mysterious allness of God is the secret of Divine Grace. Someone once proclaimed dogmatically, referring to a certain temple: "Nobody sings the Names of God there. It has no holy atmosphere." The moment I heard this remark, Mother revealed to me that Divine Reality alone has become all animate and inanimate existence. What dimension of God could be lacking holy atmosphere?

I clearly perceive all manifestations without exception as bubbles in the ocean of *satchidananda*—a shoreless ocean always at play in gigantic waves of Divine Love. Where can there be any lack or absence? Persons are like pills that are filled with indivisible Reality, Awareness, and Joy. I once ran with ecstasy into a flourishing meadow near my native village and carefully observed the small and even infinitesimal living beings it contained. This meadow was revealed to my concentrated gaze as filled to the brim with Divine Consciousness. Each conscious being is a flower in a different stage of blossoming, with a different number of petals unfolded, with a different degree of Divine Consciousness manifesting.

Ramakrishna suddenly cries out enigmatically: "I am manifest! I am here!," startling the peaceful sleepers at his feet into wakefulness. Disappearing totally into *samadhi,* he remains in this state of indescribable transparency for many extended breaths. Even though we have gone without rest the entire night, we do not feel the slightest inclination to close our eyes during this interlude of silent absorption. The living vision of the *avatara,* the full human manifestation of Divine Reality, is so satisfying that the sleep of this conventional world holds no attraction. Such sleeplessness is the mood that Ramakrishna maintained during the intense period of his contemplative exercises, or *sadhana,* as he engaged in generating liberating energy, not for himself but for all humanity. During twelve years, his eyelids did not touch each other in ordinary sleep.

The sage begins to regain subject-object awareness. He blinks several times, looks around him like a delighted child of five, and laughs. Now standing, still naked, he begins to pace back and forth, repeating: "Mother, Mother, Mother! Do not bring honor to me from the lips of men. I do not want superficial or hypocritical respect. I spit on it!" As he turns toward us, his eyes are the sun and moon of knowledge and love— radiating bliss, glistening with tremendous brightness.

The golden orb is now touching the horizon. The Great Swan lights incense and waves it gracefully before the complex array of pictures on the walls of this blessed room. These are spiritually awakened icons—living doors into Divine Presence, calling us to pass through them. Ramakrishna bows before each with unimaginable reverence. He pauses before a painting of Jesus Christ, standing miraculously upon the waters of the sea, lifting up his apostle Peter, who is sinking beneath the waves, unable to maintain the perfect lightness of the Great Master. Everyone in the room feels identified with the experience of the blessed Peter. Ramakrishna turns and fixes us with a gaze containing all the compassionate intensity of Goddess Kali. His words are directed precisely to our unspoken question. "One attains this state of transcendence, this walking on water, only after divesting from every egocentric grief and desire." Now our Master blends again into ecstasy, speaking directly with the Goddess.

RAMAKRISHNA Mother, I spit on this mere knowledge of Advaita Vedanta. When Your True Nature is realized, Vedas and Vedanta remain far below. I do not follow the abstruse reasonings of Vedanta and do not care to follow them. Please go away with Your *I am God.* Allow me to keep *Thou, Thou, Thou,* in order to enjoy the fun. A million salutations to Your famous *brahmajñana,* the experience of formless-ness. I do not want it. Give calm dispassion to those who seek it, O Mother, but make me mad with love for You. A *paramahamsa* is a child who enjoys playing with its mother, engaging in an infinite variety of games, sports, and theater. The dimension of formless radiance is real, without a doubt, but equally real are the beautiful Forms and Names of God. Equally real is Your sparkling, insubstantial universe, O playful Mother of the Universe. Philosophical reasoning about Reality must come to an end before genuine realization can occur. The intellect should burn like camphor—not leaving even a trace of ash.

The Paramahamsa now shifts into an entirely distinct atmosphere—sober, ordinary, practical. Here is the sage whose minimal possessions are always exactly in place, who sweeps his room so carefully that not a particle of dust collects, who insists that his friends find only the best buys in the bazaar, sending them back with the merchandise if the slightest defect is found, who instructs his disciples how to roll betel leaf, prepare a smoke, and trim the wick of an oil lamp to perfection.

RAMAKRISHNA A realized master cuts away the bonds of his disci-ples, no doubt, but at the moment of final fruition, he stands aside and allows the disciple to make the final steps. When felling a giant tree, the woodsman cuts through almost the entire trunk, deftly removes his saw, and steps back. The tree falls over with its own weight. The farmer laboriously digs an irrigation ditch from the river. He stands aside when only a few feet from his field. The earth gradually becomes soaked, crumbles, and is washed away. Then life-giving water pours through the open channel in torrents.

What does mere formal chanting of the Divine Name really accom-plish? One must weep with true longing. Your only responsibility is to experience profound longing—day and night, while seated, walking, or lying down, in solitude or in the household or marketplace. Suppose you repeat, like a mantra, "Wood contains fire and fire cooks rice." Can the mere repetition of these words, valid as they are, kindle the fire, prepare and serve the meal? You will enjoy bliss and gain inner strength only when you commune with God directly, only when you actually partake of the rice. Then alone can you distribute sacred nourishment to humankind. Awakened souls are profoundly affected by human suffering and long most intensely to show human beings the clear path to God-realization and to help them along the way.

Weeping with tenderness, our Master sings a single line over and over, with surprising melodic variation: "O beloved friends, how great is my relief to hear you chanting Lord Krishna's luminous Name." Once, when encountering childhood friends during a visit to his native village, Ramakrishna fell to the ground and begged them to chant the sweet Divine Names. This God-man is manifest in a mode devoid of authority, magnificence, and supernatural power, although secretly he is the full embodiment of all three. His commitment to humanity is complete. Often he exclaims: "My attitude is very simple. Look upon human beings as God and serve all their needs as the supreme form of worship." This is precisely the approach later taken by his successor, Narendra, who will be celebrated worldwide as Swami Vivekananda and who will mount the most consistent campaign of compassionate service known in India since the Mahayana Buddhist kingdoms.

We observe our Master constantly showering tenderness upon whomever he encounters, particularly those who are rejected or ignored by conventional society. Every day, he breaks the formal rules of caste separation and often disregards the traditional practices of ritual purity, although at other times he remains very strict and correct in certain aspects of his behavior, just like an orthodox brahmin priest. He moves entirely according to the moods that the Goddess mysteriously expresses through him. But Her intense Compassion always remain primary. Consider the Master's friendliness toward prostitutes, such as the well-known Ramani, to whom he always calls out his greetings as she walks through the Temple Garden. Before various conservative visitors, both men and women, the Paramahamsa proclaims: "O Mother, You alone have become the prostitute and the chaste woman." He often makes the shocking remark: "I am at the service of all, like a prostitute."

RAMAKRISHNA I beg you, dear friends, to sing the beautiful Names of God. Love God and live in the sweet companionship of the lovers of God. What else is there? The whole universe is simply the hide-and-seek of lover and Beloved, who are already one. What else can you want or need? Why attempt to improve upon perfection? One does not whitewash a wall which is already inlaid with mother-of-pearl.

The lovers of God are closer to each other than blood relations. We are all the mystically feminine companions of Radha, who is the primordial power of Awareness. We are rays from Her. Krishna is conditionless Awareness—our Supreme Beloved, our True Nature. This is the essential teaching. This is the secret of universal manifestation. Divine Reality is courting itself, seeking the supreme consummation.

Focus upon the nondual Panorama of Awareness rather than on the habitual, limited, fragmented perspectives of personal consciousness. Selfish enjoyments are the small piles of puffed rice with which Mother lures Her creatures away from Divine Bliss so that Her Cosmic Play may continue, just as merchants skillfully lure mice away from huge stores of grain.

Drop every limited motivation. Among the subjects who are fortunate enough to have an audience with the king, most persons come with various desires and petitions. The king is immensely attracted to the citizen who enters the royal presence simply with love, not requesting the slightest favor or intervention, either obviously or subtly.

This is the most powerful instruction. There is nothing that is being held back, or concealed, for some future transmission. Mother has put me into a state of mind so intense that I cannot hide Truth. Not even to the faintest degree. Feel attraction and love for this form now before you. That will be enough.

Ramakrishna now enters the mood of *avatara*. He unveils his True Nature, at Divine Mother's Command, with great humility and subtlety of spirit. Only the inner circle of lovers is present. We, too, are part of the avataric descent. This is the most secret teaching.

RAMAKRISHNA Astonishing as it may seem, only twelve realized sages recognized Rama as a full incarnation of Divinity. Out of countless human beings in Lord Rama's vast kingdom, including numerous saints and devout practitioners, only twelve persons were awakened enough to welcome the *avatara*, the full Divine Descent as Rama, Sita, Lakshmana, and Hanuman. The *avatara* is not a single figure but manifests with a holy consort and a *mandala* of intimate companions who are also expressions of the Divine Essence. Please think about the significance of this in relation to your own lives. Are you separate individuals? Do you need to practice asceticism and austerity? Are you ever apart from me?

The Only Reality plays about and sports in countless ways—as Divine Creator, as heavenly deities and subtle beings on various planes, as human souls and civilizations, as stars and atoms. The *avatara* is the sublime play of this Only Reality as a human being who consciously embraces all the other manifestations. The entire ocean of Being, Consciousness, and Bliss condenses into a genuinely human form. The *avatara* is not an apparition but a human being who eats, sleeps, and weeps. This is not easy even to accept, much less to recognize in person.

My father went on pilgrimage to Gaya where Lord Rama, under the aspect of Raghuvir, appeared to him vividly in a dream, declaring several times: "I shall be born as your son." Months later, when my revered father returned from his extended journey, my saintly mother was already pregnant. One day Divine Light had flowed into her womb from a shrine of Lord Shiva, causing her to faint on the spot. These events were witnessed and are well known in our small village of Kamarpukur. But who can correctly interpret such signs? And who can constantly bear their meaning in mind, without becoming distracted again by mundane considerations?

It is impossible to recognize the true dimensions and value of an *avatara*, unless one's mind is free from conventional calculations, whether worldly or religious. A diamond merchant showed a seller of eggplants an extremely precious gem. The owner of the vegetable stand responded immediately, with great confidence: "I will offer you up to nine pounds of eggplant for it, but not a single pound more."

My sister used to worship my feet with flowers and sandalwood paste when I was a young boy. Once, during this tender ceremony, I placed my right foot upon her head—an act of unthinkable discourtesy for a well-raised child—and proclaimed to her in a loud, mature voice: "You will die in Benares and be liberated!" If you love an *avatara*, it will be sufficient. I am an illiterate village man, but Mother supplies knowledge from behind. The Mother of the Universe speaks through these lips. I will swallow all your sorrow, all your misguided actions. If you receive even a minuscule ray of light from the Wisdom Goddess, both secular and scriptural learning will seem dim and insignificant. I pray for you all, so that you may attain God-consciousness swiftly. Again and again,

I cry inwardly, where no human being can overhear: "O Mother, may those who visit this room, feeling sincere attraction for Divine Presence alone, attain illumination during their present lifetime."

If you cannot constantly remember God, then think about me. The experiences that have occurred through this present human form transcend all those recorded by sacred history. If a person gathers his whole mind and places it upon me, he will achieve every possible spiritual ideal. Who am I? No one. Mother alone exists through this form now before you. Eventually, this holy form will be represented in many homes, in many cultures. Everyone will accept the authenticity of this manifestation.

It is easy and delightful to meditate on a human emanation of Divine Reality. Burning sunlight becomes gentle and healing when it manifests as moonlight. God descends as a human being without *samskaras*, without behavioral patterns inherited from previous lifetimes. The physical and emotional body of the *avatara* is simply a transparent covering—a glass lantern within which light is permanently blazing or a glass case in a museum where you can witness various ancient treasures right before your eyes.

The brilliant sun of tropical Bengal has now risen over the Dakshineswar Garden. The timeless day of the New Dispensation is advancing. Ramakrishna tenderly requests Narendra to sing his favorite hymn, commenting: "Narendra is a huge, red-eyed carp. Others are like minnows in comparison. I feel tremendous strength when he is with me in a gathering." We have never heard the most beloved disciple sing with such clarity and intensity of spirit, such world-transforming power.

> Within the black sky of Wisdom,
> the full moon of Love is rising.
> The floodtide of Love
> surges in a vast wave
> up the river of Love,
> inundating the countryside
> with Divine Love's ecstasy.
> The victory is Yours alone,
> O blissful Mother.
> Victory unto Thee!

Lovers shine like stars
around this tender moon,
playing with supreme Reality
as their most intimate friend.
The gates of Paradise
are open on this earth.
The victory is Yours alone,
O blissful Mother.
Victory unto Thee!

The spring wind of the New Day
stirs dynamic waves of joy,
bearing the fragrance of Love
to every heart without exception.
Mature souls who seek union
are drunk with Divine Delight.
The victory is Yours alone,
O blissful Mother.
Victory unto Thee!

The rising sun of sacred India
blossoms like a golden lotus
upon the universal ocean
of the New Dispensation.
Within its thousand petals,
the Black Goddess is enthroned.
Lovers of Truth like bees,
inebriated by delight,
sip the nectar of Her Mystery.
The victory is Yours alone,
O blissful Mother.
Victory unto Thee!

The bright face of the Goddess,
Her tender and ecstatic Gaze,
melts every heart in creation,
causing the universe to fall in love.
At Her dark blue Lotus Feet,

long-haired yogis and yoginis
are dancing with abandon,
transcending all convention.
The victory is Yours alone,
O blissful Mother.
Victory unto Thee!

What ineffable loveliness!
What peace pervades all worlds
when She unveils Her Form,
seated in meditation or dancing
within the heart of Consciousness.
The victory is Yours alone,
O blissful Mother.
Victory unto Thee!

The slave of ecstatic love
who sings this song
cries out to everyone:
I beg you, sisters and brothers,
to sing the Mother's praises.
Victory to Kali! *Jai Kali!*
Victory unto Thee!

RAMAKRISHNA You young persons are precious flints. There is fire in you. A flint can be kept under the ocean for a thousand years, yet the moment you strike it, there are sparks. You will ignite the entire world this time. I promise you. But no one can get any sparks from me. What is there to strike against in this empty frame?

Exhausted yet extremely happy, we spread sleeping mats on the veranda. The Paramahamsa is still fresh. White cloth around his waist, white towel over one shoulder, skin shining with a luminous golden color, he strolls toward the holy river for his morning bath. The Great Swan is reeling with inebriation. I steady him as he walks, lightly holding his right arm, whispering: "Step up here, sir. Step down here." We are heading toward the more intimate bathing ghat to the north of the Master's room, where his beloved wife and mystic consort, Mother Sarada, takes her holy bath every morning, bearing a lantern through the darkness before predawn.

She used to come without a light, until she almost stepped on a crocodile, resting underwater upon one of the stone steps of the ghat.

We can see Sarada's small, delicate figure standing in the doorway of the music pavilion where she resides—red-bordered sari thrown casually over her head, slipping back slightly to reveal her beautiful hair, brilliant black like the image of Goddess Kali. Ramakrishna unveiled her Divine Identity as Mahakali when she was only nineteen, awakening her through esoteric tantric rites, then offering his rosary and the fruits of his contemplative practices at her feet. This original worship was only the beginning. Daily, Ramakrishna reconsecrates his efforts for all humanity at the feet of Mother Sarada—his twin emanation, the sacred chalice of his realization for future generations. The God-man often comments simply about his sublime partner: "She is my power!"

Sarada Ma is now saluting her noble husband, her head gracefully tilting to one side, palms joined, fingers slightly interlaced. She is surrounded by an atmosphere of selfless devotion, yet transcendent insight streams from her steady gaze. Ramakrishna enters deep ecstasy at the very sight of her. He stands perfectly still, palms joined at his heart. Finally, inclining his head with reverence in her direction, he sings very softly, voice like the humming of a bee in the depth of a blossom: "The victory is Yours alone, O blissful Mother. Victory unto Thee!" As we continue to stroll together, the Master comments: "Have no doubt. The one over there in the Nahabat and the one here are exactly the same manifestation."

Suddenly, the Great Swan becomes annoyed at me for supporting him and scolds: "If you hold me by the arm, people will think I am drunk. I can walk by myself." The mode of his ecstasy changes. He begins to stride rapidly, singing aloud: "Behold my blissful Mother playing with Her Consort, Lord Shiva, both lost in joy. Drunk with celestial wine, She reels yet does not fall."

I cannot keep abreast. The Paramahamsa walks with almost supernatural speed. For some mysterious reason, he is now moving east toward the main Temple Gate. The road, lined with flowering trees, is covered by red brick-dust, contrasting beautifully with the sage's white cloth and polished black slippers. Above his head, the golden morning sun is suspended. As I stand and watch, the dynamic figure suddenly turns bright black against the red road. It is Goddess Kali—infinite power, infinite wisdom, infinite peace, infinite delight. She is approaching the ornamental gates of Her magnificent Temple Garden. Her Divine Intensity is fully focused. The

Wisdom Goddess is prepared to go forth from Her sanctuary and transform the modern world.

One of the signs of God-realization is joy. There is absolutely no hesitancy in such a person, who is like an ocean in joyous waves. But deep beneath the surface, there is profound silence and peace.

—*Ramakrishna Paramahamsa*

OM SHANTI SHANTI SHANTI

PEACE BE UNTO ALL LIVING BEINGS!

Index

Adhar, 70–71
Advaita Vedanta, 36, 107–10
Akhanda satchidananda, 11, 17, 169, 173, 214, 229, 281, 295, 297
Allah, 255, 256
Amrita, 222, 224
Ananda, 233
Anandamayi Ma, 163
Ant, 106
Arhat, 235
Arjuna, 90, 230, 281
Arrow, magical, 265
Asana, 46
Ashrama, 272
Ashtavakra Samhita, 108
Asiatic Museum, 167
Atman, 36, 178, 180, 189, 216
Avatara, 9, 45, 155, 156, 156–57, 159, 173–74, 174–75, 180, 224–25, 230–31, 267, 301–3
Avidya, 26. *See also* Ignorance
Awakening, 29
Awareness, 216

Baba, Pavhari, 35
Babu, Mathur, 90, 91, 129, 150
Babu, Ram, 155, 157, 159–60
Balaram, 56–61
Bhagavad Gita, 80, 142, 278
Bhagavan, 36, 79. *See also* God
Bhagavata, 79
Bhairava, 187

Bhairavi, 187
Bhakta, 79
Bhakti, 42, 79, 154, 291. *See also* Love, Divine; Prema
Bhava, 291
Bhava samadhi, 124
Bhavatarini, 182
Bholanath, 84
Birth signs, 302
Bodha, 235
Bodhgaya, 233, 237
Bodhisattva, 235
Boiling rice, 176
Bondage, 66, 110, 258
Brahmajñana, 163, 175, 296
Brahmamayi, 162
Brahman, 26–27, 36, 283, 288; Nirakara Brahman, 160; Nirguna Brahman, 184; Saguna Brahman, 184
Brahmananda, Swami, 15, 80–81, 89, 90
Brahmani, Bhairavi, 9
Brahmin priest, 87, 252, 300
Brahmo Samaj, 38, 128, 272
Buddha, Gautama, 235, 236–37, 246
Buddhism, 235

Campbell, Joseph, xiii
Cancer, 245
Car Festival, 194
Caste, 89, 281, 300
Cat and kittens, 102–3

Chaitanya, 8, 40–41, 94. *See also* Panihati festival
Chakras, 15, 146, 246, 261, 264
Chandramani, 101
Chatterji, Bankim Chandra, 71–74, 76–79
Chosen ideal, 184, 259
Christianity, 289
Christian monk, 272
Clay pots, 175
Coins, 288
Communion. *See* Mystic union
Companionship, spiritual, 170–71, 214
Condensed Gospel of Sri Ramakrishna, The, xiv
Contemplation. *See* Mystic union
Cosmic play, 67–68, 73, 203. *See also* Lila
Cossipore garden house, 245

Dakshineswar, 2–13, 81, 90
"Damn," 74
Darshan, 94
Datta, Ramchandra, 98, 242
Daya, 111
Dayananda, 137–38
Death, 130–31, 135, 248–49
Diamond essence, 288
Differentiation, 125
Diksha, 94
Discrimination, 164–65
Divine drunkenness, 306
Divine energy, 239–40
Divine fisherman, 49
Divine forms, 68–69
Divine humor, 136
Divine Incarnation. *See* Avatara
Divine Love. *See* Love, Divine
Divine madness, 273–74
Divine Presence, 30, 31
Doctrine, 227, 278, 280
Dualism, 171
Durga, 266

Ecstasy, xi–xii, 131, 203
Ego, 176–77
Egocentricity, 50, 131, 143, 216–17
Elephant, mad, 228
Enlightenment, 215, 288

Faith, 146
Fana, 256
Faqir, 242
Feminine devotion, 90–91, 153–54
Fish soup, 40–41
Four modes of experience, 48
Freedom, 143, 258

Ganga, 80
Gauranga. *See* Chaitanya
Gauri, Pandit, 116–18, 252
Gayatri, 80
God, 31, 173–74. *See also* Bhagavan
Goddess worship, 87, 88, 180
God-man. *See* Avatara
Good works, 24, 258–59
Gopis, 152–53, 296
Gosh, Girish, 226, 246
Gospel of Sri Ramakrishna, The, xii, xiv
Goswami, Navadvip, 95
Grace, 165, 242, 257, 284, 297
Great Master, The, xiii
Greed, 77
Gupta, Mahendranath, xiii, 21, 51–52, 161–62, 234, 290
Guru. *See* Teacher

Hanuman, 301
Hazra, 82–83
Heart, 35
Holy Mother, xv
Hriday, 111, 132

Ignorance, 270–71
Illness, 132–33, 135
Image-worship, 266–67
Ishtadeva. *See* Chosen ideal

Ishvarakoti, 81
Islam, 256, 289

Jafar, 255
Japa, 185, 190
Jatila, 147
Jesus Christ, 28, 173, 246, 271–72, 298
Jivanmukta, 141, 259
Jñana, 154, 178–79, 203, 214, 230
Jñani, 36, 177–79, 282–83

Kaaba, 255
Kali, 28, 183–84, 306–7; Lotus Feet of, 282; mantra, 167, 248, 294, 295; as Shyama, 251; will of, 132, 251; worship, 182–85
Kalipada, 242
Kamini kanchan, xiii
Karma, 104, 156
Karmanasha, 130
Kathamrita, xii
Kedar, 28
Kirtan, 93–99
Krishna, 3, 8, 71–72, 73, 89, 154, 230, 281, 301; in Arjuna's chariot, 90; as English boy, 88–89; as Gopala and Govinda, 80, 262; as Madhusudana, 147, 148
Krishnakishore, 109
Kundalini, 91, 170, 172, 239–40, 261, 284
Kuthi, 90

Lakshmana, 301
Lamp, 138–39
Latu, 149, 243, 247
Liberation, 258, 259
Lila, 73, 203. *See also* Mahamaya
Lilaprasanga, xiii
Living room of God, 35
Love, Divine, 17, 29–30, 129, 291, 297. *See also* Prema
Lover and Beloved, 69, 133, 152–53, 176, 216–17, 288, 301
Lust, 77

Ma, 130, 149, 167, 226, 286, 287, 306
Mahakali, 6, 85, 133, 259. *See also* Kali
Mahakali murti, 182–83
Mahamantra, 3, 41, 96–98
Mahamaya, 66, 168, 277–8, 286, 293
Mahanirvana Tantra, 145
Mahasamadhi, 248–49, 296
Mahasiddha, 29, 220, 265, 276, 285, 292
Mahatma, 114
Mahavayu, 239. *See also* Kundalini
Mahayana, 235, 300
Mahendra. *See* Gupta, Mahendranath
Mahimacharan, 145
Mallik, Mani, 155
Mandala, 9, 118, 148, 284, 301
Mantra, 94, 103, 122, 141, 157, 248, 249, 265, 279, 286, 294, 295, 299, 307
Maya, 26, 68, 111, 144, 169, 231–32, 281, 282
Meditation, 185, 222–23
Mind, 32
Moffitt, John, xiii
Money, 142
Mosque, 256
Mother, The, 160, 166, 248, 258, 263, 275
Mudfish, 142–43
Mudra, 158
Muhammad, 28, 247, 256
Muni, 115
Muslim, 29, 255
Mystic union, 62–64, 72, 186, 187, 248, 254–55, 291

Namaz, 256
Name, Divine, 190, 262, 278
Name and form, 73
Namo narayana, 257
Nanak, Guru, 59, 262. *See also* Sikh
Nangta, 223. *See also* Totapuri
Narada, 49
Naralila, 84, 257
Narendra. *See* Vivekananda, Swami
Neti, neti, 36, 178, 254

New Day, 59, 304
New Dispensation, 59, 246–47, 303, 304
New Dispensation, 56
Nikhilananda, Swami, xiii
Niranjan, 242, 247
Nirvana, 237
Nistarini, 243
Nitya, 68, 203
Nityashuddhabodharupa, 215
Nonduality, 109–10, 125–26, 136, 158, 164, 176, 203, 228–29, 238, 260, 283

Ocean of Nectar, xii
Om, 107–108, 141, 159, 196–97, 294
Oneness. *See* Nonduality
One-sidedness, 258

Panchavati, 139
Pandit, 10, 198
Panihati festival, 93–99
Paramahamsa, 1, 78, 220, 277, 288, 299
Path of love, 194
Paths, many, 257
Persian book, 256
Philosophy, 282
Pilgrimage, 259
Pillowcases, 275
Pir, 250
Pleasure-seeking, 187
Polarities, 109
Practical concerns, 234
Prakriti, 126, 282. *See also* Purusha
Prasad, 137, 203
Prayer, 63–64, 116, 165
Preaching, 74–76
Pregnancy, 196
Prema, 17, 256, 258, 269–70, 291. *See also* Love, Divine
Prostitute, 82, 88, 300
Puranas, 27, 216
Purna, 107, 179, 249

Purna, companion of Kamakrishna, 220
Purusha, 36, 126, 282. *See also* Prakriti

Queen Victoria, 127
Questions, 62–69
Quran, 256

Radha, 8, 28, 72–73, 96–98, 100, 274, 301
Raga, 29
Rai, Govinda, 255
Rajas, 41, 42
Rakhal. *See* Brahmananda, Swami
Rama, 87, 265, 289, 295, 301
Ramakrishna
   arm fracture, 161–62, 167
   birthday, 51–55
   dancing, 14–15, 91–92, 96
   ecstatic states, 33–34, 35, 69, 96, 123
   final days, 241–49
   as handmaiden of Divine Mother, 90
   intimate experiences of, 81–91
   linguistic style, xi
   mahasamadhi, 248–49
   marriage, 85
   pain at touch of gold, 150
   passing of, 245–49
   as Radha, 90
   as Rama and Krishna, 89
   responding to questions, 62–69, 142–43, 253
   sadhana, 51
   in samadhi, 121–22
   suffering of, 132, 212–13, 247
   tantric transmission, 202–11
   throat cancer, 212, 220
   visions, 83–90, 220, 221, 281
Ramakrishnaloka, 236, 250
Ramakrishnananda, Swami, 89, 247
Rama worship, 89, 289
Ramprasad, 16–17
Rasagolla, 102

Rasmani, Rani, 8, 90, 150–51, 252, 259

Rational analysis, 286–87

Reality, 26–27, 36, 276

Realization, 191, 292

Red toy, 259

Reincarnation, 76, 175

Relativity, 185–86, 225

Relics, 247

Religions, 15–16, 30, 294

Religious ritual, 7, 28–29, 141, 195, 196, 197, 269, 285

Remembrance, inward, 188, 195

Renunciation, 64, 109–10, 143–44, 164–65, 284

Rishi, 107, 161, 171, 189

Rudraksha, 42, 194

Sadhaka, 87, 275, 285

Sadhana, 21, 51

Sadhu, meeting with, 157–59

Salaam, 192

Samadhi, 11, 29, 72, 84, 121–22, 152–53, 187, 244, 296–97; nirvikalpa, 237, 255

Samskara, 303

Sandals, 143

Sannyasa, 65, 109

Sannyasi, 65

Sarada, Mother, xv, 82, 305–6
  appearance, 100
  and children, 11–12
  chores, 100, 251
  as Holy Mother, 94, 306
  marriage, 85–86
  and Panihati festival, 93
  in samadhi, 103–4
  service of, 92, 234
  speaks about Ramakrishna, 101–3, 104–5
  stringing garland, 86

Saradananda, Swami, xiii

Saraswati, 8, 198

Sarkar, Doctor, 212, 218, 219, 222, 226, 227, 231

Sarod, 29

Sashi. *See* Ramakrishnananda, Swami

Satchidananda. *See* Akhanda Satchidananda

Sattva, 41, 42

Scholarship, 25, 116, 285

Scripture, 194–95

Self-consciousness, 52, 213–14

Sen, Keshab, 242; death of, 139; last meeting with, 120–29

Sexuality, 65–66, 144, 186–87, 281

Shakti, xvi, 125, 126, 158, 187, 283

Shanti, 2, 15, 307

Shashadhar, Pandit, and Tantric transmission, 202–11; visit to, 193–201

Shiva, 8, 174, 187; mantra of, 157

Shiva and Shakti, 104

Shivananda, Swami, 247

Shivanath, 38

Sickroom, 236

Siddha, 24

Siddhi, 10

Sikh, 262. *See also* Nanak, Guru

Single-pointedness, 151

Sita, 28, 87–88, 295–96, 301; mystic identity with, 153

Sleeplessness, 298

Soham, 108. *See also* Mantra

Soul, 48–50; evolution of, 156

Spiritual guidance, 145–48, 264–65, 277

Suffering, 105

Sufis, 255, 256

Sufi saint, 260

Suicide, 47–48

Swan, 78

Tabla, 273

Tagore, Devendranath, 149, 150

Tagore, Kalikrishna, 217

Tagore, Rabindranath, 149

Tamas, 41, 42

Tantra, 9, 27, 216

Tantric practitioner, 46–47, 252

Tantric transmission, 202–11

Tapasya, 190

Tara, 182. *See also* Bhavatarini

Tarak. *See* Shivananda, Swami

Teacher, 198–99, 228, 267–69

Terminal illness, 212

Thoughts, 170

Three brides, 103

Throat cancer, 212, 220

Tide, 262–63

Totapuri, 9. *See also* Nangta

Trailokya, 81

Transcendent experiences, 81–91

Truth, 139, 290–91

Tulsi, 117, 157

Tyagi, 278

Understanding, levels of, 129–30

Uma, 216

Upadhi, 125

Vajrayana, 202, 235. *See also* Tantra

Vasishta, 289–90

Vedanta. *See* Advaita Vedanta

Vedas, 27, 107, 216

Vidya, 24, 26. *See also* Jñana

Vidyasagar, Pandit, 20–27, 125

Vijaya Day, 232, 249

Vijñana, 214

Vijñani, 178–79, 282–83

Vina, 8

Virgin Mother, 271

Vishnu, 174

Visions, 83–90; of Divine Mother, 83, 85, 221; of reservoir, 281; of six-teen-year-old boy, 220

Viveka, 233

Vivekananda, Swami, xi, 84, 111–12, 113, 240, 247, 249, 255, 280, 290, 300, 303

attributes, 116

and avatara doctrine, 238–39

and Buddhism, 233, 235, 236–37

as emanation of celestial sage, 115

meeting Ramakrishna, 114

at parliament of religions, xi, 114

singing, 57–61

Vow of completion, 118–19

Vrindavan, 289

Way of Honey, 153

Wilson, Margaret, xiii

Women disciples, 87, 102, 103, 151, 180, 241, 243. *See also* Rasmani, Rani

Women mystics, 153, 154. *See also* Brahmani, Bhairavi

World and self, 284

Worldliness, 261

Worldly life, 64–65, 142–43

Worship, 185, 266–67, 269

Yoga, 140

ALSO IN SHAMBHALA DRAGON EDITIONS

The Art of War, by Sun Tzu. Translated by Thomas Cleary.

Bodhisattva of Compassion: The Mystical Tradition of Kuan Yin, by John Blofeld.

Buddha in the Palm of Your Hand, by Ösel Tendzin. Foreword by Chögyam Trungpa.

The Buddhist I Ching, by Chih-hsu Ou-i. Translated by Thomas Cleary.

Cutting Through Spiritual Materialism, by Chögyam Trungpa.

Dakini Teachings: Padmasambhava's Oral Instructions to Lady Tsogyal, by Padmasambhava. Translated by Erik Pema Kunsang.

The Dawn of Tantra, by Herbert V. Guenther & Chögyam Trungpa.

The Diamond Sutra and The Sutra of Hui-neng. Translated by A. F. Price & Wong Mou-lam. Forewords by W. Y. Evans-Wentz & Christmas Humphreys.

The Experience of Insight: A Simple and Direct Guide to Buddhist Meditation, by Joseph Goldstein.

Glimpses of Abhidharma, by Chögyam Trungpa.

The Heart of Awareness: A Translation of the Ashtavakra Gita. Translated by Thomas Byrom

The Hundred Thousand Songs of Milarepa (two volumes). Translated by Garma C. C. Chang.

I Am Wind, You Are Fire: The Life and Work of Rumi, by Annemarie Schimmel.

I Ching: The Tao of Organization, by Cheng Yi. Translated by Thomas Cleary.

I Ching Mandalas: A Program of Study for The Book of Changes. Translated & edited by Thomas Cleary.

Mastering the Art of War, by Zhuge Liang & Liu Ji. Translated & edited by Thomas Cleary.

The Myth of Freedom, by Chögyam Trungpa.

Nine Headed Dragon River, by Peter Matthiessen.

Returning to Silence: Zen Practice in Daily Life, by Dainin Katagiri. Foreword by Robert Thurman.

Seeking the Heart of Wisdom: The Path of Insight Meditation, by Joseph Goldstein & Jack Kornfield. Foreword by H. H. the Dalai Lama.

Shambhala: The Sacred Path of the Warrior, by Chögyam Trungpa.

The Spiritual Teaching of Ramana Maharshi, by Ramana Maharshi. Foreword by C. G. Jung.

Tao Teh Ching, by Lao Tzu. Translated by John C. H. Wu.

(continued on next page)

The Tibetan Book of the Dead: The Great Liberation through Hearing in the Bardo. Translated with commentary by Francesca Fremantle & Chögyam Trungpa.

The Vimalakirti Nirdesa Sutra. Translated & edited by Charles Luk. Foreword by Taizan Maizumi Roshi.

Vitality, Energy, Spirit: A Taoist Sourcebook. Translated & edited by Thomas Cleary.

The Way of the White Clouds: A Buddhist Pilgrim in Tibet, by Lama Anagarika Govinda. Foreword by Peter Matthiessen.

The Wheel of Life: The Autobiography of a Western Buddhist, by John Blofeld. Foreword by Huston Smith.

Worldly Vision: Confucian Teachings of the Ming Dynasty. Translated & edited by J. C. Cleary.

Zen Dawn: Early Zen Texts from Tun Huang. Translated by J. C. Cleary.

Zen Essence. The Science of Freedom. Translated & edited by Thomas Cleary.